REPORTING
HONG KONG

REPORTING HONG KONG

FOREIGN MEDIA AND THE HANDOVER

Edited by

Alan Knight

and

Yoshiko Nakano

St. Martin's Press
New York

St. Martin's Press, Scholarly and Reference Division, 175 Fifth Avenue, New York, N.Y. 10010

First published in the United States of America in 1999
Printed in Great Britain

ISBN: 0–312–22429–X

Library of Congress Cataloging in Publication Data

Reporting Hong Kong : Foreign media and the handover / edited by Alan Knight and Yoshiko Nakano.
p. cm.
Includes bibliographical references and index.
ISBN 0–312–22429–X
1. Hong Kong (China)–History–Transfer of Sovereignty from Great Britain, 1997–Press coverage. 2. Hong Kong (China)–History– Transfer of Sovereignty from Great Britain, 1997–Public opinion. 3. Foreign correspondents–China–Hong Kong. 4. Journalism–China– Hong Kong. 5. Mass media–Hong Kong. I Knight, Alan. II. Nakano, Yoshiko.
DS796.H757R46   1999
070.4'499512505–dc21   99-11038
                                 CIP

To Geoff Wade
for his unstinting advice and support

CONTENTS

CONTENTS

CONTENTS

CONTENTS

ACKNOWLEDGEMENTS

This project has been supported by research grants from City University of Hong Kong, the Public Discourse Research Group of its Department of English, and the Contemporary China Research Centre.

We would like to thank the Hong Kong Foreign Correspondents' Club and the members who took time for interviews and discussion. In particular, Francis Moriarty gave us the benefit of his extensive local media knowledge. Kathy Wilhelm allowed us access to the Freedom Forum Asia Center with its computers, files, and library; Janet Cheung was of great assistance there.

Alan Knight would like to thank the Centre of Asian Studies at the University of Hong Kong where he visited as an Honorary Research Fellow in 1997. Help was also provided by the University of Technology in Sydney which allowed sabbatical leave during the project. In Hong Kong, support came from May Ting, Margaret Prisca Lo, and Terry Nealon, Head of English Language News and Current Affairs at RTHK. In Guangdong, the staff and management of the *Guangzhou Daily* opened their doors to outside inquiries.

Yoshiko Nakano would like to thank Ron Scollon who has been a constant source of advice and inspiration. She has also benefited from discussions with Suzanne Wong Scollon, Mariko Watanabe, Yuling Pan, Anthony Y.H. Fung, David C.S. Li, Maggie O.Y. Leung, Ken Rose, and Jim Kelman. Daniel Reeves and Rachel Scollon provided editorial assistance. In Tokyo, NHK Radio Center generously provided support, and gave permission to print a translation of their radio script in Chapter Six. She also remains deeply grateful to Deborah Tannen, her mentor at Georgetown University.

Andrew Taylor, Acting Head of the Department of English at City University of Hong Kong provided indispensable support and wisdom.

We thank our research assistants: Winnie W.F. Or, Zhou Linong, Stephanie Chan Mei-na, Cheung Pak-chuen, Daniel Luk, Beatrice Chan Sau-ki, Woo Ka-yin, and Charlotte To Kit-yi. Without their language skills and meticulously organised archives, this project would not have been possible.

Marie Lenstrup of Curzon Press, Brian Moeran and Lise Skov provided invaluable support during the production process.

We are particularly grateful to Geoff Wade, who read the manuscript in one of its earlier versions and gave us detailed suggestions for revision. While this book owes much to the support of these organisations and people, none of them is responsible for the problems which remain.

ACKNOWLEDGEMENTS

The Hong Kong Democratic Party: page 44.

The Frontier: page 105.

Cheung Pak-chuen: page 22, page 51, and page 83.

Alan Knight: page 34.

Yoshiko Nakano: page 61 and page 81.

Kazuaki Hanada: page 132.

Every effort has been made to trace the copyright of the illustrations reproduced in this book. Unfortunately, in some cases this has proved to be impossible. The authors and publisher would be pleased to hear from any copyright holders whom they have been unable to contact, and to print due acknowledgements in the next edition.

-

Parachute journalism reinforces a pack mentality which has always plagued foreign reporting. Correspondents who hurry off to a new place stick together, interviewing friends who arrived earlier and competing to find the most dramatic angle of the story. Wherever there are a few resident correspondents, a Parkinson's law of journalism holds that news increases in direct proportion to the number of visiting reporters in town.

Mort Rosenblum in *Coups and Earthquakes* (1981:12)

PREFACE

Millions of people switched on the television to see the end of colonialism, live on global newscast. They watched the last governor of Hong Kong as his Rolls Royce wheeled out of Government House. News teams who had flown in from across the world to eyewitness the event told viewers that the governor's car had gone three times around the driveway. Narrators said that Governor Patten was carrying out an old Chinese tradition which meant that he would return. But they were merely quoting from a government press release issued the day before. They ignored the inconvenient fact that Governor Patten did not complete the circuit. A scripted photo opportunity had triumphed over what people on the spot really saw. The 'news' was picked up by reporters from the United States, Britain, mainland China, Singapore, Australia and places beyond. The handover coverage frequently became little more than a media release.

In the summer of 1997, thousands of foreign journalists converged on Hong Kong for a few days to record one of the last episodes in Western colonialism. They outnumbered the People's Liberation Army troops that marched across the Chinese border. In a downpour, 29.6 degree heat, and 94 per cent humidity, the journalists recorded the end of 156 years of British rule, and Hong Kong's return to China. *Guangzhou Daily*, a newspaper in the city of Guangzhou or old Canton where British and Chinese fought the Opium War in 1839–42, described the handover coverage as 'The Battle of the Century for Chinese and Foreign Media':

The solemn ceremony of Hong Kong's handover has become the focus of the world's media. By yesterday's count, nearly 8,400 journalists from 775 news organisations are in Hong Kong to report on this historic event of Hong Kong's handover. This media battle of the century is heating up.

Yesterday, CCTV, Hong Kong TV stations, CNN, BBC, NHK and others, began their live coverage which ranges from six to seventy-two hours. The human resources mobilised, equipment used and the amount of money spent are nearly astronomical.

(Guangzhou Daily July 1, 1997:62)[1]

The Hong Kong handover was a series of staged spectacles, but unlike the Olympic Games that are portable from Sarajevo to Lillihammer to Nagano, it was deeply rooted in the Crown colony. It was an event to mark the handover for the world. Mental and physical preparation for the event began with the 1984 Sino-British Joint Declaration. Media study researchers Daniel Dayan and Elihu Katz (1992) distinguish media events as planned symbolic performances from unplanned incidents such as earthquakes. They suggest that media, television in particular, presents such events as narratives. In the case of the handover, Governor Chris Patten was portrayed as Britain's approved hero and the People's Liberation Army (PLA) as the threatening villain. Democrat Martin Lee starred in a sub-plot in Hong Kong coverage. But in the Beijing-controlled media, he was nowhere to be seen, and the PLA was heralded in a celebration of Chinese sovereignty after long humiliation.

How foreign journalists chose to report the handover, and what they decided to ignore about it, reveals much about foreign news agendas and how they are framed by ideological and cultural assumptions. How did different nations' correspondents report the same strictly stage-managed event? How did media handlers construct and stage the events?

When we examine the work of journalists, we are tempted to examine only the product of the journalistic process: the published stories in the newspapers, or perhaps reports on radio and television. This certainly provides insights into news agendas. But this method ignores the process of reporting, the ideological and cultural context from which the correspondents emerge, not to mention the views of the correspondents themselves. In their book on the Falklands War, David Morrison and Howard Tumber (1988:viii) stress the need to include the voices of the journalists involved. The approach, they claim, not only gives outsiders a clear view of the journalistic process, but also opens the eyes of the journalists themselves, turning them into reflective witnesses of their occupation:

> Reading the academic literature, one cannot help but feel sympathy with the journalists' claim that the 'outsider' has failed to get inside the trade; it is all too formalistic, too sterile, too serious; and it is not surprising therefore, that working journalists fail to recognise the world they are supposed to inhabit.

At the same time, foreign correspondents' own reflections do not necessarily provide insights into their own ideological and cultural frames. Many of them engage in an exclusive club within the wider journalism culture. Their mythologies are often enshrined in biographies, which purport to tell the stories behind the news, but which more often recount tales of drinking, danger, humour and frequently sex. Anthropologist Mark Pedelty (1995:128–29), who examined the work of war correspondents in El Salvador, sees this behaviour as ritualised recreational rites which 'filled the void between myth and practice'. Anecdotes and biographies which accentuate *machismo* often mask the conflict between correspondents' self-image, and the routine of filing reports framed in 'objectivity', directed by office news priorities and cramped by mainstream news agendas. Such behaviour, according to Pedelty, allows reporters to fit their new experiences into the narrative of legendary correspondents.

In this book, three communication researchers with journalistic backgrounds illustrate the process of media reporting as well as the product. We attempt to bridge the gap between media analyses in living-rooms and anecdotes from the field by interviewing journalists and media strategists, by observing them in their work contexts, and by comparing their reports against each other, against local coverage and against the official record.

On the media handler side, we track strategies of the Hong Kong Government Information Services and the Hong Kong Democratic Party. On the media side, we take snapshots of the handover day through the eyes of journalists from Britain, mainland China, Japan, the United States, Australia, Vietnam, Italy, and Hong Kong, and lay out a collage of 'on the record' interviews, imagery, and analyses to reflect on the diverse nature of reportage. The book pays particular attention to reporting by journalists from three countries – Britain, China, and Japan – whose interests have been intertwined in Hong Kong. For

Britain, the event was tinged with nostalgia for past greatness. For China, it was the much heralded icon of its emergence as a world power. For Japan, it was an event that might affect the economic climate in Asia as well as the future of the favourite holiday destination. For many journalists, it represented a new fault line between libertarian and authoritarian modes of reporting, between notions of free speech and state censorship.

The huge volume of reports about Hong Kong's decolonisation meant that the study, in order to be completed some time this century, centred on the day itself, excluding the thousands of stories written and broadcast in the run-up period. However, in retrospect, it is obvious that the handover was a media event where spectacle frequently obscured the issues. The large number of journalists pressed the limits of access to principal characters and events. And yet, media organisations operated under the contemporary demands for instant and constant coverage. To meet this, the Hong Kong government provided abundant visual and press releases in live feeds, as hardcopy and on web sites. V.G. Kulkarni, the *Far Eastern Economic Review*'s news editor, commented on the handover coverage:

> Once this sort of mob journalism gets rolling you can't stop it. Somebody who just logged onto the Hong Kong web sites or watched it on TV, probably could have written the story from Argentina or Peru or London as well as some of the people who came here and talked to others. I suppose this is inevitable when you have such a jamboree.[2]

This book considers how a 'reality' is constructed through press releases and visual spectacles. It also features Insiders' Insights: interviews with thirteen Hong Kong-based journalists from seven countries who took part in this media jamboree. The voices range from CNN's China-watcher, Mike Chinoy to a Vietnamese journalist who was one of a few non-Chinese Communists on the scene. They discuss the restrictions that they worked under including the pressure for colourful stories, self-censorship, and the inability to pose questions to the key players. These pieces serve as interludes between chapters, and can be read individually.

Overview of Chapters

In Chapter One, Alan Knight introduces Hong Kong which has served as a base for Western journalists for more than 150 years. Hong Kong plays a critical and central role in Asian-Pacific media and remains the most important window on greater China. The chapter reviews this history, and profiles the vibrant press and diverse population of foreign correspondents who despatch stories from Hong Kong. Reference is also made to the 1993 Cambodian elections, which was the last major media event in Asia before the Hong Kong handover.

Chapter Two illustrates how Hong Kong Government Information Services (GIS) handled the over 8,000 domestic and foreign journalists who signed up to cover the handover. Various GIS officers explain their strategies for 'press marshalling': the process of accreditation, the creation of a live satellite television feed service, and the distribution of press releases by Internet.

Chapter Three shifts the focus to coverage of a non-government event. Yoshiko Nakano describes Martin Lee's speech at the balcony of the Legislative Council building through the eyes of a young Hong Konger who drafted the speech. The widely covered English speech was significantly different from the Cantonese version which was delivered back to back with the English version, reflecting the ideological divide within the Democratic Party. In addition, many English-language newspapers and magazines relied on English press releases, and quoted Lee from a prepared draft speech rather than from his actual speeches. The chapter illustrates multiple realities in 'bilingual' Hong Kong. It also points to the gap between American and Hong Kong Chinese perceptions of Martin Lee.

The interlude following Chapter Three considers construction of images. It includes an examination of how *Newsweek* packaged Hong Kong stories differently for its American and Asian audiences.

In Chapter Four, Knight looks at a major Cantonese newspaper in mainland China, the *Guangzhou Daily*. It has the most modern production facilities in the region, and is already one of China's leading newspapers and a model for the new wave of news outlets driven by advertising profit. The *Guangzhou Daily* sent a team of ten reporters to Hong Kong, and put out a ninety-seven-page special issue on July 1. While the paper covered human interest stories extensively, it was also obliged to print official Chinese political reports including a *People's Daily* editorial which said, 'It is time for the Chinese nation to wash away one hundred years of shame.' The chapter also depicts the paper's coverage of the British military forces and Governor Patten.

In Chapter Five, Barry Lowe looks at the way a major British television network, ITN, constructed the narrative of the climactic event of Britain's colonial legacy. The chapter examines the sentimental values that Britain attached to its last major colony, and how the coverage reflects the anachronistic and contradictory nature of Britain's lingering colonial presence. It compares and contrasts ITN's report of Patten's departure from Government House with the report by its rival network, the BBC. In the following subsection, Alan Knight shows how the BBC – BBC World's twenty-four hour news service and national news bulletins – reported the effective end of the British Empire.

Chapter Six focuses on an operation by visiting Japanese journalists showing how public radio NHK attempted to cover the visual spectacle with radio voices. The producers flew in six days before the handover, and broadcast for a total of over five hours of live programming from Hong Kong. Nakano, who was a reporter for the coverage, shows how NHK Radio carried local voices within the constraints of limited access and information, getting around the parachuter's paradox by providing a more in-depth view of conflicting Hong Kong identities.

The book concludes with Chapter Seven which draws together earlier analyses. A press release reality, or reporting based on official handouts, was a salient feature of the handover coverage. The chapter also presents differing views on 'negative' Western media reports and Beijing's media control by politicians, entrepreneurs, and both local and foreign journalists. Reference is also made to some changes in Hong Kong's local media scene. For foreign correspondents, the transition to Chinese sovereignty raises practical and intellectual questions about media coverage of Asia.

Reporting Hong Kong explores the movement of text and image from scripted performance, to news, to mythology. It documents how journalistic prisms shape the 'truth' in socialist as well as in free societies.

Alan Knight
Yoshiko Nakano
Hong Kong

THE PEARL OF THE ORIENT

Alan Knight

When I started out as a journalist twenty-five years ago, on a Hong Kong newspaper where as you began writing your story a large cockroach would crawl out of the typewriter, my boss, a grizzly Australian veteran of pre-War Shanghai, gave me two pieces of advice. The first was to get myself into a suit. The second was to remember at all times that news consists of the unexpected. In other words, if you know something is going to happen, it isn't a story when it does.

Tim Luard, BBC World Service (1997)

Hong Kong was a high-water mark for European influence on China. Founded on sordid contraband and conquest, it became a glittering nexus for East and West, a global communications centre whose free market of ideas shaped world opinions on Asia. Its return to the Chinese motherland, doggedly ruled by an authoritarian regime intolerant of criticism, meant more for journalists than just another British colony being handed back to the indigenes. It represented the closure of the last privileged outpost for those who in earlier days defined themselves as the advocates of colonialism; the Western foreign correspondents who interpreted the Orient for metropolitan consumption. Now it seemed that there would be no more tea parties for selected Westerners on the lawns of Government House. The intelligence agents, who had been so helpful in the past, spent their last days in the colony burning the files which had provided so many of the deep backgrounders. There would be no more English-speaking insiders leaking policies at the bar of the Foreign Correspondents' Club. The last of the old European empires had ebbed away, leaving the remaining China-watchers beached and isolated. The new order would favour Chinese-speaking reporters and presume Chinese priorities.

The handover had the elements of one last sensational news story. A local Chinese entrepreneur marked the colony's return to the embrace of the motherland by selling a special edition T-shirt showing a scrawny Mick Jagger figure slouching away with the Union Jack over his shoulder. He was being replaced by a smiling Attila the Hun, riding in on a pony decorated with human skulls. The perceived potential for conflict helped make the reunification the region's media event of the decade.

A Borrowed Place

Hong Kong stands at the mouth of the Pearl River, China's southern artery for commerce with the outside world. It was the creation of nineteenth century trade wars, prosecuted by Britain so that the Indian Empire's opium might continue to reach a ready Chinese market. The military humiliation forced the isolated Qing Dynasty (1644–1912) to cede the then barren and largely deserted Hong Kong island to Britain in perpetuity. The excellent moorings lying between the town of Victoria and the shores of Kowloon allowed the British fleet's Far Eastern Squadron to force the door which had been closed to the opium traders expelled from Canton (Guangzhou) upriver. Beijing subsequently allowed occupation of Hong Kong's 'New Territories', through a ninety-nine year lease whose expiry of which proved the catalyst for the 1997 'reunification with the motherland'.

It seemed a colonial acquisition of questionable value, with a reputation for shady dealings, violence, piracy and tropical diseases which regularly disposed of large sections of the European community. Yet under British rule of law, businesses prospered, with the population isolated from the religious fervour of the Taiping rebellion, the supernationalism of the Boxer Uprising, the disruption of the Republican revolution and the chaos of the warlords. But the Royal Navy's 9.2 inch gun batteries could not protect the colony from the Japanese Imperial Army, whose China War veterans mopped up the English, Scottish, Canadian, Indian and local defenders in a matter of weeks in 1941. The brutality of the occupation of Hong Kong contributed to more enduring injuries sustained by Chinese nationalist sensitivities. The obliteration of European forces, followed by the creation of Japan's Co-Prosperity Sphere, signalled the end of Western colonialism throughout most of Asia.

2

Handover Ceremony

Yet British colonial authority, which was swiftly re-introduced after the hostilities were declared over, would linger for another half-century in Hong Kong. The territory became a haven for refugees from the 1949 Communist Revolution. Displaced entrepreneurs from Shanghai and other mainland centres provided the expertise for post-war industrialisation. Nearly half the Chinese population was born outside Hong Kong. Workers fleeing the famines of the Great Leap Forward and the persecutions of the Cultural Revolution filled the factory assembly lines.

Capitalist Hong Kong became the key entry port for Communist China as its economy slowly revived. When the Korean War resulted in a US-organised trade embargo on China, Hong Kong became Beijing's most important conduit to the outside world. The Communist Party remained underground in Hong Kong and kept its membership secret. However, diplomatic representation was conducted by 'journalists' employed by Xinhua or the New China News Agency. These operatives, based just across the road from the Happy Valley race-course, reported directly to the Beijing leadership rather than to a wider Chinese audience, maintaining a web of pro-communist community groups and unions. The actual Xinhua news, meanwhile, was processed in a small newsroom hidden nearby in the back streets of Wanchai.

During this time, the Beijing financed pro-Communist newspapers preached anti-imperialism while practising pragmatism and waited for the lease to expire. In 1979, Governor Murray MacLehose was told that the paramount leader, Deng Xiaoping, was determined that there would be no extension of the lease. The handover of the entire territory was confirmed at talks which began with British Prime Minister, Margaret Thatcher, in 1982. There was agreement that Hong Kong's special status should be preserved under Deng's policy of 'one country, two systems'. Under this policy, Hong Kong people would retain their British-conceived institutions and practices while continuing to act as a dynamo driving China's modernisation.

This tidy arrangement between mandarins was upset by the uncontrolled events in Tiananmen Square in 1989. Thousands of Beijing students and workers filled the streets, demanding that economic reforms be matched by political freedoms which would cleanse corruption from the ranks of the gerontocracy. Uncensored television reports of the subsequent massacre prompted massive demonstrations in the colony and sparked the establishment of a highly motivated and articulate pro-democracy movement. Distrust of Beijing's intentions led the British government to discontinue the practice of selecting supine civil servants as their gubernatorial representatives;

4

appointing instead Chris Patten, a former politician with his own agenda for last minute democratic reforms. The subsequent elections instituted by Patten resulted in a sweeping victory for Hong Kong's pro-democracy politicians and a rupture with Beijing which claimed that the agreement for an easy handover had been breached.

Hong Kong's handover to China brought an end to the long British adventure in Asia. An unsympathetic Australian cartoonist depicted Britain's heir apparent, Prince Charles, standing dejected on the stern deck of the Royal Yacht Britannia, as the Hong Kong skyline sank on the horizon. Charles, resplendent in a full dress Royal Navy uniform, was clutching bags of duty free souvenirs. The cartoon was titled, 'The last of the boat people'. The return of Hong Kong represented opportunities lost and ultimately an end to British notions of superiority. Public school boys would no longer get rich in the Orient, in doing so coining the acronym 'FILTH': Failed In London Try Hong Kong.

Hong Kong Media

Hong Kong had served as base for media China-watchers for more than 150 years. Those sympathetic to Western interests had almost always been free to work there. Morrison of *The Times* of London passed this way to report on the Boxers. Sun Yat-sen, the founder of modern China, took refuge under the Union Jack, as he prepared the arguments for a republican constitution. In more recent years, Hong Kong became a staging centre for coverage of the Vietnam War and a listening post on the turmoil of the Cultural Revolution. The former editor of the Hong Kong-based *Far Eastern Economic Review*, Derek Davies (1997) claimed that the colonial government had been generally uninterested in the work of Western journalists in Hong Kong. 'Journalists all over the region envied the contempt in which we were held,' he said.

It must not be forgotten that, for many years, Hong Kong had possibly the freest press in the whole region. Even the Japanese press went in for a curious process of self-censorship, eschewing news which did not fit Japan's self-image. It was impossible to read an even-handed analysis of a trade dispute, or an in-depth piece on Japan's untouchables, the *eta* or *burakumin*, or evidence that Japan's sun-god-emperor mythology came from Korea (even academics filled in archaeological digs which revealed such unwelcome evidence). Elsewhere, the communist/socialist bloc regarded the press as an instrument of the Party; the military dictators regarded it as subversive and to be controlled or suppressed. Other newly-independent Third World governments regarded it as an instrument for nation-building, its journalists' patriotic duties requiring solidarity with the nation – or more correctly, its government – all of which spawned the appalling phenomenon of what was euphemistically known as 'developmental journalism.'[1]

(Davies 1997)

While developmental journalism became a state creed in Singapore, Indonesia and Malaysia, the laissez-faire approach taken by the Hong Kong authorities allowed the *Far Eastern Economic Review* to criticise these countries with impunity; establishing its reputation as the region's leading journal of news analysis. Davies said that in Hong Kong, the pre-Patten government simply ignored most journalists who were regarded as socially and therefore politically insignificant. 'Any criticism was by definition uninformed, because the critic had not seen the files,' he said.

If any criticism did penetrate the official thick skin, it ran the risk of being damned with the worst condemnation a government spokesman could offer: it was described as being 'unhelpful.' Protestations that it was not a journalist's function to be helpful met with puzzlement.... However, although there was a certain non-responsive arrogance about the hermetically-sealed bureaucracy, I would argue that at the same time the Hong Kong government was one of the region's most responsive governments to its perceptions of the popular will. Precisely because they were aware of their own anachronism – the questionable legitimacy of an alien, non-elected government – they strove not to alienate the population. Their nervousness made them sensitive.... I have argued that Hong Kong enjoyed a free press largely because the bureaucrats ignored it and assumed that everyone, like them, paid the press and its opinions no attention.

(Davies 1997)

Such attitudes allowed Hong Kong to become the most important centre for Western foreign correspondents operating in East and Southeast Asia, with more than six hundred foreign journalists based there. It was the regional headquarters for international wire services, weekly news magazines, television and radio media. The last governor,

Chris Patten, saw a continuing open media as a key element in the success of Hong Kong's free market economy:

> It seems to me that it is no accident that a place which has the largest number of newspapers and the highest readership levels per head of population is also the world's most open economy and one of the most stable societies. Market freedom and media freedom go together. Free markets need prompt access to reliable information if they are to function. They need public scrutiny to keep them healthy. So, too, do governments. As Justice Sutherland observed in 1935, 'A free press stands as one of the great interpreters between government and the people. To allow it to be fettered is to be fettered ourselves.' Furthermore, the sharing of information and ideas through the news and lively discussion through radio and television debates or editorial columns, all help to meld a community together.
>
> (Patten 1997)

Patten told Commonwealth journalists that freedom of speech ought to survive the transition of sovereignty. He said whether the government of the People's Republic of China would allow the people of Hong Kong to be masters in their own house was a question that others would have to answer. Whether freedom of speech survived would determine the way China was regarded by the world, he said. It would determine how far the hopes and possibilities that Hong Kong had created, were given reality in the next decade.

> It ought to survive, ought to survive because the story of Hong Kong after 1997, the story of this extraordinary construct of Chinese people and Western law, of Scots and Indian people, of Shanghainese and Cantonese entrepreneurs and newspaper proprietors, this model for Asia of what the future might be like, the story of when this city steps out of the old clothes of colonial rule and puts on the new garb of a Special Administrative Region of China, will be a more important, more interesting story than anything that has happened here before.
>
> (Patten 1997)

Under the British, a diversified and complex local media had been permitted to flourish. By 1997, it included fifty-nine daily newspapers, 675 periodicals, two commercial television companies, a subscription television service, a regional satellite television service, and two commercial radio stations. The government broadcaster, Radio

Television Hong Kong, which began transmitting in 1928, operated seven radio channels in English and Cantonese. Its television service produced programs which were carried on both commercial television stations.

Yet Britain kept tight controls on the Hong Kong Chinese press during the early years of the colony. Pro-Communist publications were strictly suppressed after the People's Republic gained control of mainland China in 1949. Tsang Tak-sing, Editor in Chief of the Beijing-backed Hong Kong newspaper *Ta Kung Pao*, was once arrested and jailed for distributing anti-colonial tracts.

> You may only need to look back into your own history to understand how little democracy and freedom of the press one could have in reality under colonial rule. You can find earlier Chinese newspapers in Hong Kong with little blank spaces where the censors had deleted the contents, or worse they won't allow the appearance of blank spaces, the sentences had to be arbitrarily joined together making readers at a loss to understand. For over a hundred years we never had democracy. We never had freedom of the press.
>
> (Tsang 1997)

Tsang said that China's 'one country, two systems' policy implied that a free flow of information would exist in Hong Kong. 'We realise that the operation of the press is different in the two systems.' 'Properly managed, this can only be of benefit to China,' he said. However, he predicted things would change after Tung Chee-hwa became Chief Executive. Tsang denigrated what he saw as the submissive and flippant nature of the colonial press:

> When Mr Patten arrived in Hong Kong to be governor, the press here covered it, writing about how he dressed in his suit, how cute his daughters looked in their hats, how Mrs Patten was impressed with so many rooms in Government House, and how 'Whiskey' and 'Soda' were the names of their two dogs. None of the coward press even raised the questions: What right does Mr Patten have to govern over Hong Kong? How much did he know about Hong Kong and how much did the people of Hong Kong know about him? (The answers to both questions is practically nil). This was the 'free' and 'lively' press after 150 years of colonial rule.
>
> (Tsang 1997)

Of course, Tsang could himself be accused of highly selective journalism if not censorship. While his own newspaper regularly reported on the often tiny demonstrations staged against the British by pro-China groups, it neglected to record criticisms made by major local politicians of Beijing. Although a leader of the Democratic Alliance for the Betterment of Hong Kong, which had failed dismally in the democratic Hong Kong Legislative Council elections, Tsang came second only to the Xinhua [Chinese national official news agency] Director in the selection for the Chinese National People's Congress representatives for Hong Kong.

His paper, *Ta Kung Pao*, also followed the party line from China. Like the official Chinese Hong Kong web site, it chose to ignore the more than 40,000 Hong Kong people who held a candle-light vigil one month before the handover to mark the anniversary of the Tiananmen massacre. It is worth recalling that the Xinhua web site chose to lead its news summary that day with a story about a slight fall in the gold price, followed by a report about a Chinese province which was to present a suitably grateful Special Administrative Region (SAR) with a specially-engraved clam shell. Was this a submissive and flippant treatment of a serious issue?

But Tsang did have a point. In the declining years of British colonial rule, restrictions imposed on local publishers became more relaxed, allowing the local Chinese reporters and editors many of the same freedoms enjoyed by their Western colleagues. Mr Tsang attributed this change to the influence of China and the Basic Law agreement, which he said guaranteed free expression. Freedom of the press in Hong Kong was enshrined in the Basic Law which provided the constitution for the new Special Administrative Region. It was adopted on 4 April 1990 by the Seventh National People's Congress in Beijing. In Chapter Three of the Law, 'The Fundamental Rights and Duties of Residents', it specified protection of freedom of speech, of the press and publications. The same Article Twenty-seven protected freedom of association, assembly, procession, demonstration and the right to strike and form unions. There was also the protection of the freedom to engage in academic research, literary and artistic creation and other cultural activities. Academic institutions were also promised autonomy. Article Thirty-nine promised to maintain an international system for the protection of human rights. But questions remained about how those freedoms would be defined in practice.

Hong Kong journalists were only too aware that China, the sovereign power which administered the Basic Law, also had a constitution which appeared to guarantee freedom of speech. According to Dr Yash Ghai, Professor of Constitutional Law at Hong Kong University, the Chinese constitution was an inspirational and ideological document rather than a bedrock platform on which laws and practices were based.

> China's constitution provides for many freedoms and many rights, including the freedom of expression, but the Chinese constitution is not directly operable. It requires legislation to become effective. China has in recent years been passing legislation, regulating the press and the media. So the rights are to be gathered from the legislation and not the constitution. We argue in Hong Kong that the Basic Law is directly enforceable and it doesn't require any further legislation. So if you look at China, there are many provisions which allow the government to suppress papers, to apply censorship, to punish journalists. I could not say that China has an effective system for protection of freedom of the press.[2]

> (Quoted in Knight 1997b)

Hong Kong's Basic Law, like the Chinese constitution, guaranteed freedom of speech. But the exercise of such freedoms depended on those who created and administered those documents; the members of the Beijing government. In 1997, it remained to be seen whether these authoritarian and elderly rulers would allow the formerly 'British' Chinese to be regulated by the rule of law. Their decisions would ultimately be made on political rather than legal grounds. Even the best of the Hong Kong lawyers could not predict the outcome.

The Flood

The uncertainty about Hong Kong's future whetted editors' appetites for what might be a sensational story. The colony braced for a flood of foreign journalists arriving to cover the handover. Six thousand media people were expected; that is more than five times the number who were in Cambodia to cover the 1993 elections, or about twice those who went to South Africa to witness Nelson Mandela's accession to power. No one really knew how the correspondents would behave in Hong Kong.

Foreign reporters are frequently depicted in the cinema as courageous interpreters of dangerous events, filing stories for Western consumption from exotic locations. Former *Far Eastern Economic Review* columnist, Richard Hughes, whose bronze bust still adorns the main bar of the Hong Kong Foreign Correspondents' Club, was seen as such a stereotypical figure. A heavy drinker who styled himself as a 'China Watcher-watcher', Hughes provided the basis for journalist characters employed in Hong Kong-based works by spy writers John LeCarre and Ian Fleming. In fiction, he was a crafty, if jocular individualist, with excellent contacts among local Chinese people. In fact, his former editor, Derek Davies, came to believe that Hughes, increasingly befuddled by alcohol, often recycled apocryphal tales that he had heard some years before. Richard Hughes Junior further claimed that his father had been a double agent, who supplied and benefited from Soviet and British intelligence (Hughes 1994). He was so impoverished in his final years in Hong Kong that fellow journalists appealed to the Australian government to make him eligible for the old age pension.

In contrast, the elite of Hong Kong's foreign reporters, the resident correspondents, led privileged and affluent lives. Sent by major news organisations to be based in the area covered, they were on full staff salary, received substantial allowances and were often provided with accommodation packages which sometimes included domestic helpers. In Hong Kong, where living costs were as high as New York or Tokyo, it was usually only major organisations from relatively wealthy countries which were capable of establishing bureaux. Predominately American, Japanese and much less frequently British or Australians, these reporters continue to enjoy access to the powerful and newsworthy, as well as automatic accreditation to major events. Long periods of residence in Asia allowed them to develop networks of contacts. However, news organisations seeking to defray costs frequently gave these correspondents regional responsibility, expecting them to travel at short notice to breaking stories in distant localities. Such regions could be very large indeed, stretching from Korea in the north to Kashmir in the west. As reunification approached, some organisations chose to cover Hong Kong from Beijing which, as the capital, was seen to be the source of the most important stories about China. However, in practice, censorship, a different system of government and Chinese dialect differences, made the first-hand gathering of information on Hong Kong even more difficult. As a result, resident correspondents frequently relied on news agencies for tip-offs and Hong Kong-based English language media for background information.

The news agencies and their usually anonymous reporters and editors continued to dominate international news coverage. Reuters, Agence France-Presse and the Associated Press all maintained substantial bureaux in Hong Kong prior to and during the handover. They wholesaled news consumed by other reporters, their editors and their publications, who often used their material with attribution, unthinkingly magnifying the agencies' unseen influence. Agencies operated around the clock though a seamless web of computer consoles, satellite links and telephones which allowed them to flash urgent stories around the world in seconds. Such a process could allow little time for reflection by reporters and even less for margin for checking by sub-editors. Reuters Asian News Editor, Rodney Pinder, admitted that the speed and pressure of constant agency news processing created a constant potential for mistakes which could be repeated with virtually infinite variations. Pinder said that Reuters sought to maintain quality by seeking to hire experienced staff:

> Asia is important enough to have its own group of specialists and all of our people here are in some way or another specialists in Asia. They want to visit Asian countries. They travel on assignments. These central desks are reservoirs for re-inforce-ments on stories. They are handling Asia copy. We are in the same time zone as the rest of Asia and we are all here because we are interested in Asia. I think if you move that away to London or wherever, you will lose that core interest which is a great benefit to the file. We have people on the desk who are a great resource for bureaux. They catch mistakes because they know the story. They are all experts in one way or another.
>
> (Quoted in Knight 1997b)

However, lower salaries, shift work, strict time constraints and little recognition meant that talented agency journalists were continuously tempted to move on to more accommodating employers. The agencies in turn sought to recruit replacements from local news organisations and where that failed, from the fluctuating pool of freelance journalists.

Hong Kong had been a magnet for freelance journalists since before the American intervention in the Vietnam War. English-language government, low tax, and a large local press helped make the colony a starting point for many journalists wishing to make their names in the Orient. Freelance journalists try to sell their stories to the highest bidder. But income from such sources can be unpredictable, so that many freelancers were in the practice of taking casual work with news organisations to help cover expenses. Prior to the handover, many were employed by visiting news teams to help find contacts, arrange interviews and even write the questions to be asked.

The last and largest group of journalists covering Hong Kong's handover were visitors, known in the trade as parachute reporters. These included the many television and radio anchors, who were flown in to place a recognisable face before the exotic backdrop. The London *Daily Telegraph* was not the only newspaper which brought a squad of senior executives, lodged and fed them handsomely at one of the colony's best hotels, while seeking entry for them to the key events. V.G. Kulkarni, the *Far Eastern Economic Review*'s news editor, said that many of the visitors sought help from local journalists. This resulted in the same sources being repeatedly quoted, he said:

> Almost everybody wrote almost the same things. Visiting journalists were sceptical to the point of being cynical. They were looking for the darker side of the story but none of that happened. It went off very smoothly. Many reporters did the same story; cage men [impoverished people living in shared rooms], the housing estates [public housing projects] and the Wanchai bars. In fact, social workers involved with the cage men were inundated with calls. They were overloaded with requests and it became difficult to get their cage men to talk. They [journalists] talked to the same old politicians and businessmen who had been newsmakers in stories in the past. In the end, some of them just interviewed other journalists.[3]

The Club

The Hong Kong Foreign Correspondents' Club (FCC) hoped the wave of visitors would act in a predictable manner, wolfing down enough food, wine and beer to revive its shaky finances. For some years, the Club has leased a three-story building in Hong Kong's Central business district, offering journalists a dining room, two bars, a gym and a work room. Famous news photographs from the Vietnam War grace the walls of the non-smokers' library. In the spirit of Hong Kong free enterprise, visiting journalists were given a complimentary handover diary and notebook, sponsored by the clients of a public relations agency. The club office augmented its usual stock of FCC silk ties, woolly jumpers and umbrellas by selling souvenir T-shirts, coffee mugs and other memorabilia. For those with professional questions in mind, the FCC held a series of seminars, discussing how the handover might affect questions of freedom of speech. Speakers included Rita Fan, the President of the Beijing-appointed Provisional Legislature, as well as legislators Allen Lee, David Chu, Christine Loh, and Emily Lau. Hong Kong's most popular elected politician, Martin Lee, also accepted an invitation to speak. Beijing's new Chief Executive, Tung Chee-hwa declined.

Meanwhile, the FCC's main bar stayed open all night during the handover, offering liquid solace to those who failed to get into the main events and breakfast to those that did. Many of the visitors were veterans of the 1993 Cambodian elections, the most recent big Asian media event on the foreign reporters' schedule. Some clearly saw Hong Kong as a similar story and appeared at the FCC dressed accordingly, rigged out in camouflage combat vests and hiking gear.

Live from Hong Kong

Wall-to-wall coverage was another characteristic of media events in 1997. China Central Television (CCTV) boasted a seventy-two-hour special beginning on the handover eve. CNN and other news channels of TV giants such as BBC, American NBC and Japanese NHK enjoyed flexibility to cut live on the cable or satellite airwaves. However, multifaceted events such as the handover pose particular problems for live television coverage.

American CNBC's coverage of the Handover Ceremony was technically excellent with split screen live coverage of Beijing and Hong Kong in festive red. While the visuals were exemplary, they had a little more difficulty with the textual information. On the stage, the Union Jack was lowered just before midnight, and the Chinese red flag went up. While the commentators waited for Chinese President Jiang Zemin's speech to begin, they filled in time by discussing what they could see of the events from their fixed broadcast points.

> *Male Reporter:* The cheering is still going on. You can still hear people on the streets.
> *Male Anchor:* Yes, I suspect that they will cheer until their throats wear out.
> *Female Anchor:* As will the people in Tiananmen Square, as we can see with our live shots from Beijing, and Beijing's Tiananmen Square.
> (CNBC: July1, 1997)

In the Convention Centre, two masters of ceremony announced to the audience, 'Please be seated. His Excellency, Mr Jiang Zemin, President of People's Republic of China will now speak,' – first in Mandarin and then in English – reversing the order of the languages after the stroke of the midnight. The split screen showed both Jiang in Hong Kong and fireworks in Beijing. On CNBC, however, Jiang was to speak in Mandarin for more than forty seconds without translation. When the English translation began at last, it was fragmented and given in a halting voice.

Female Voice-over: According to the joint declar ... Sorry ... yeah ... Just go all right ... Just ... It is the ... the ... just ... it is the ... the historical event of China and also it is the 1997 ... people will remember this date forever ... after one hundred years ... Hong Kong will finally come back to China ... Hong Kong people finally become the master of the China ... Hong Kong finally entering the new era.

(CNBC: July 1, 1997)

An embargoed English translation of Jiang's speech was not made available before it was delivered. What Jiang Zemin actually said was as follows:

The national flag of the People's Republic of China and the regional flag of the Hong Kong Special Administrative Region of the People's Republic of China have now solemnly risen over this land. At this moment, people of all countries in the world are casting their eyes on Hong Kong. In accordance with the Sino-British Joint Declaration on the question of Hong Kong, the two governments have held on schedule the handover ceremony to mark China's resumption of the exercise of sovereignty over Hong Kong and the official establishment of the Hong Kong Special Administrative Region of the People's Republic of China. This is both a festival for the Chinese nation and a victory for the universal cause of peace and justice.

Thus, July 1, 1997 will go down in the annals of history as a day that merits eternal memory. The return of Hong Kong to the motherland after going through a century of vicissitudes indicates that from now on, the Hong Kong compatriots have become true masters of this Chinese land and that Hong Kong has now entered a new era of development.

Not only the handover events were staged, their broadcast coverage was also staged. And some acts failed to materialise. Presenters may be as near as possible to the action, and present the illusion of being all-seeing, but are in fact transfixed by the glare of their own lights, usually remaining in a fixed location before their cameras, producing words to cover the vision, under the time constraints and pressures of live broadcast. To find out what is going on around them, they often rely on

Source: Hong Kong Government

President Jiang Zemin Speaks

THE PEARL OF THE ORIENT

their producers to filter and interpret what their reporters and news agencies collect, and like people half a globe away, what may or may not be revealed by their own television monitors.

Cambodian Prelude

Many of the foreign reporters covering the handover had also attended a curtain-raiser event; the United Nations-sponsored elections held in Cambodia in 1993. Just as the handover closed the last great European colony in Asia, the Cambodian elections signalled a formal end to the most recent European military intervention in Asia, the Vietnam and Indochina Wars.

Cambodia had been a magnet for foreign adventurers, hoping to emulate journalists who had made their reputations covering the war. Most had seen the movie *The Killing Fields*, and more than some identified with the romantic representation of Western journalists pitted against the evil 'other', in this case the Khmer Rouge. Unfortunately for their ambitions, the war was, by 1993, little more than an insurgency on the border with Thailand. The resulting clash between reporters' expectations and what proved to be an orderly election, proved a public relations nightmare for the United Nations Transitional Administration of Cambodia. Reporters who failed to confirm Khmer Rouge violence accused the UN PR people of withholding information. Eric Falt, the UN PR co-ordinator had the unenviable task of telling reporters that the story they expected simply did not exist. He said many journalists appeared to see themselves as actors in an adventure movie 'showing in their heads'. Falt said the demand for sensationalism led to gross inaccuracies in reporting:

> Before the election we had a core group, so to speak, of about fifty people, which was fairly easy to deal with. One of the problems we have experienced in Cambodia where there are many freelance journalists and when you are a freelance you have to sell your copy. Unfortunately there is a need to sensationalise, to make it a little more attractive, so that your words are going to be printed. We have an abnormally high number of freelance journalists and probably not the best ones. I have nothing against freelance journalists – there are some excellent ones – but some times they are here to make a name for themselves.[4]

(Quoted in Knight 1997a)

Phnom Penh rumours became more exotic as they simmered in the heat at the favourite reporters' bars in USSR Boulevard. Parachute journalists

17

on big expense accounts and even bigger ego trips became desperate as the event unfolded without major disruptions. Reporters began interviewing each other; a sure sign that hardly anyone understood what was really going on. A fist fight broke out between Japanese film crews over an official press release almost devoid of information. Later, there was a frantic rush to a phantom news conference which brought more than 100 correspondents to a darkened Phnom Penh back street for news that wasn't there. When the wet season arrived on election day with a pre-dawn thunderstorm, many awoke believing the long awaited Khmer Rouge artillery barrage had begun. Falt left Cambodia thoroughly disillusioned about media practices. He had given up any desire to go back to being a journalist, he said.

> Do I want to be part of the crowd? I am not sure any more. All throughout my youth, I wanted to be a journalist, but I always thought I would make a difference if I reported on the news. Now I find myself on the other side of the fence for a few years and I don't understand. I am shocked. I am traumatised. I don't exaggerate. I don't know if I want to go back into the field of the media because what I see I don't like.[5]
>
> (Quoted in Knight 1997a)

He wasn't the only one. The Asian correspondent for Britain's ITN television news, Mark Austin, covered both the Cambodian elections and the Mandela victory. He said that many journalists arrived in both places expecting the wrong story:

> There are parallels. Both elections went off quite well. Things didn't go quite so well later in Cambodia. But the elections were a success. The irony about South Africa was you had two or three thousand journalists who came for this mind-blowing story, when really the mind-blowing story was happening in Rwanda, at the very time when everyone was in South Africa. It [South Africa] was still an epic story and I got the feeling that when it [violence] didn't happen people left very quickly. There was an unseemly departure. I am sure that there are people here [in Hong Kong] who think the handover will be marred by demonstrations and the whole democracy story will be about the communist beast which is coming to dominate a free Hong Kong. Journalists have that perception and they will probably come looking for that kind of story.[6]
>
> (Quoted in Knight 1997b)

INSIDERS' INSIGHTS

China Watchers

Reporters came to Hong Kong looking for stories and ultimately reputations. The three represented here played different roles within the same performance. Diane Stormont, the veteran correspondent, worked for the oldest and largest of the international news agencies, Reuters. Based in Hong Kong, she had been expected to give priority to hard news; information wholesaled to newspapers and television stations around the world.

Dan Boylan was at the beginning of his career as a reporter. He came to Hong Kong inspired by the examples of correspondents who had eked out an existence before making their names with big news from the Orient.

Ichiro Yoshida, a Hong Kong hand, this time spent more time being quoted by reporters than reporting himself. He was a valuable source for the parachutists who arrived for the handover, and a recognised voice for distant tabloid editors seeking sexy stories.

Interviews

The Tourists of History

Diane Stormont, Hong Kong Bureau Chief, Reuters

Diane Stormont was Reuters news agency Bureau Chief in Hong Kong from 1995 to 1997. She resigned from the agency in that year, later becoming the correspondent for the British Daily Telegraph. *The British-founded agency was the world's oldest and largest operation news wholesaler, supplying text and video material to newspapers, radio and television stations around the globe. Reuters moved its regional headquarters from Hong Kong to Singapore after the handover, citing 'cost pressures'. Stormont was elected President of the Hong Kong Foreign Correspondents' Club in 1998.*

Stormont: Reuters set up a team of writers who sat at terminals. They set up a system of copy takers [to deal with] the reporters in the field who would phone or modem their stories in. Then the main writer of the day would be wrapping up the big elements into what they call a 'Leadall'. Newspaper journalists usually write one overall view. We actually build up a story like building blocks and then do a final wrap.

Speed is the biggest difference [in working for a wire service]. It's probably more akin to working for radio, but even they only have broadcasts every hour or half hour. When I first started in wire services a beat was measured in minutes. When I finished, it was measured in tenths of seconds.

Knight: *What sort of pressure does that place on reporters?*

Stormont: Accuracy always comes first, they say. You are breaking it [the story] down into elements. You are on a mobile phone.

You have to be able to think very fast. You wouldn't take a risk on the first story. But when the story is out, you can get a second bite of the cherry where you can rewrite and polish it a bit.

So much of the handover news was visual, where did that leave text-based agency journalists?

Stormont: I did Patten leaving Government House which was a pool event. [Reporters were balloted for a permission to attend]. In spite of the television reports, he didn't drive around the house three times. Although that has become the perceived reality, it's not true. They gave us the GIS [Government Information Services] press release five minutes before it happened.

It [three times around the house] has become a sort of manufactured tradition here. Sir David Wilson [Patten's predecessor] did it when he left.

Did the live feed affect reporters' perceptions of events?

Stormont: Sure. Let's take the Patten incident. When whoever was doing the commentary said that it happened, another wire service picked it up, and reported it as given. [In doing so the agency would have passed the story on to its thousands of subscribers.] You say that we can be spoon-fed.

One of the dangers these days [is that] they send off a TV camera [to record an event], and write the story off the TV when he comes back. That's happening more and more. They call it multi-media in co-operation, but it's a dangerous trend.

What impact did the parachutist correspondents have on reportage?

Stormont: Personally, it made me grate my teeth. Many came with preconceived ideas. Others were genuinely interested in what was going on, but clearly had to follow an agenda set by their editors back at home. You could almost divide the coverage into national characteristics. The British certainly went for nostalgia, as one would expect. The Americans banged the democracy drum. The Chinese did whatever they were told, although they were a lot less passive than many people expected.

The good side is that they [parachutists] bring a fresh eye to a story. The down side is that they don't have all the facts at their fingertips, so they make dreadful errors. They get names wrong. They get the balance wrong.

The handover was a set event. It wasn't like covering a war or some of the other beanfests I have been at, say for instance, the first Cambodian Peace conference in Jakarta. There were hundreds of us there and none of us knew what was going on. The people who actually knew were those who had been covering Cambodia from Thailand.

What was the satisfying work for you during the handover?

Stormont: The handover day was the culmination of years of counting down.

I had been covering it since the Sino-British talks. Things started moving in 1997. Until then, things had been happening at snail's pace because of lack of co-operation. Once things started moving you could see where it was all going to fit in. On the day itself, you couldn't be everywhere. But as Bureau Chief, I put myself down for all the big events. So I got to go to the flag ceremony, Patten's departure from Government House, and then I watched the PLA coming across the border.

Yet they were all stage-managed events weren't they?

Stormont: Yes, but I just wanted to see it. We are really tourists of history, aren't we?[1]

(Knight)

The Visual Media Pack in Action   Source: Cheung Pak-chuen

It was a Fun Story

Dan Boylan, American journalist

Dan Boylan was in Beijing in 1989 as a freshman visitor when he witnessed the Tiananmen Square demonstrations. What he saw and how he saw it reported made him determined to return to Asia as a foreign correspondent. He got his first job in journalism in 1995 as an intern on a small local paper in Salem, Massachusetts, USA. Jobs as a sports writer and as a 'nuts and bolts' wire service reporter followed.

Boylan: I always wanted to be a writer. But after seeing so many journalists there [Tiananmen Square] and seeing the impact that television and the press had, showing people standing up to tyranny, I thought reporting could be something worthwhile I could do with my life.

Knight: *What did you think of the reporting [of Tiananmen] you saw when you went home?*

Boylan: My father collected a tremendous amount of stuff for me, ranging from the *Economist* to the *New York Times*, all the way down to

22

the tabloid papers. I was struck by how Americans viewed the whole thing. They were comparing the students in Tiananmen Square to American activists in the sixties. When I was over there, it was evident they were working on a long-standing Chinese tradition for students. The correspondents, whether they were obeying their editors or not, seemed to be making the news palatable and digestible for an American public. In fact the story stood on its own. These courageous kids were taking a stand against tyranny.

Why did you want to be a foreign correspondent?

Boylan: I studied East Asian history at college. I have always liked reading stories with a bit of history in them. There is certainly a market out there for people who focus a little more on history and who don't speak to their audience like they are fools.

Why did you choose Hong Kong?

Boylan: After I got my [writing] speed up, I thought that this would be a great place to jump off from. I knew a little bit about the story here and had done some reading on it. I thought if it was my first venture, I should go some place where I could definitely sell some stuff. I needed a big story I could get a lot of features out of. I didn't want to thrust myself someplace where there is an extreme story like Cambodia, that I had no background at all. I wanted to take my virgin experience where things wouldn't be too crazy. I didn't think the tanks would roll in here on July1.

How did you live here?

Boylan: I was down to about HK$3.00 (US¢39) for about three and a half days. If I took the Star Ferry over to Kowloon, I wouldn't have enough to get back. My buddies lent me some dough. I had some chicken soup I watered down a lot and I had some rice. That was quite lean. I began losing weight then. What was really critical was that I ran out of smokes. When I finally did get paid, I lived like a goddamn king for a few days. I have gone through ups and downs. I came with US$2,000 which was quickly eaten up by getting my flat. But I figured I could get a lot of local work.

So what did you write about the handover?

Boylan: The only two big events I covered were the June 4 memorial and I filed about 1,200 words on the actual day of the handover. In the period between, I did four features.

23

There was a story I was really proud of. I heard UPI had a bureau here and I went there looking for a job. There was a woman who had just come back from Boston. I told her I was Dan Boylan and I filed some stories for the *Boston Herald*. She said, 'Oh you are Dan Boylan! I read one of your stories. It was about the Opium Wars and it was great!' It made me feel good. It was a fun story.

(Knight)

Will Hong Kong People Wear Mao Suits?

Ichiro Yoshida, Editor-in-chief, *Hong Kong Tsushin* Monthly

Ichiro Yoshida was a frequently quoted commentator in the Japanese media during the handover. He first came to Hong Kong as a student in 1985, and lived in the Kowloon Walled City – a massive slum known for its prostitutes, unlicensed clinics, and opium dens. 'It was safer than I thought. The rent was half the market price. And after all, people were living there,' Yoshida said. After a few years back in Japan, he returned to Hong Kong in 1990 as a writer and editor for Hong Kong-based Japanese-language publications. His Hong Kong Tsushin *magazine featured Hong Kong politics, movie stars, and details of Cantonese life such as public housing and tourist guide operations. It had a cult following in Hong Kong as well as in Japan until it folded in May 1998.*

Before the handover, Japanese journalists asked Yoshida many absurd questions. These often came from tabloid reporters who had never set foot in Hong Kong.

Nakano: *Which Japanese media outlets asked for your comments during the handover hype?*

Yoshida: There were so many, I don't think I can remember all of them. Among networks, I was interviewed by NHK, TBS, Fuji TV, and TV Asahi. I also gave sound bites for quiz and variety shows through TV production companies. I don't know who broadcast them. Among newspapers, I talked to *Asahi*, *Sankei*, and *Nikkei* [*Nihon Keizai Shimbun*]. And a Kyodo [wire services] reporter came, and various local papers printed his article. A *Saitama Shimbun* reporter also came to talk to me. For magazines, I wrote a few pieces of my own, and in addition, more than ten magazines called for telephone interviews in May and June alone. It ranged from men's weeklies that feature nude photos like *Asahi Geinō* and *Shūkan Taishū*, to women's weekly

24

tabloids like *Shūkan Jyosei*, and to those which stick to hard news like *AERA*.

What were some of the questions that surprised you?

Yoshida: They had their own preconceived image [of the handover], and kept building their work around it. I thought that was scary.

For example, one of the most frequently asked questions was: 'What's going to happen to brand-name goods? Can we shop for them [after the handover]?'; and 'Can we still enjoy sharks-fin soup after the handover?' I wondered what made them think of these questions.

Who asked these questions? TV variety shows?

Yoshida: These came from women's tabloids.

Other frequently asked ones were: 'Will the Democrats get arrested when Hong Kong returns to China?'; and 'After midnight strikes [on July 1], will there be a riot?' These questions came from serious publications, for example, *Chinese Dragon* which is a newspaper that specialises in China affairs. I thought to myself 'What makes them think that there will be a riot?'

What, do you think, made them think of these questions? What's missing in their picture?

Yoshida: What's special about the Hong Kong handover was that nothing was going to change. That's why it was unusual. They didn't seem to understand this principle. But at the same time, as a magazine editor, I know mass media needs to stir interest. If nothing extraordinary happens, stories won't be sexy.

They also seem to be obsessed with the idea that Hong Kong would return to 'Communist China.' It's true that China is under one party rule and socialism, but as you know, it has pursued economic reforms, and taken an open-door policy and market economy. And Japanese media people know this. Many Japanese companies have been operating in China, and many have had business dealings with the Chinese. And they know that Chinese people don't wear Mao suits, and instead dress like many of us. And yet when the Hong Kong handover came, many [interviewers] asked, 'Will private properties be frozen? Will foreign enterprises be confiscated? Will private assets be taken? Will the sale of brand-name goods be banned?'

These questions came from many magazines, including *SAPIO* [a bi-weekly which calls itself an 'international intelligence magazine']. If these [interviewers] did not know anything about China, that's one thing. But their magazines have published articles on China, and have written about [China's economic reforms]. They have run photos of girls walking around in Beijing in T-shirts and mini-skirts. And yet, when Hong Kong was about to return to China, they were asking, 'Will Hong Kong people wear Mao suits?' What made them think of this? I think they hadn't really sat down and thought [the handover] through.

Would you say it was tabloid people who seemed to have the least grasp?

Yoshida: I think so. Overall more magazine people asked absurd questions, while newspaper people seemed to know what they were doing. These papers have correspondents based in Hong Kong, and they conduct their own interviews and research. So I did not hear questions that were totally off the point from them. But at the same time, newspapers are more limited in terms of subjects compared with magazines. They can't write from a bizarre angle. For radio and TV, I had thorough discussions [with producers] beforehand, so there were no surprises during live broadcasts.

Did you give the same answers to all interviewers?

Yoshida: No. On one day in June, *Asahi Shimbun* and *Sankei Shimbun* printed my interview pieces with totally different angles. I told *Asahi* [a paper known for its liberal stance] that, 'When Hong Kong returns to communist China, freedom and human rights could be gradually curtailed, especially in the area of freedom of speech. They are guaranteed under the Basic Law, but I'm concerned because the communist way of doing things has begun to filter into Hong Kong.'

I gave a totally different analysis to *Sankei* [a paper known for its conservative stance]. I basically said, 'Hong Kong has been a colony, and there has not been much social welfare or human rights. In Hong Kong, there are old women who collect trash to make a living. If they were in Japan, they would be eligible for social welfare. But they have no pension or medical insurance, and need to support themselves. This is a result of colonial rule. But Hong Kong will be reunited with people of the same nationality. And under the communists, I think social welfare will improve and Hong Kong will be an easier place to live for its citizens.'

I gave these interviews separately in May, but they printed them on the same day in June. I didn't mean to contradict myself. When there were ten elements to the story, I gave three to one interviewer, and another three to another interviewer. And the result was two totally different pictures.[1]

(Nakano)

CHANNELLING THE FLOOD
Government Information Services
Alan Knight and Yoshiko Nakano

The Sunset

The sun was setting for the last time in British colonial Hong Kong. At the British Farewell Ceremony, Chris Patten delivered his last speech as the Governor in pouring rain that blocked the sunset:

> I am the twenty-eighth governor. The last governor. Like all the other governors and their families, my wife, my children and myself will take Hong Kong home in our hearts. You have been kind to us. You have made us welcome. It has been the greatest honour and privilege of my life to share your home for five years, and to have some responsibility for your future. Now Hong Kong people are to run Hong Kong. That is the promise. And that is the unshakeable destiny.

Patten's voice echoed at the Prince of Wales Barracks at East Tamar Base where some 10,000 people gathered for the Farewell Ceremony. Also present were 1,000 journalists from forty-eight countries and territories including Nigeria, Qatar, and Vietnam.

An Australian documentary maker, Phillip Robertson was behind a camera filming the Ceremony from a floating pad on a scaffolding. His crew was one of twenty foreign TV crews that were given access to the event. To reach his assigned position, Robertson obtained a press accreditation, negotiated with his fellow journalists from Australia and New Zealand to represent them as the pool crew, and then went through three security check points:

Since we had never seen the place before, we didn't know where we were. It turns out we were on a scaffolding, very high, six stories high. In fact, we couldn't see people, stands, anything like that. You were miles away, and it was like filming a rock concert.[1]

The Hong Kong Government designed the Ceremony to be photographed, and assigned camera positions to photograph it. Robertson was caged up during the Ceremony, and was not allowed to wander down to film faces in the crowd:

> It was done deliberately, I think, so that you were excluded from covering, so that you would take their [official] footage. And that was my main feeling that they organised a spectacle. They had six to eight cameras. That was only wide spectacle shot. No human interest there. Close shots of Charles, and the Governor, but no close shots of ordinary people, no audience shots whatsoever. If you took the feed, what you got was spectacle.

The task of handling the diverse and competitive media which would descend on Hong Kong fell largely to a department of the rather prim and proper civil service, the Hong Kong Government Information Services (GIS). The Farewell Ceremony was one of the official events whose coverage was tightly controlled by the GIS. Founded and run on

Governor Patten at the Farewell Ceremony   Source: Hong Kong Government

British lines, GIS's News Division had in colonial times sought to influence domestic and international opinions about what Government House defined as Hong Kong's aims and achievements. It did so by channelling information by teleprinter to the press, and dealing with press inquiries. The GIS sought to continue this tradition at the biggest and last colonial event, the handover.

The GIS was not merely a public relations department that produced glossy annual reports. It also had direct access to the public itself by preparing local news bulletins broadcast on Hong Kong's radio and television stations. By 1966, it was responsible for eleven radio bulletins in English and eight bulletins in Chinese each day. These included ten-minute news bulletins, as well as one-minute news summaries. This service evolved into the BBC-style news and current affairs produced by the SAR's Radio Television Hong Kong (HKGP 1966:208).

Meanwhile, the Hong Kong civil service provided cradle to grave support for the families of GIS senior employees; offering a package which included private schooling for children, medical care, housing and even a burial plot for those who died in the course of duty. The GIS training manual promised an exciting career, with civil service security:

> On any given day, GIS staff might find themselves locked in meetings discussing high level government policy, dealing with the media at the scene of a major disaster, conducting visiting journalists round a refugee camp, planning a major advertising campaign, out with a camera crew making a promotional film, or even travelling abroad to attend an international conference or exhibition. Through all these activities GIS carries out its task – helping the government communicate with the people of Hong Kong. The message is put across through press releases, films, television and radio announcements, posters, leaflets and books. GIS also organises community activities such as outdoor rallies and stage shows.
>
> (GIS undated)

The handover project would seek to draw together these diverse skills, becoming the GIS's top priority and involving all of its 350 staff. A bureaucracy of career information officers, it had been asked to transform itself into a modern media handler during the governorship of Chris Patten.

Patten arrived in Hong Kong on 9 July 1992 – five years before the handover. The last governor, a politician accustomed to playing to the Westminster Gallery, thought the GIS lacked a sense of direction, not to mention professional skills. At his first governor's news conference, journalists were herded together by a GIS which seemed incapable of even getting the microphones to work. It ended in a shambles. To an extent, the smug behaviour of the information officers reflected that of an anachronistic colonial government which saw little need to court public opinion or even communicate effectively through a media which was expected to dutifully wait for official news from Government House. Many GIS information officers were recruited directly from university, with negligible experience in journalism and apparently even less concern about journalists' need for quick, accurate and colourful material.

Patten the politician thought that GIS was 'hopeless' at conveying the confronting messages he had to make through the period of transition. 'The operation tends to be fire fighting and damage limitation, rather than getting out and selling what we are trying to do,' Patten said later (Dimbleby 1997:76). He moved quickly to create the position of Governor's press secretary, to play the media more effectively. The last person to hold the job, Kerry McGlynn, a former Australian journalist known as an astute political operator, became GIS's Deputy Director (Overseas) after transition to Chinese sovereignty. Before the handover, he was undoubtedly the best connected conduit for information available to foreign correspondents in Hong Kong: a certain source of off the record information, a talented fixer, and a well-regarded raconteur at the bar of the Foreign Correspondents' Club. Afterwards, he was to keep his job, but lose most of his high-level connections.

Some journalists were relieved to see GIS in control of the handover ceremonies. Prior to the handover, the independent Hong Kong Journalists Association (HKJA) was concerned that GIS could be taken over by Xinhua, the Chinese central government's media muscle. Although both organisations were engaged in promoting the views of arms of the Chinese government, the Association believed there were obvious differences in news handling by the two organisations. In China, media outlets were part of the Party machinery and consequently expected privileged access to information and events. In post-handover Hong Kong, there was still a line drawn between media operations and government interests. Even at Radio Television Hong Kong (RTHK), a civil service broadcaster directed by a former GIS official, journalists operated independently and sought to criticise government.

The HKJA saw the appointment of career civil servant, Thomas Chan, as GIS Director as evidence that the organisation would continue to operate as an informer rather than an enforcer of Hong Kong media.

It asked Mr Chan how he responded to China Central Television (CCTV) reporters who were used to privileged access in mainland China. They complained they had not received special treatment in coverage of handover events:

> I told them: there is a notice board over there and press activities are announced there. There will not be special notifications. If you want to sign up, you should do so at the right time. This is the rule of the game in Hong Kong. Later on, people from CCTV were used to this system, and were happy during the whole process of interviews...
>
> The media knows exactly what the standpoint of the [Hong Kong] government is. They respond to the policy and information released by the government. Both sides accept the working style of each other. The media does not want to see stringent press restrictions being imposed on reporters; the government does not want self-censorship of the media due to commercial or other reasons.
>
> (HKJA 1997)

Under the spotlight of the world media, mainland journalists were at least supposed to be seen to be playing by the same rules of access. There were supposed to be no unwritten rules requiring Hong Kong reporters to write their stories in officially approved ways, thereby engaging in self-censorship.

The Rules of the Game

The GIS was, however, determined to weed out unruly freelancers. It sought to control press reporting through a system of accreditation which it initiated in 1995. An Australian GIS information officer, Jonathan Lange, conducted a survey of international and local media organisations he thought might be interested in covering the events. Lange said that the Hong Kong Government prepared an extensive list of official contacts from which journalists could be accredited:

> We sent out the survey to all of the foreign correspondent representatives we know about in Hong Kong and all of the local media. We sent it to our overseas offices. We have ten and they can distribute it to their contacts. We sent it to the European Broadcasting Union, the Asian Broadcasting Union, the North American Broadcasters Association and all of the agencies.

It followed that the GIS process of selection relied on journalists' employers rather than journalists' own organisations to identify legitimate reporters. Since accreditation was initially by invitation only; the process inevitably resulted in unexpected applications as freelance journalists arrived from around the world to cover the story. In addition, all journalists covering the event were subjected to a security check made with the police in their home countries. Accreditation, therefore, was sometimes flatly denied to latecomers. They received a letter from the Handover Ceremony Coordination Office which said:

> At the close of application deadline on 7 April, we have received about 8,500 submissions for accreditation. Unfortunately the number has far exceeded our anticipation. Accreditation will give access only to the Press and Broadcast Centre from where journalists/broadcasters file their stories. Coverage of events such as Handover and Farewell Ceremonies will require separate and additional accreditation. Since space at these venues are very limited, I regret to inform you that your application is unsuccessful.

Chief Information Officer Daniel Sin said these last minute applications ironically caused the GIS the most problems:

> Even in the last week of June we were still getting calls from people wanting accreditation. Some media staff who had not applied for accreditation with us thought they could arrive on June 29 or June 30, get accredited and walk straight into the Handover Ceremony. However, we tried to help them as much as we could and short of giving them accreditation, ensured that most could make use of the facilities at the PBC [Press and Broadcast Centre] and receive all of the information available to accredited media workers.

(Free 1997)

Unaccredited journalists were subsequently allowed limited access to the PBC, and could collect press releases there. However, they had to wait in a queue to reapply each time they sought to enter the premises. They were denied press kits, and were unable to attend press briefings, ask questions or take part in the organised visits. They were also automatically excluded from the pooling system organised for access to the key events.

Marshalling

The Hong Kong GIS had quietly assumed the right to decide who could work as a journalist in the opening hours of the Special Administrative Region. This approach contrasted strongly with media handling in other international news events. In Cambodia, the United Nations provided accreditation to reporters who could prove membership of the International Federation of Journalists. In South Africa, individual political parties such as the African National Congress provided accreditation. The result was an open if somewhat anarchic coverage of the Mandela inauguration. In South Africa everybody got in, but most people had to wait a long time. ITN News producer, Glenda Spiro, was caught in the media scrum.

> It was over the top. We had to stay up the whole night to get into something that started at noon. [Journalists had to queue for media buses which left at 5 a.m.] If you have to go from one event to another it becomes impossible. Traditionally here [Hong Kong] they want you to be early to all the events. But not that early.
>
> (Quoted in Knight 1997b)

The 300 media employers' responses to the Hong Kong GIS survey were used in planning for the Press and Broadcasting Centre (PBC), which was located at Hall Seven in the Hong Kong Exhibition and Convention Centre. The responses formed the basis for selecting a list of media organisations which were invited to nominate journalists who would be considered for accreditation, allowing them security passes to at least get them into the PBC. From these accredited journalists, GIS selected an elite group to directly cover the key events such as the handover event and the subsequent British departure.

GIS described its mass media handling as 'press marshalling'. 'We had to strike a balance between giving the photographers and reporters access to events while making sure their presence did not interfere,' according to Assistant Director (News), Mak Kwok-wah, who was responsible for the press marshalling teams:

> We have never dealt with such large groups of media before, but I'm happy to say that we managed pretty well. We encountered the usual problems such as reporters or photographers trying to get beyond cordon lines or jostling for better positions, but we expected this and could deal with it quickly and effectively.

The GIS identified four major events for journalists: the Farewell Ceremony, the Handover Ceremony, the Inauguration Ceremony and the Celebration. Among 1,000 seats available for media at the Farewell, half of the places went to Britain and Hong Kong. The remainder of the seats were allocated proportionally to foreign countries whose press corps balloted for spaces. 'It was a very tedious process,' Mak said later.

> The media were not unruly. Most of them were very under-standing. Those who came to Hong Kong to cover the handover understood our problem. They realised the efforts Hong Kong had put into organising these events. From the experience that I got from individual media sessions with them, they deserved some praise from us.

Control through Support

During the peak period from June 28 to July 2, more than half of the Information Services Department were on duty in the Press and Broadcasting Centre (PBC). The HK$85 million PBC had space for about 600 reporters at any one time, as well as providing 160 booths for individual broadcasters. It was staffed around the clock by the GIS to field questions and provide answers on subjects ranging from the Maipo

Journalists making news by videotaping the source of their press releases

Source: Alan Knight

Marshes to the new Chek Lap Kok airport; from the economy to the social welfare system; or from the price of flats to the cost of a beer. GIS Assistant Director, Ella Tam, led the team of officers seconded to the Handover Ceremony Office:

> There was heavy interest in a lot of the nitty-gritty about the events such as the exact timing and program rundown of the Farewell Ceremony and the Handover Ceremony.... There were also technical aspects which had to be handled such as making sure radio journalists could get good, clear sound, ensuring TV broadcasters were able to transmit their signals by satellite or helping print journalists send their stories by modem.

GIS staff organised a program of seventy package tours for visiting media which included thirty briefings and forty visits over a three week period. Some 1,900 journalists attended the briefings and 1,200 took part in the visits. The most popular tours were those to see the border that divided Hong Kong from China, and the new airport under construction.

Journalists who came to the PBC were greeted with a bagful of souvenirs – a polo shirt, a designer watch, and a binder containing fact sheets including biographies of Governor Patten and Chief Secretary Anson Chan, but not one of incoming Chief Executive Tung Chee-hwa. The journalists also received copies of the Basic Law and the Joint Declaration, and *The Hong Kong Advantage* – a positive portrayal of Hong Kong's economic future by academics. However, some Japanese visiting journalists saw no use for them, because they could not read English. They simply gave their copies to their local assistants.

Press releases were made available in printed form, on a continuous news feed supplied to news organisations and on a special Internet home page. GIS began an Internet service in 1995, progressively providing separate pages for individual departments. It established two home pages for the handover; a general information page for the public and a specialist service for journalists which included a search function with access to speeches and press releases. The unit operated twenty-four hours a day during the handover, providing updated information within minutes of release. An accurate transcript of Governor Patten's speech at the Farewell Ceremony was available to anybody who logged on to the site. Internet team leader Christine Cheung said that the graphics had been intentionally simplified to allow quick downloads for impatient reporters:

> We found that many of the overseas journalists were tapping into the web site quite often because it had all the information as soon

Chief Secretary Anson Chan visits Press and
Broadcast Centre

Source: Hong Kong Government

as it was available. In the end, we had almost 190,000 hits on the
web site over a three week period, which was encouraging.

Just over a decade ago, according to Hedrick Smith (1988:409), the
Reagan White House toyed with the idea of setting up its own press
agency. It was, however, vetoed by David Gergen, a spin-master who
was a speech writer for Nixon, the communications director for
Reagan, and later a counselor for Clinton, because Gergen thought that
it was 'dangerous'. The United States was not going to degrade itself to
control news using the tactics of the Soviet news agency, Tass, or the
Chinese news agency, Xinhua. Yet in 1997, with home pages on the
Internet, any computer user was able to set up his or her own press
agency. The 'official' stories were readily available in cyberspace.

Digitalised photographs were also available on the Internet site.
GIS's team of twenty-six photographers attended and recorded all of
the major events, working more than twelve hours a day for the five-day
peak period. Unit leader Samuel Pang said that the photographs were
shot in 35 mm and scanned for digital transmission:

> We used more than 600 rolls of film during that period – that is
> over 20,000 frames. Our biggest problem now is that we have to

do all the filing, which will take much longer than to take all the photos.

The Press and Broadcast Centre provided live television links to all major events. RTHK acted as host broadcaster, heading a consortium which included 200 staff from the Hong Kong commercial stations ATV, TVB and Wharf Cable. To aid coverage, ten outside broadcast units were set up, using 103 cameras to cover more than twenty-five events. The core feed was beamed over a continuous ninety-six hours to satellites covering 80 per cent of the globe. The service was free of charge.

In practice, this meant that news organisations could cover the multifaceted events from their news rooms; drawing as RTHK Radio did, on the television live feed, news agency material, electronically delivered speeches and news releases. With access to the main events strictly controlled, a limited number of journalists was able to actually witness the events on which they were reporting. There were very few opportunities to ask questions. Those outside the pool relied on the GIS information feed supplied on giant screens in the PBC to create the 'on the spot' reports on events happening elsewhere. These journalists, many of whom were presenting live coverage, were as a result heavily dependant on the material fed to them. They might pretend that they were on the site, but many were just as isolated from the action as their news editors half a world away. Indeed, some journalists even came to believe that what they were seeing was real, rather than a selective view – a confection created for their consumption.

This control of information and access gave GIS unprecedented leverage over how the drama was reported as it unfolded. The Joint Liaison Group had written the plot some time previously. The public relations teams attached to the respective leaders supplied the scripted dialogue for their respected news actors. The event planners provided the spectacle for the cameras. RTHK made sure that the microphones worked this time.

The official message to be sold by GIS had already been outlined by Hong Kong's Chief Secretary, Anson Chan, in a speech delivered to the Pacific Basin Economic Council in Manila in May 1997. If Hong Kong could survive the media onslaught, it could survive anything, she said:

> Of course we know that a lot of journalists will be looking for a juicy story and Hong Kong has already had its fair share of those. But the headline I'll be looking for, at least in sub-text, will say: 'Hong Kong goes back to China; Nothing happens.'
>
> (Chan 1997)

INSIDERS' INSIGHTS

Media Handled

All journalists who wanted to get near the major events found themselves handled in some way by the Government Information Services. Stephen Vines had an established reputation for independence, as an editor and correspondent willing to criticise both the British and Chinese governments. Vines identified ubiquitous but often clumsy attempts to marshall the news.

Dermot Tatlow, a Westerner who grew up in Hong Kong, was also familiar with the way stories were spun by the colonial government and its opponents in Xinhua. A rising photojournalist on the Asia beat, he knew the need to penetrate the tangle of official 'public relations' to capture the images he needed.

Interviews

Goodbye Hong Kong

Stephen Vines, correspondent, *The Independent*

> News stands in the streets near Hong Kong's Convention Centre, where the handover was taking place, were shut down by the police during the five day period set aside to mark the event ... Hawkers were told that the closure was prompted by fears that they would display sensitive publications which might offend guests participating in the handover events ... It appears to be part of a process of placing a ring of steel around the Convention Centre, both for the purposes of security and to ensure that the Chinese government participants are not aware of any protests or any form of activity which can be regarded as critical of the new government.
>
> 'News Stands are Closed in Police Clamp Down' Stephen Vines
> The British *Independent,* July 1, 1997

*Stephen Vines was one of the most pessimistic foreign correspondents
when it came to questions of freedom of information in Hong Kong. He
claimed that the process of self-censorship began in Hong Kong before
the handover itself, as media owners sought to protect their investments
on the mainland. Vines had been editor of the* Eastern Express, *a
quality English-language broadsheet which closed in 1994, after failing
to attract advertising from Hong Kong corporations. He believes that
the Civil Service, including Hong Kong Government Information
Services, have rapidly returned to the tight-lipped practices common
before the term of Governor Patten.*

Vines: Patten forced them [GIS] to act against their natures, as far as they
were concerned. There was a big relief and as soon as he was out the
door. They bolted it. I can tell you that for the most elementary things, I
have the most trouble getting things these days. People don't want to go
on the record. You have to speak to flunky number six. You are not
allowed to speak to whoever is doing whatever it is. Of course, they
whinge like drains if you say anything they don't like. They complain that
you haven't given their point of view which they haven't given to you.

By the time of the actual handover, and by that I mean the period
from May until June, they were already in China mode. The quality of
information you got from them went very sharply into decline. There
was one very anal retentive person who wouldn't even tell you what the
time of day was without qualifying it very heavily and telling you that it
wasn't really his business to tell you. They were working very much with
an eye to the new masters at that time. [Incoming Chief Executive] Tung
[Chee-hwa]'s office had been installed and the gravity of power had
already moved out of Government House. They saw from Tung's office
which had the most shambolic public relations known to personkind,
that they didn't really have to communicate [anything important].

... Mountains of trees throughout the world must have been
destroyed for these so called information sheets. But elementary pieces
of information such as when is Jiang Zemin arriving, is Li Peng
coming, what will the Handover Ceremony consist of and the things
you needed to do your job, had to be squeezed out and you would get it
at the last moment. They criticised us for what might happen. But when
you have a set piece like this, what might happen [rather than what's on
the agenda] is what is interesting.

I think they did make a genuine effort to arrange these enormously
wide-ranging briefings. They were useful for the people who were not
based here. But it is up to the journalists, even if they are spoon-feeding

you, to go out and get other stuff. It is not incumbent on the government to supply it. It's up to the journalist to go and find it.

Obviously you must have a process of accreditation. But did you have to corral the journalists who were, for example, covering the demonstrations? It seemed to be a complete overreaction. Was it necessary to be so tight with simple operational details?'

(Knight)

Propaganda Came First and the Troops Second

Dermot Tatlow, photojournalist

> PLA troops were very friendly towards media personnel, and were constantly waving and saluting. They were all wearing very neat military attire and white gloves, and were not carrying arms.
> 'Neatly Dressed and Without Arms'
> (*Apple Daily* July 1, 1997:A4)[1]

Dermot Tatlow is a freelance photojournalist who has lived most of his life in Hong Kong. He uses the former colony as a base for assignments which take him to Southeast Asia, Indochina, China and North Korea. Tatlow uses conventional 35 mm cameras to produce photographs which he scans and delivers digitally to customers world wide. During the handover, he was employed by the German Springer press to cover events including the arrival of the People's Liberation Army at the Hong Kong border. In this interview he describes what it means to be 'marshalled'.

Tatlow: There was a bus stop near the Convention Centre where everyone was corralled. They [GIS] had a check list and you had to previously apply for the trip up there. The buses were completely air-conditioned and they wouldn't turn down the air-conditioning. It was about an hour's drive up and the day was extremely hot and humid. You had been in cold air-conditioning so your equipment is buggered because of the condensation. So all of the photographers spent about twenty minutes panicking to get their equipment right. But we had plenty of time up there. We were put into a section along the main roadway just after customs.

Knight: *Were you allowed to move from the designated press area?*

Tatlow: Not really. We couldn't cross the road. There were police lined across the corral where we squeezed to take photographs. We knew the troops would come in there. We didn't know whether they would spend any time there in front of us or just roar right past.

Did any of the international journalists try to leave the corral?

Tatlow: Not that I was aware of. We were separated from at least some of the mainland journalists. On the other side of the road, there was a large CCTV truck linked up by satellite dishes. We weren't allowed into their area.

What happened when the troops came across the border?

Tatlow: There were two occasions. One was at 9 p.m. the night prior and then at 6 a.m. The first troops to come across were in four-wheel drives and then there were trucks with troops. It was pretty strange. It was a show. Leading the armour, there was a big, black convertible limousine and they [mainland Chinese] were filming everything from this limousine. Propaganda came first and the troops second. I haven't seen the images they produced. They were obviously for Chinese domestic consumption. A lot of people argued beforehand whether armour should be brought into Hong Kong at all. It's not needed strategically to defend Hong Kong. Obviously they wanted Chinese people to see the armour roll in. I don't think they gave two hoots about whether Hong Kong sensibilities were offended by seeing armour. [Only about a month before the handover, more than 40,000 Hong Kong people took to the streets to mark the massacre at Tiananmen Square where the PLA used armoured vehicles to suppress demonstrations.] There was a Swedish guy who had a very tight deadline who was using a sat [Satellite] phone to send his material directly back. He plugged in his digital camera to his laptop, added captions and then dialled his newspaper direct.

Everything was so thoroughly organised. There was such a difference between the official events and the unofficial things like Martin Lee's demonstration, scrabbling around Legco [Legislative Council] delivering his speech.

What did the GIS control of events mean for your photographs?

Tatlow: Everyone got the same pictures which were very flat. If you are being kept x metres from your subject, there is only one type of image you can get. I didn't feel I was getting the best image.

At least you didn't have to fight to get a shot.

Tatlow: I don't really mind the fighting. It's part of the job.

(Knight)

41

THREE

SETTING THE STAGE FOR A DEMOCRATIC HERO

Yoshiko Nakano

Martin Lee, chairman of the Democratic Party, was the hero in a sub-plot of the handover coverage. The Democratic Party had set the stage to make the most of the international spotlight on Hong Kong. Approximately forty minutes after Hong Kong returned to China, Lee appeared on the balcony of the Legislative Council building. He presented a speech in Cantonese and in English campaigning for democracy and freedom. Amid cheers and applause, he led nineteen other elected lawmakers who had lost their seats in the Legislative Council to a Beijing-appointed body. They declared, 'We shall return!'

The timely message from the democratic hero attracted extensive coverage. Indeed, the day after the handover, Lee was more frequently quoted in English-language newspapers than two principals who occupied centre stage – Prince Charles and the incoming Chief Executive Tung Chee-hwa. Democratic media strategists understood what the local and foreign media needed and carefully constructed the event. In fact, what Martin Lee said that night depended on who he was talking to. In addition, the quotations from his speech in the next day's paper were not necessarily what he said at the balcony.

The Speech Writer

'All the things [that] happened on June 30 at night were for the foreign press. That was our tactics,' said Lau Sai-leung, then Senior Executive Officer of the Democratic Party, an equivalent of the Chief of Staff in Washington.[1] It was 31 year-old Lau who had drafted the July 1

Declaration for Martin Lee. 'You know, the foreign press expected "something will happen,"' he continued:

> In the local media, interest was not in the Democratic Party. Their interest was in the ceremony. And we were just a story for the local press. But if you were foreign press, maybe the ceremony was one of the stories, the main story may be the Democratic Party.... We wanted foreign coverage, foreign coverage on 'we were forced to leave the Legco [Legislative Council]'.

The Democratic Party, therefore, had prepared meticulous plans. Lau and other strategists were highly aware of foreign media perceptions of the Democratic Party and Martin Lee:

> They think we are anti-Communists. Communist means evil empire, and Martin Lee is a martyr.

Then Lau pointed to a photograph that showed a cover of the *Sunday Morning Post Magazine*. The illustration depicted a towering Greco-Roman figure in front of the Legislative Council building with the headline 'Martyr Lee'.[2] 'American press project [an image] like this. It reflects foreigners' projection of Martin Lee,' said Lau. The Hong Kong handover to 'Communist China' sparked negative coverage elsewhere, but especially in the United States. According to Frank Ching (1997), the *Far Eastern Economic Review*'s senior editor, America's influential press was spreading 'the message of gloom and doom about Hong Kong' – often ignoring the fact that Hong Kong had been a colony without much democracy. Ching notes that, for example, Tung Chee-hwa's election by 400 elite Hong Kongers could be certainly called 'non-democratic', and yet, it was more democratic than Governor Chris Patten's appointment by one British Prime Minister. In the communist oppression scenario, it was Martin Lee who was the fighter for freedom and democracy.

As a Democratic Party strategist, Lau had been involved in the process of creating and nurturing Lee's image for seven years, and yet he was quite cynical about the product. 'They [foreign media] kind of package us as anti-China. It's a good sell,' said Lau, who resigned from his Democratic Party post in December 1997.

The Democratic Party is the most prominent political party in Hong Kong. In the 1995 elections, the Party scored a landslide victory, winning nineteen out of sixty seats in the Legislative Council. For the first time in Hong Kong's history, all the Council members were elected – directly or indirectly. The Council was, however, about to be replaced

Martin Lee and the Democrats at the
Legislative Council Balcony

Source: Hong Kong Democratic Party

by a Beijing-appointed Provisional Legislative Council. Accordingly, the party members decided to focus on the message, in Lau's words: 'People's mandate for representative was replaced by rubberstamp'. In other words, the Democratic Party appealed on the grounds that the people's right to representation had been taken away, and that the Provisional Legislature was illegal. They also agreed on two party slogans: 'Support the Return of Sovereignty' and 'Fight for Democracy'. For a few months leading up to the handover, the leaders of the Democratic Party – Martin Lee, Szeto Wah, and Lau himself – gave numerous interviews to feed the background to reporters.

For the site of the rally, they chose the balcony of the Legislative Council building to which they would technically lose access at midnight on July 1. Lee rejected a request from Chief Executive-designate Tung Chee-hwa to abandon the plan, and announced that he would climb up a ladder if necessary. The Democrats would not submit an application to use the balcony to the Provisional Legislature because it had not been sworn in.

When the historic day came, about nine hours before his balcony speech, Lee gave a press conference to some 150 reporters who packed the Foreign Correspondents' Club. For the reporters who could not fit into the room, the Club set up a TV on the verandah to relay the press conference live. Lee rehearsed some of the key concepts from the speech including the idea that 'freedom' was that which gave lustre to 'the Pearl of the Orient'. Later, in his address from the balcony, he said:

> Hong Kong is called, and rightly called, the Pearl of the Orient. Where does the lustre come from? It comes from our freedom. Hundreds of thousands of Chinese people come to Hong Kong precisely for freedom.

The reporters had stories, but needed photogenic protests to convey the message. 'Why we chose the balcony? Why we needed to struggle with C.H. Tung and [Provisional Legislature president] Rita Fan to get onto the balcony? Because we wanted coverage in the international press – good photos and good quotations,' said Lau. There were other rallies that were competing for media attention such as the one led by Emily Lau, an outspoken pro-democracy legislator who was also forced to leave the Legislative Council. But the Democrats' organised struggle successfully diverted many journalists' attention away from other protestors.

The balcony speech was a superb 'visual press release'. In the Reagan White House, media strategist Michael Deaver perfected the art of staged news. His team produced such events for the TV network news by providing action and drama to Reagan's policy. In each episode, the White House selected a hot issue, and had officials and agency spokespersons repeat a message until it sank in. The script was carefully edited in the White House so that some executive producer in New York would not edit the story-line. For the climax, their leading actor delivered the message against a compelling backdrop (Smith 1988:392–450). Visual press releases were not pre-packaged PR videos that were handed to the media, but they were seamless media events that created a reality.

In the appeal for democracy, the Legislative Council was the most compelling film location. As a result, Lee's words and the image on the balcony prevailed in reports from Hong Kong. CNN carried Lee's English speech live with two captions, 'Martin Lee, Democracy Advocate' and 'Pro-democracy Rally'. *The New York Times* wrote, 'From the balcony of the Legislative Council building, Martin Lee, the leader of the pro-democracy forces in the disbanded legislature, told thousands of demonstrators that democracy would return to Hong Kong'.[3] *The Washington Post* ran an article titled, 'Activists Vow to Press Fight for Freedoms'.[4] Both the *New York Times* and the

Washington Post quoted Lee extensively. *The Times* of London printed an 8.4 x 5.2 inch photo of Lee and his fellow Democrats on the balcony with their fists up. A part of the caption read, 'Mr. Lee ignored fears that he would be prevented from speaking and gave a warning that Hong Kong was losing its freedoms'.[5] The Japanese press was also receptive. Almost six months after the handover, an *Asahi Shimbun* reporter wrote in an essay:

> ... the chairman of the Democratic Party [Martin] Lee Chu-ming appealed to the public, 'As Hong Kong returns to its motherland, why must we pay such a high price for democracy?' It was persuasive. I thought he was exactly right.
>
> *(Asahi Shimbun* December 27, 1997:7)[6]

Below the Legislative Council balcony, a Democratic Party platform exhibited two slogans in Chinese: 'Support the Return of Sovereignty' on the left, and 'Fight for Democracy' on the right. As might be expected, of these slogans, 'Fight for Democracy' was far more popular in the Western press.

Ironically, Singapore's *Straits Times*, which under-reported the scale of the rally, was among the few foreign journals to report the two slogans with an equal emphasis. While two Hong Kong local papers, the *South China Morning Post* and the *Hong Kong Economic Times*, estimated the crowd at 'more than 3,000 people', the *Straits Times* estimated it at 'about 800 people'.[7] The article entitled, 'Isolated Protests as Clock Ticks Away: but host of festivities go on [sic.]', said:

> Democratic Party chairman Martin Lee was set to join the rally at 1 a.m., after attending the handover ceremony, to express support for China's resumption of sovereignty while vowing to continue the fight for democracy.
>
> *(The Straits Times* July 1, 1997:7)[8]

In the Western media, however, Martin Lee was the defender of a struggling democracy. On the handover eve, a headline in the *Washington Post* read 'One Man's Anti-Communist Crusade: Opposition Leader Vows to Continue Campaigning for Democracy'.[9]

One Speech, Two Versions

In the territory where 95.2 per cent of the residents speak Cantonese, Lee gave the July 1 Declaration in both Cantonese and English. Lau wrote the speech in Cantonese after consultation with Lee, and it was endorsed by the Democratic Party Central Standing Committee about ten days prior to the handover. The speech then was handed over to Minky Worden, an American special assistant to Lee, who was responsible for setting up Lee's meeting with President Clinton at the White House in April 1997. She rewrote the English speech for a foreign audience. In other words, Lee's Cantonese speech and English speech followed the same theme, but were not identical. Lau explained, 'We didn't want word for word translation. It's so boring, if you're translating word by word. So we maintained the autonomy of the different language versions to address different people.'

For example, Lee opened his English speech with a reference to the global movement toward democracy.

(*English Speech*)
My dear friends,
As we approach the end of the twentieth century, the world community is looking at Hong Kong at this very moment. The whole world is looking at us. The world has never seen so many countries marching towards democracy, the rule of law, and freedom. As Hong Kong returns to China, and puts an end to more than 150 years of colonial rule, we are proud to be a part of China again. This is the most glorious day for all Chinese people in every corner of the world. We begin a new era of Hong Kong as part of China.

Lau had never heard the English version. He could not bear to see his seven years of efforts to legislate bills go down the drain under the new administration, and he therefore left Hong Kong and secluded himself in Bali during the handover. When I read the opening lines aloud for him, he did not recognise the first three sentences, and said:

Return of sovereignty is China and Hong Kong's. 'World trend toward democracy?', I think, has no meaning at this moment. I think it's detached. Detached. You separate Hong Kong people and Chinese.

The Cantonese version which he drafted made no reference to the attention from the world community and the global movement toward democracy:

(*Cantonese Speech – Translation*)
My dear friends, friends who love democracy, hello. Forty minutes ago, we put an end to colonial rule. Hong Kong became a

Special Administrative Region of China. I believe Chinese people in every corner of the world are proud of it, and find it glorious. The Democratic Party was actually the first to advocate the return of Hong Kong's sovereignty. That's why we have been looking forward to this day. Now that Hong Kong is part of China again, now that we have returned to the embrace of our motherland, we want Hong Kong and China to advance together, and not step back together.

In the Cantonese version, Lee used the greeting: 'friends who love democracy'. But while the English version elaborated the slogan 'Fight for Democracy', the Cantonese version launched into the other slogan of 'Support the Return of Sovereignty'.

When Lee said, 'The Democratic Party was actually the first to advocate the return of Hong Kong's sovereignty', he was referring to a faction in the Democratic Party, the Meeting Point. Unlike Lee who was hesitant to support the 1984 Joint Declaration at first, the Meeting Point members quickly expressed their support for it. They had a record of anti-colonialist and nationalist movements. Their basic values were also shared by other major factions in the party: the Hong Kong Alliance in Support of Patriotic Democratic Movements in China (the Alliance) which organised the annual candle-light vigil for victims of the 1989 Tiananmen Square massacre, some 1970s student and social activists, and some 1989 Tiananmen student activists. Lau, a 1989 student activist, explained, 'The English version reflects what he [Martin Lee] thinks. The Chinese version reflects what I want Hong Kong people to think'.

Lost in Translation: Japanese World War II Aggression

Two sections in the Cantonese speech were completely edited out in the English version. They addressed ties between China and Hong Kong developing along the theme of 'Support the Return of Sovereignty'. The first section referred to Japanese atrocities during World War II. Approximately six and a half minutes into his twelve minute speech, Lee spelled out why he and other ousted lawmakers chose the Legislative Council balcony to express their determination:

(*Cantonese Speech – Translation*)
Here we make this declaration to all of you. Actually, there is history behind this. During World War II, in the basement of this

building, Japanese soldiers secretly tortured Hong Kong people. Many brave Hong Kong people suffered from the torture, [but] insisted on their principles. They refused to surrender. We chose this place to let everybody know that we are Chinese who love our country and love Hong Kong. We will definitely continue to fight for democracy for all of us. 'Fight for democracy! Long live democracy!'

The Legislative Council building was a witness to Hong Kong people who suffered from Japanese atrocities but would not give in, and therefore the Democrats found it the most appropriate place to declare their determination not to give in to pressure. This line of argument was remarkably similar to the Alliance's pledge of action after July 1, 1997:

We are unintimidated. We will steadfastly uphold our original principles and maintain our original level of activities without yielding to the forces of oppression.

(Hong Kong Alliance Web Site)

In Lee's English speech, the reference to World War II and nationality was reduced to one sentence, 'We are proud to be Chinese – more proud than ever before'. Instead, he gave the following explanation as to why the Democrats had gathered in the Legislative Council building:

(*English Speech*)
It [the Provisional Legislature] is against the Joint Declaration, and against the Basic Law. That is why we are gathered here today in this building to make our strongest possible protest against it.

When I asked Lau why the reference to Japanese atrocities was present in the Cantonese version, but absent in the English version, he answered, 'I don't know. Because I didn't write the English version. Maybe they considered the Japanese'. He, however, made reference to the Japanese occupation in Cantonese because it was 'a part of Hong Kong history'. Then I asked whether he was trying to appeal to the nationalistic feelings of Hong Kong people. He answered:

It's not addressed to nationalism, but we just want to make the message strong, and convey to the people that DP [the Democratic Party] is not anti-return of sovereignty. It's not nationalism but it [China] is our nation.

You know before 1997, during the Sino-British negotiation of constitutional reform, pro-Beijing newspapers, their propaganda is to say DP [the Democratic Party] is anti-China, and anti-return of sovereignty. We don't want to [be] confuse[d].

Lau added, 'This is for the local press'. The reference to World War II was covered by Hong Kong's local media including the *South China Morning Post*, the *Hong Kong Economic Times*, the *Oriental Daily News* and the *Express News*. To my knowledge, among the English-language media outside of Hong Kong and Japanese-language media, *Time* magazine was the only one to report it.[10]

Another remark in the tradition of 'Support the Return of Sovereignty' was edited out in the English version:

> (*Cantonese Speech – Translation*)
> In fact, Hong Kong's contribution to our motherland is not limited to economic areas, as some people suggest. Hong Kong may serve as a model for China in many other areas: our developing democracy, the rule of law that has been in force, freedom that we all cherish, our corruption-free society, and Hong Kong people's eagerness to make progress. All of these make up Hong Kong's success.

Lau studied history as an undergraduate student at the Chinese University of Hong Kong, and believes that Hong Kong has served an important role in Chinese democracy since the time of Dr Sun Yat-sen. For him, without political reforms in China, Hong Kong's democracy has no future:

> When I drafted the speech from the balcony, because it was a historical event, I wanted to address this issue from a historical dimension, and to prove Hong Kong is part of China. But I know this thinking is not popular in Hong Kong.

Lau took only half an hour to write the speech which Lee took almost twelve minutes to deliver. He said that it is 'because I wasn't writing for somebody. I just followed what I thought'.

For those who tend to associate the Democrats with liberalism and human rights, it is difficult to understand why Lee would make a statement imbued with nationalistic sentiment. Lau clarified that it was a reflection of the activist side of the Democratic Party represented by Vice-Chairman Szeto Wah, a schoolmaster and former president of the Professional Teachers' Union.

When *Time* magazine selected 'The 25 Most Influential People in the New Hong Kong' on June 23, 1997, it listed Martin Lee and Szeto Wah as two opposition leaders. It called Lee 'Democracy's Statesman,' and

Szeto Wah and Fellow Activists   Source: Cheung Pak-chuen

Szeto 'Democracy's Foot Soldier'.[11] But Szeto Wah was not a familiar name for many visiting foreign journalists. For the handover, the three American networks and CNN sent their anchors to Hong Kong: NBC's Tom Brokaw, ABC's Peter Jennings, CBS's Dan Rather, and CNN's Bernard Shaw. When asked about Szeto Wah, the *South China Morning Post* reported, none of the four anchormen knew who he was.[12] Anti-Japanese militarism and nationalistic movements within the Democratic Party were not widely known among the visiting journalists either:

> A lot of foreigners ask why Japanese occupation era? You know, Szeto Wah participated a lot in anti-Japanese militarism: about the students' history textbook [issue], invasion of China, and also Diaoyu Tai [Islands] movement. So the Diaoyu Tai incident happened in late 1996, at that time, a lot of foreign press [was] here too. They wondered why. Nationalism and liberalism are two ways. From the projection, DP [the Democratic Party] is liberalism, support democracy, civil rights, but they don't understand why you participate in nationalistic [movements]. You know my explanation is DP [the Democratic Party] is just like a hybrid – different elements put together.

51

Lau concluded, 'For the foreign press, it's hard to understand DP. It's very complicated.'

Szeto Wah and Martin Lee

The gap in the Cantonese and English speeches originated from the ideological divide within the Democratic Party, according to Lau. To illustrate the divide, he drew this diagram:

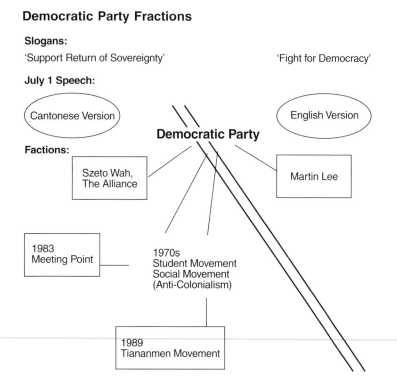

Democratic Party Fractions

Slogans:
'Support Return of Sovereignty'   'Fight for Democracy'

July 1 Speech:

Cantonese Version   English Version

Democratic Party

Factions:

Szeto Wah, The Alliance   Martin Lee

1983 Meeting Point   1970s Student Movement Social Movement (Anti-Colonialism)

1989 Tiananmen Movement

The differences are in relative, not absolute focuses. I am not, therefore, suggesting that Martin Lee does not support reunification with China, or that Szeto Wah is not interested in the fight for democracy in Hong Kong. Nonetheless, Lau said that the slogan 'Support Return of Sovereignty' was more in the tradition of the Alliance led by Szeto Wah, the Meeting Point, the 1970s activists, and the 1989 Tiananmen activists.

The Alliance was established in 1989 in order to support democratic movements, and listed the following five 'objectives' for 1997:

1. Release the dissidents;
2. Rehabilitate the pro-democracy movement of 1989;
3. Whoever ordered the massacre be held accountable;
4. End one-party dictatorship;
5. Build a democratic China.

(Szeto 1997)

The urge to build a democratic China was more evident in the Cantonese speech, and also in the concluding remarks in both Cantonese and English speeches, but was rarely cited by the Western media:

(*Cantonese Speech – Translation*)
Finally, I would like to tell you that, as a Chinese, I hope very much to see China, our motherland, become a truly great nation, and that in our great nation, the human rights of every Chinese will be respected and protected by law.

(*English Speech*)
Finally, my wish today is that our country China, which is a big country, will soon become a truly great nation – where the human rights of every single individual citizen will be respected and protected by law.

On the other hand, the slogan 'Fight for Democracy' reflected Lee's thinking more strongly. According to Lau, Lee, a British-trained barrister, was more comfortable with British elements in Hong Kong including 'rule of law, partial democracy, and civil service bureaucracy'. His inclination toward Western-style democracy was more evident in statements in his English speech: 'But we ask ourselves this question: why is it that our leaders in China will not give us more democracy? Why must they take away the modest democracy that we have fought so hard to win from the British government?' – a section frequently quoted by the Western media.

'Martin Lee is an odd man in the party,' said Lau. However, he went on to explain that:

As a party, you need different hands. It's not like two-line struggle. This hybrid is a positive side. [It] gives the party room to manoeuvre, to face the Chinese government or to face the Hong Kong people.

When the foreign media sought interviews from Democrats, the American and British media overwhelmingly went for Lee. According to Lau, 'Martin Lee was very interesting, they found. Good English, good manner, like a British gentleman.' But only a handful including the media from India, Denmark, Sweden, the Czech Republic, Japan and Korea showed interest in Szeto:

> Every time the foreign press interviewed Szeto Wah, he asked me to be a translator in my office. The foreign press found the interview very dry, because they had no such understanding of DP [the Democratic Party].

Media Favourite

How, then, did the international media cover Martin Lee? We have studied the July 1 edition of the following eighteen newspapers and July 14 edition of two news magazines:

Newspapers, July 1

1. *Apple Daily*	Hong Kong	Chinese
2. *Ming Pao*	Hong Kong	Chinese
3. *South China Morning Post*	Hong Kong	English
4. *Wen Wei Po*	Hong Kong	Chinese
5. *People's Daily* (Mainland Edition)	PRC	Chinese
6. *People's Daily* (Overseas Edition)	PRC	Chinese
7. *Guangzhou Daily*	PRC	Chinese
8. *China Daily*	PRC	English
9. *China Times*	Taiwan	Chinese
10. *China News*	Taiwan	English
11. *The Times*	England	English
12. *New York Times*	USA	English
13. *Washington Post*	USA	English
14. *Sydney Morning Herald*	Australia	English
15. *Yomiuri Shimbun* (Tokyo Morning Edition)	Japan	Japanese
16. *Asahi Shimbun* (International Satellite Edition)	Japan	Japanese
17. *Straits Times*	Singapore	English
18. *Bangkok Post*	Thailand	English

Magazines, July 14 issue

19.	*Time*, Asia Edition	USA	English
20.	*Newsweek,* International Edition	USA	English

Among those papers and magazines, fifteen publications carried stories about Martin Lee. The five papers that ignored Lee were all based in or supported by mainland China: Hong Kong's *Wen Wei Po*, the *Guangzhou Daily, People's Daily* (Overseas Edition), *People's Daily* (mainland edition), and the *China Daily*. On the other hand, when Lee appeared in news stories, he was not simply mentioned but often quoted and, as the Democratic strategists had intended, thirteen out of fifteen publications quoted Lee's statements. The two that did not quote Lee were the *Sydney Morning Herald,* whose first edition went to press before the balcony rally occurred, and Singapore's *Straits Times* which nevertheless mentioned the rally. Two other newspapers in Asian time zones – the *China News* and *Yomiuri Shimbun* – did not cover the rally, but quoted Lee from earlier appearances on June 29 and 30.

If we limit the scope to the twelve publications outside of Hong Kong and mainland China, Martin Lee's voice was just as prominent as the British and Chinese leaders in the official ceremony. Overall, the most frequently quoted person was President Jiang Zemin (11 out of 12), followed by Martin Lee (10) and Chris Patten (10), Prince Charles (9), and Tung Chee-hwa (8). Among the pro-democracy politicians, Lee stood out. While all twelve media mentioned Lee, only three – the *China Times*, the *Sydney Morning Herald*, and the *Bangkok Post* – quoted Szeto Wah. Similarly, Emily Lau was only quoted in the *Sydney Morning Herald,* and mentioned in the *Bangkok Post,* which devoted a large space to pro-democracy activities.

'For the foreign press,' the former Democratic Party officer Lau Sai-leung said, 'we won this battle. We were not just a side story on July 1. In the foreign press, we were the focus. That was our intention'.

Press Release Reality

Where did Martin Lee's quotes come from? Many news organisations relied on a press release from the Democratic Party rather than on what Lee actually said from the balcony of the Legislative Council. The Democrats were media savvy. It was a part of their media strategy to provide the English transcript of speeches on-site to gain international publicity.[13] They distributed the 'July 1 Declaration' in Chinese and English right after Martin Lee made his address from the balcony. It was, however, prepared before the speech, and Lee did not read faithfully from his script. As a result, there were four July 1 Declarations to quote from: Cantonese speech, Cantonese press release, English speech and English press release. In the race against time, many foreign press based their reports on the English press release. For example, one article from the *Washington Post* quoted thirteen sentences from the Declaration: ten from the English press release (77 per cent), and three from the English speech (33 per cent). The following is an excerpt:

> 'This is a glorious day for all Chinese people everywhere, for we are leaving behind the legacy of more than 150 years of British colonial rule,' said Lee, who attended the handover ceremony, then skipped the new government's inauguration. But Lee asked, 'Why must we pay such a high price to become Chinese again?'
>
> (*The Washington Post* July 1, 1997:A13)[14]

The two quotations in the paragraph were from the following English press release, and are highlighted in bold letters:

(*English Press Release*)
This is a glorious day for all Chinese people everywhere, for we are leaving behind the legacy of more than 150 years of British colonial rule.
   ... We are Chinese. We are proud to be Chinese and that Hong Kong is no longer ruled by Britain. But we ask ourselves this question: **why must we pay such a high price to become Chinese again?**

These were popular quotes. *Time* magazine quoted from the first sentence in bold letters, and *The Times* of London quoted the second sentence from the press release.[15] Lee, however, actually phrased these ideas differently in his speech:

(*English Speech*)
As Hong Kong returns to China, and puts an end to more than 150 years of colonial rule, we are proud to be a part of China again. **This is the most glorious day for all Chinese people in every corner of the world.** We begin a new era of Hong Kong as part of China.
   ... We are proud to be Chinese – more proud than ever before. But we ask ourselves this question: **Why is it that our leaders in China will not give us more democracy? Why must they take**

away the modest democracy that we have fought so hard to win from the British government?

The press release had phrases that were more snappy. The sentence in the press release, 'Why must we pay such a high price to become Chinese again?', was more compact and emotionally ridden than 'Why is it that our leaders in China will not give us more democracy? Why must they take away the modest democracy that we have fought so hard to win from the British Government?'

The press release was also used by a wire service. A report from Reuters used the following quote:

'**In the eyes of the world, we call on the Chinese government to allow free, fair and democratic elections immediately,**' said leading democracy campaigner Martin Lee.

(Reuters July 1, 1997)[16]

In the speech, however, Lee did not mention 'the eyes of the world'. Instead he said:

(*English Speech*)
We call upon our own Chinese leaders to give us democracy. Elections – fair and open and democratic elections – guarantee stability and freedom.

Newsweek used another frequently quoted segment from the press release:

'**The flame of democracy has been ignited and is burning in the hearts of our people,**' Lee said to a crowd of several thousand supporters and journalists. '**It will not be extinguished. We shall return!**'

(*Newsweek* July 14, 1997:18)[17]

The two sentences in bold letters were from the press release. Once again, Lee spoke these sentences in the following way:

(*English Speech*)
As we stand here this early morning in democratic solidarity, I will say to the whole world that **the flame of democracy has been ignited in Hong Kong. It will not be snuffed out because the flame of democracy is burning in the hearts of every person in Hong Kong.**

Some reporters combined the press release and the actual speech in one sentence. For example, the *Bangkok Post* wrote:

57

Emotional Democratic Party chief Martin Lee told 1,500 supporters from the balcony: '**We are prepared to defend the freedoms we cherish. The flame of democracy has been ignited and is burning in the hearts of our people. It will not be snuffed out.**'

(The *Bangkok Post* July 1, 1997:5)[18]

Here the reporter used two sentences from the press release as the base, but replaced 'extinguished' with 'snuffed out,' as Lee actually said.

The Times of London quoted six sentences from the press release. The Asia Editor of *The Times*, Jonathan Mirsky, said later that *The Times* had only two reporters covering the handover, himself and another, and that they were fully occupied covering the official events.[19]

Among ten English-language news organisations that quoted from Lee's speech, seven organisations – *Time* magazine, *Newsweek*, *The Times*, the *Washington Post*, the *Los Angeles Times*, Reuters and the *Bangkok Post* – based their quotations on the English press release. Only three organisations – the *New York Times*, Associated Press, and the *South China Morning Post* – cited solely from their own transcription of Lee's speech.[20]

Some may ask: so what? The published versions were only slightly different in wording, and after all, they were from an official statement from the Democratic Party. One Japanese journalist even argues that press releases are sometimes more accurate than what has actually been said. Kathy Wilhelm, who was a reporter for Associated Press covering the balcony speech, disagrees. She said that a press release is 'just a guideline but it's no substitute for reality'.

> The readers are going to assume that those are the words that actually came out of his mouth. And there isn't going to be any room for explanation on how it's actually from a press release.[21]

The question then is what constitutes reality? And which version of reality does one report – what is officially sanctioned, or what actually happens? Many foreign reporters chose the official version of reality based on the blueprint which Ron and Suzanne Scollon (1997) call 'press release reality'. In other words, 'what was expected to happen' entered the historical record, masking what actually happened. And in the end, written record weighs more than spoken account.

In the age of the information superhighway, press releases are ever more visible in cyberspace. The *South China Morning Post* published the entire English press release on their web site as, 'The "July 1 Declaration" by Martin Lee Chu-ming, Democratic Party chairman, from the balcony of the Legislative Council building'.[22] The English press release is also ready for download at Martin Lee's web site.[23] Unlike the Hong Kong Government Information Services which released the actual transcripts of speeches by Governor Patten and Prince Charles, many media-handlers do not have the human resources to change their drafts instantly. Reporters are under 1990s pressure for instant and constant news, and many news organisations simply do not have the time and the resources to check the press release against the delivery. As a result, we are likely to see more press release reality in print.

In the Hong Kong context, this practice poses a particular problem, because in this somewhat 'bilingual' society, English speeches often deviate from the Cantonese version, giving the newsmakers freedom to create more than one reality. And although English remains an official language, the British departure meant that, in Hong Kong politics, English began to be upstaged by the language of photo opportunities for international media.

When I pointed out the heavy reliance on the press release to the speech writer, Lau Sai-leung, he grinned:

> Basically we use the same tactics: when he [Martin Lee] makes a speech. There is press release, it's handed out on site. And then people can quote from that.

Local Reactions

Anthony Fung (1998), who studied media coverage of the 1995 election, writes in his article that the Hong Kong media tends to be more critical of the Democrats than the pro-China politicians. He explains that most of the political beat reporters in Hong Kong are former student activists who are sympathetic to democratic values. As a result, the Hong Kong media holds the Democrats to a higher standard. At the same time the Democrats are relatively open about their plans and operations, and therefore the Party has become an easy target.

The Hong Kong media were not kind to the foreign press that followed Martin Lee either. When Taiwan's *China News* printed an Associated Press story reporting a Democratic forum on June 29, it said, 'Democratic Party Leader Martin Lee acknowledges a packed crowd of supporters during a democracy forum in Hong Kong's Tsim Sha Tsui on Sunday'.[24] A column in the *Apple Daily*, however, satirised the forum as attracting 'a mass of *gweilo* [foreign] reporters':

> [Hong Kong] Chinese and foreigners seem to live in different worlds. The forum which the Democrats organised before the handover was attended by several hundred people. Only a few Chinese reporters were present.
>
> *(Apple Daily* June 30, 1997:A11)[25]

Similarly, many foreign publications, including *The Times* of London, the *Washington Post* and *Yomiuri Shimbun*, reported Lee's determination to deliver his July 1 Declaration from the Legislative Council balcony, referring to his remark, 'I'll climb up a ladder,' if necessary.[26] The *Hong Kong Economic Times,* however, quoted Lee saying that his appearance at the Legislative Council building would be 'anti-climactic', although everyone was expecting a 'martyr' to climb up a thirty-foot ladder to the balcony 'under the pressure of the Provisional Legislature':

> he [Martin Lee] seems to know that his opponents would not give him the chance to run his 'show', and predicted that [the rally] would be 'anti-climactic' at the Legislative Council at midnight.
>
> *(Hong Kong Economic Times* July 2, 1997:A8)[27]

The article also offered reasons why he was popular among foreign journalists:

> Martin Lee is fluent in both Chinese and English, responds quickly to questions asked, needs no script for his speeches; for foreign journalists looking for a democratic voice after China resumed sovereignty of Hong Kong, he would be an obvious choice.
>
> *(Hong Kong Economic Times* July 2, 1997:A8)[28]

Martin Lee became an even greater icon of democracy after the balcony speech. Lau Sai-leung, who worked so hard to set the stage for Lee, is no longer the Senior Executive Officer at the Democratic Party. 'I belong to the wrong historical moment in Hong Kong,' Lau said. Being an anti-colonial activist, he devoted his seven years to bringing democracy to the British colony. But the Democrats lost their seats to Beijing-appointed politicians, and because of the struggle, many labelled him as anti-Chinese and as Patten's running dog. He was caught in a double-bind, even with his boss:

Former Democratic Party Official Lau Sai-leung   Source: Yoshiko Nakano

I wrote for him [Lee] for a long time. All his Chinese speeches in Legco, and [his articles that] appeared in Chinese[-language] newspapers and Chinese[-language] magazines, I was the writer. So I know what he thinks. I understand what he thinks. But I didn't agree with him sometimes. So I used my name to write for newspapers and magazines. Because I needed a balance. [*Lau broke into laughter.*]

Lau has begun his second career writing for a Chinese-language magazine covering Hong Kong politics.

Martin Lee's eloquence in English and the Democrats' media strategies made them more accessible to foreign media. But these media skills bypassed the complexities of Cantonese politics, resulting in journalists showing only a fragmented picture of 'Martyr Lee'.

INSIDERS' INSIGHTS

Constructing Images

Journalists are themselves caught up in the cycle of image making which infiltrates the modern media. As an experienced correspondent, Kathy Wilhelm witnessed the way in which the Democrats sought to benefit from world attention by constructing their own mini media event. The relaxed and festival atmosphere she saw outside the Legislative Council contrasted with the rhetoric of the press releases, which were distributed and later reported.

The international magazine, *Newsweek*, sought to market the expected confrontation by producing two covers wrapped around the same stories. In the United States, *Newsweek* readers had their fears of Communism confirmed. In Hong Kong, the magazine pandered to the readers' hopes for continued prosperity.

As a television journalist, Mike Chinoy was keenly aware of how images can dominate stories. He talks of the Chinese leadership and its unsophisticated attempts to control the message from Hong Kong. But he admits that television news can be held hostage to its own need for drama.

Interview

The Party at the Barricade

Kathy Wilhelm, News editor, Associated Press

Kathy Wilhelm has covered Asia since 1987. She was an Associated Press news editor in Hong Kong during the handover. On the handover night, she was assigned to cover Martin Lee's July 1 Declaration at the Legislative Council [Legco] building. Wilhelm later resigned from AP, and became the director of the Freedom Forum Asia Center in Hong Kong.

Nakano: *What was the mood that day when you were at the Legco building? Was there a sense that something was going to happen?*

Wilhelm: No. Everybody understood very clearly by that afternoon, there was not going to be any kind of confrontation at the Legco – although the main problem was that Tung [Chee-hwa]'s office was still not saying whether or not he [Martin Lee] was formally given permission. My recollection was that as late as that afternoon, I was calling Simon [spokesman for the Provisional Legislature] frequently. He just kept saying that it wouldn't be permitted. So he was taking the rigid stance of not allowing this rally to go on, while it was clear that Martin was going to move with it. And that fed the impression that there would be conflict. But in fact, that was just one person, Simon, creating that impression.

When I went over to the Legco, and I talked to the guards, they had no intention [to intervene] whatsoever. They were not young strong men armed with weapons. And they had no intention whatsoever of using any kind of physical force, or trying to bother him [Lee] by standing in front of him. As far as they were concerned, their job was to quietly sit in the gallery during Legco sessions. So they weren't going to block him. It was a very laid-back atmosphere.

The people from the Democratic Party set up a platform in front of the building. It was like a festival atmosphere. And the party supporters who came out, I talked to a lot of them in the crowd. They had their song sheets, and they were there for a pep-rally. They were there to support Martin in this critical hour, but they certainly didn't expect him to get arrested. And they weren't there to get arrested. They were not all young people either. There were housewives and workers. And most of the crowd was reporters and tourists, and a lot of *gweilo* [foreign] party goers, young teenage *gweilos* [foreigners] out to roam around between parties and between bars, coming to see the action.

When they [the Democrats] set up stage, the police were setting up crowd barriers to cut off traffic. The police were very relaxed. I saw a lot of scenes where foreigners were all dressed up for a New Year's Eve party, draped in flags. They'd come along and they'd give their Instamatic to a policeman and say, 'Take my picture with Legco in the back', and the policemen were taking the pictures! It was obvious that their instructions were to be very relaxed. They were not there for an intense confrontation on the scene. So the whole atmosphere was very relaxed. And I think the reporters knew that, too.

The Hong Kong Economic Times on *July 2 quoted Lee in Cantonese saying that his appearance at the Legco would be 'anti-*

climactic'. But it wasn't necessarily how foreign media characterised the event.

Wilhelm: But it *was* very anti-climactic. Because there had been that whole build-up. He [Lee] made remarks about how he would climb up on the ladder. Whether he intended it or not, all of that gave the cameramen a lot of hope. [It was a] very good image, because so many of them had been closed out of the Ceremony, and they had no other images to shoot, [but] they didn't just want to shoot the parties. So this gave them an alternative, but by and large, people were not excited.

Of course, the place for the rally and a lot of faces [on the balcony] were not internationally known. So that was not great. And the slogans were in Chinese. So that was no good. And the rally was Chinese chants and Chinese songs. And that was not useful for international TV.

The only moment that mattered really was when he [Lee] came out, he shot out his arm. That was visual. That worked, although he looked very uncomfortable. There was a cuff link [on his sleeve]. You know when you have a cuff link, you cannot quite get your arm [high]. He is not a rabble-rouser at all; he is a barrister.

How did you report the speech?

Wilhelm: When I called my quotes in to the office, there wasn't any feeling that 'this is worth a separate story'. So we didn't do a separate story. It was a quote to put somewhere in a story.

I was glad I went out, even though it wasn't a big deal. From a historical point of view, it was an emblematic moment anyway. From that point of view of understanding Hong Kong's political system and the way the political leaders relate to their public, it was an interesting evening. From the point of view of news – something dramatic happening – it was far less interesting.[1]

(Nakano)

Essay

One Magazine, Two Editions
How Newsweek Transformed Articles for the US Edition

YOSHIKO NAKANO

Political media strategists were not the only ones who were spinning the events. *Newsweek* used a clever marketing strategy for the pre-handover special: it gave two entirely different portrayals to its Asian and American audiences. For the Asian readers, *Newsweek* published a special commemorative edition entitled, 'Hong Kong, The City of Survivors: What does the Future Hold?' The golden cover was festive with the big Chinese characters 'Hong Kong' in red and the English title in white. This edition framed Hong Kong people as survivors. The editor-in-chief, Richard M. Smith, wrote:

> A year ago *Newsweek* International started planning a special issue to mark the changing of the guard. Hong Kong-based Asia Editor Steven Strasser and Hong Kong bureau chief Dorinda Elliott took charge, and hit upon a theme – "The City of Survivors" – that captured the resilience of Hong Kong's people.
>
> (*Newsweek* 1997a:4)[1]

The theme, however, did not make it to the US edition. The US *Newsweek* carried an adaptation of seven articles from the Asian edition in its May 19, 1997 issue as a Special Report Issue. They were, however, sold in a completely different package. The headline said, 'China Takes Over: Can Hong Kong Survive?' 'China Takes Over' echoes the 'Chinese communist takeover' under Mao Zedong in 1949, which is an expression many Americans use with condemnation. The phrase, 'takeover', was rarely seen or heard in Hong Kong where people commonly used the term 'handover'. The graphics were also changed from festive to provocative. The US cover was dark blue with a bust shot of a woman blindfolded with a Chinese red flag. A small caption said, 'Model at a Hong Kong Fashion Show.'

The cover story 'Why the World Watches' bore the same title and the same stunning nightline picture in both editions, but they were completely rewritten with the assistance of an additional author. The lead for the Asian version was 'Forget most of the hype and remember this. Once you have been to Hong Kong, you never quite leave'. The piece ended with praise for the resilience of Hong Kong people:

> It is the beauty of a population most of whose parents arrived there with nothing. It is the spirit of a people who, with little outside assistance and with few natural resources, but by the sweat of their brow, have built one of the great cities of the world. It is the strength of those who have survived through all that fate has hurled at them, hammering away, building a better life for themselves and their families – and who will meet whatever lies in front of them with yet more hard work. *That's* why everyone

Newsweek Asian Edition   American Edition   Source: Newsweek

comes to Hong Kong, and why, once they have come, they never quite leave.

(*Newsweek* 1997a:7)[2]

On the other hand, the US version revolved around the theme that China might threaten the future Hong Kong. It began with the subtitle, 'How China treats Hong Kong will reveal its true face', and concluded:

For Hong Kong's people, who have built one of the world's most amazing places with little outside assistance, it will be the beginning of a new, unknown era. With luck, they, too, will soon be able to look back at that stroke of the clock with pride. The rest of the world will be watching, fingers crossed.

(*Newsweek* 1997b:35)[3]

Among the seven articles that were adapted from the Asian edition, five articles had different titles in the US edition. For example, the Asian edition featured a profile of the Shanghainese population in Hong Kong:

Refugees to Riches: The flamboyant dreamers of Shanghai gave Hong Kong some of its grandest ambitions

(*Newsweek* 1997a:40)

This 2,156-word piece was whittled down to 1,835 words in the US edition with some minor editing such as the Chief Executive Tung Chee-hwa becoming C.H. Tung. The biggest difference, however, was the title. It was changed to:

> Revenge of the Refugees: The Tungs and other Shanghai dreamers taught Hong Kong how to be grandly ambitious
>
> (*Newsweek* 1997b:36)

This transformation reportedly angered the main character of this piece – Tung Chee-hwa.

Anyone who has written articles for magazines knows that the authors often do not have control over the titles, and are sometimes stunned by sensational titles that bear no resemblance to the original. Sociolinguist Deborah Tannen (1998:46) notes that '[e]ditors, producers, and advertisers need to stir audience interest, which means arousing emotions'. The packaging of two *Newsweek*s arouse different emotions. In the United States, fear of communism is easy to provoke.

Six months later, when *Newsweek* ran the Pictures of the Year for 1997, it published a two-page photo of the Handover Ceremony. The caption in both US and Asian editions said:

> Changing of the Guard: After 156 years the British returned Hong Kong to China. The day after the July 1 handover, the Chinese began dissolving some of the former colony's democratic institutions.
>
> (*Newsweek* 1997c:22)[4]

After reading this, one Hong Konger snapped, 'What democratic institutions? Life is just the same here.'

Interview

Live Television and Foreign Reporting

Mike Chinoy, Hong Kong Bureau Chief, CNN

Mike Chinoy, CNN's Hong Kong bureau chief, began China-watching in 1976. He provided much of the live global television coverage of the Tiananmen Square massacre; an event which provides the core of his book, China Live.

Chinoy: Television is fantastic at conveying movement, action and emotion. Powerful visual images were the great strength of television. China is a visually powerful place. There are all kinds of wonderful images. The handover in Hong Kong ... was scripted for the cameras. There was the contrasting symbolism of the disappearing British colonial presence and the looming Chinese presence. Hong Kong itself is spectacular. In that sense TV was very good in allowing people to share some of the physical and emotional process of the experience. But it's much more difficult to convey difficult and complex ideas, the subtleties and nuances.

Knight: *After seeing a lot of television coverage, you get the feeling that the images overwhelmed the story.*

Chinoy: That is always a problem. The images were very powerful here. You had the governor departing, the bagpipes and the guys in kilts, and the Royal Yacht. It contrasted with the symbolism of an emerging China with the Chinese leadership, the People's Liberation Army arriving and the replaying of images from Tiananmen Square. Both television and print coverage focused very heavily on China's determination to send in the troops with all the jitters that raised. There were thousands of soldiers, ramrod stiff, coming across the border. That was a classic case of the image and the underlying reality not being the same. One of the conclusions I have come to about the whole process of the handover, which the press did not give enough weight to, is the degree to which the dynamic between the British and the Chinese was so poisonous, that the two sides dealt with each other in a way which distorted the reality on the ground. They related to each other like a couple in a bad marriage. They dealt with each other by fighting all the time. The extreme gestures on both sides exacerbated that. Once the British left, the atmosphere changed markedly.

The PLA's arrival showed how images of the same event were interpreted totally differently by two cultures. To people who had been allowed to see the images of Tiananmen Square, the sight of the PLA coming across the border was menacing. The Chinese meanwhile played up these images.

Chinoy: They played it up not to intimidate the Hong Kong people. They were playing them up to celebrate Chinese sovereignty. But I had friends in the States who called up and thought there was martial law in Hong Kong after that.

The PLA's arrival was interpreted incorrectly by many people as China imposing its writ on Hong Kong and sending an intimidating signal to a place that was still jittery about memories about Tiananmen Square. I feel the reason for what they did was deeply rooted in questions of national pride and humiliations dating back to the Opium Wars. The Chinese leadership was driven by the sense that this was a piece of Chinese territory stolen through military force by the wicked British imperialists. They decided to put their soldiers in to show that they had taken it back. It's a bit like a dog peeing on a tree. Having made that point the PLA have disappeared. They are invisible. They take the lowest possible public profile in every situation.

These conflicting interpretations surely highlight one of the key weaknesses of live television. What can you do as a journalist to counter what you know must be a false impression generated by what you are showing?

Chinoy: Sometimes there's not much you can do. The images do exist. As an honest journalist you try to be fair about what you say about it. You don't cut from a shot of tanks in 1989 to the PLA on the Hong Kong border. There were some American television programs which really gave the impression that the butchers of Beijing were arriving. When the Chinese send 5,000 troops across the border, you have to show it.

But you can include your own analysis, commentators and juxtapose other images like the thousands of happy residents in the New Territories who welcomed the PLA. Just witness all these people out in the rain cheering, holding garlands.

Is it true that Western representations of Chinese policies can be hindered by the Beijing leadership's reluctance to appear on television?

Chinoy: Sure. Even when the Chinese might have a legitimate case, they are so inept at making it. Their system discourages the sort of relationship with the media that will allow them to put their case. They don't understand the concepts of spin. There are all sorts of reasons rooted in the Chinese system. More often than not, they don't understand what we want, the deadline pressure, the importance of actual pictures and the value of sound bites. They complain the coverage is biased. Whereas if they made people available to respond to specific circumstances, they would be able to make their case. But instead they really hurt themselves.

PLA Drives Across the Border

Tung Chee-hwa has been getting Western media advice on media appearance and accessibility.

Chinoy: Tung had a very hard lesson. He got hammered. I think he acknowledged he was not accessible enough. He got better the closer it came to the handover. His perceptions of the press were different to those in Beijing. He just thought it was a bother at first. He thought he had more important things to do than waste his time with journalists. I don't think he appreciated the impact of public opinion around the world and the way that can have concrete, negative implications for Hong Kong. When he did appear on CNN, he was very effective. People asked why he didn't do more appearances. Even so, he took some convincing [to appear on CNN].

In the Chinese case it's a bit different. Their policies are so rigidly worked out. There's a party line and you can't deviate from it. It's issued in a written form and only a few people are allowed to articulate it. Lower ranking people don't want to risk their necks by doing something which may or may not come off. Whereas Tung may see the [Western] media as a pain in the neck, they see them as the enemy. To them it's something to be controlled and not a tool to be used.

What sort of demands do they make on you as a reporter?

Chinoy: They always want questions in advance. It is always a difficult point in negotiations. Sometimes you can give them topics and not questions. They are control freaks. They want everything scripted and no surprises. There's no easy give and take. It's the nature of that authoritarian system. They are learning. Look at Jiang Zemin in the States. He was a little stilted but he got there. A side of him came out which you would never see in China.

The Western press had an overdone but not entirely unreasonable view of the threat to Hong Kong. It had been fuelled by the very nasty rhetoric which went back and forth between the British and the Chinese. If Patten had said it was Tuesday, Beijing would have said it was Wednesday. When he left it was like a thorn being removed from the Chinese foot.

(Knight)

CHAPTER FOUR

WASHING AWAY ONE HUNDRED YEARS OF SHAME
Chinese Press and the New Consumerism

Alan Knight

> The *Guangzhou Daily* Press Group ... takes as its responsibility the tasks of pushing forward the development of the Chinese newspaper industry and the reform of journalism.
>
> Li Yunjiang, *Guangzhou Daily*'s President and Editor in Chief

Chinese press coverage of the end of the colonial occupation of Hong Kong could be expected to be enthusiastic and nationalistic in tone and content. But behind the wooden rhetoric and propaganda slogans that preceded the handover, there was genuine celebration of the end of what was seen as a period of humiliation for China. The British may have created China's wealthiest and best-governed city, but they had done so at the expense of Chinese national pride.

Much of the mainland Chinese press had acted as a government voice since imperial times. The introduction of Western printing technology in the nineteenth century encouraged the development of some independent newspapers; but these were harassed by the Qing regime, frequently muzzled by the Kuomintang and finally snuffed out by the People's Republic of China in 1949 (Zhang 1997:59–91). Since then, all major press operations have been under the control of, or operated by, the Communist Party. Uniformity of opinion within the party press peaked during the Cultural Revolution, was relaxed during the early Deng era and then tightened again after the Tiananmen Square massacre in 1989 (CPJ 1993). Since that time, economic reforms initiated by the central government resulted in a diversification of business ownership and rapid growth in individual and family wealth.

But the vexed question remained. Would economic liberalisation allow for more intellectual and ultimately political diversity? When it came to the handover, would the Chinese press still speak with one voice?

If the official propaganda were to be believed, lingering resentments about the Opium Wars could be expected to be found where the one-sided battles were fought; along the Pearl River where the Royal Navy men of war routed the Qing war junks so that British Marines could storm ashore to proselytise free trade at the point of the bayonet. Anti-British feelings might be presumed to be strongest at the city of Guangzhou where the Chinese authorities closed and sacked the foreign opium factories and where some time later the British military used the magistrate's palace for target practice before occupying and looting the city.

China's Wild East

One hundred and fifty years later, Guangzhou had again become one of mainland China's richest cities. It had done so through remitted earnings, trade and ultimately joint ventures with Hong Kong, the colonial sister city which had grown on territory ceded after China's defeat in the Anglo-Chinese wars. The two cities shared a common Cantonese language and, with time, the knowledge that somehow the oppressed colonial subjects enjoyed a lifestyle infinitely more affluent than the worthy citizens of the liberated motherland across the barbed wired border.

When the *Guangzhou Daily* became the first of China's state-owned newspapers to be reconstituted as a news group, it was able to harvest the tide of wealth flooding into the Pearl River Delta with economic liberalisation. By looking to Hong Kong and the West for style and, to some extent, issues, it rapidly developed into one of the most modern newspapers in China, with a daily circulation of more than 800,000 copies. By creating its own distribution system, it has freed itself of the slow and inefficient postal bureaucracy and is mostly sold directly to readers, instead of being bundled out to state-controlled work units. As a rapidly diversifying corporation, it developed both vertically, initiating new print facilities, production centres and distribution outlets, and horizontally, building apartment blocks, entertainment centres and even establishing at least one subsidiary in Hong Kong. The enormous revenues generated from rising circulation and the exploitation of affluence are creating a Chinese news corporation of unprecedented wealth and, inevitably, political power.

The group's total income grew from 122 million yuan (US$14.7 million) in 1992 to 1.2 billion yuan (US$144.7 million) in 1996; an increase of more than 800 per cent. At the same time, advertising income jumped from 39 million yuan (US$4.7 million) in 1991, and 510 million yuan (US$61.5 million) in 1996; a 1,200 per cent increase. In 1996, profits had increased to 362 million yuan (US$43.6 million) requiring a payout of 98 million yuan in taxes. In the same year, the total assets of *Guangzhou Daily* amounted to 1.61 billion yuan (US$194.1 million), the net assets 1.12 billion yuan (US$135.1 million). Madam He, the Managing Editor of the *Guangzhou Daily*, said that the paper, founded in 1952, had originally served the industrial and commercial sectors, government organisations, schools and enterprises.

When we entered the 1990s, our newspaper began making a lot of changes. As a result of China's economic reforms, the entire economic system of Guangzhou region has shifted substantially from the planned economy to a market economy. [To meet] this change, we widened our audience to [appeal to] the general public and ordinary citizens. Our current circulation not only covers the Guangzhou area, but also the Pearl River Delta cities which surround Guangzhou.[1]

Sales of the paper were booming in the year of the Hong Kong handover. The circulation was about 810,000 copies in March 1997, increasing to 840,000 copies by the first week of April. Compared with that of March in the previous year, the circulation had increased by more than 100,000 copies. About 80 per cent of the newspapers went to personal subscribers while the remainder were subscribed to companies and public organisations. About 65 per cent of the papers were circulated in the Guangzhou urban area, 30 per cent in the Pearl River Delta and the remaining 5 per cent outside Guangdong and even outside the country. President Li Yunjiang:

These are some promises to our readers. Firstly, the distribution of today's newspapers will be finished before 8:00 a.m. We have our own distribution trucks. That means you can get our newspapers at your breakfast table. But it is not early enough, because Chinese people begin their work at eight o'clock in the morning. If we can make it one hour earlier, it will be much better. Now our goal is to close the distribution of our newspapers sixty or seventy-five minutes earlier. Secondly, *Guangzhou Daily* publishes the most pages in China, with twenty to thirty-two pages every day, many of which are colour pages.... Thirdly, we promise to deliver newspaper to where readers live. We have also set up hotlines and readers can complain about our services.[2]

The *Guangzhou Daily* was produced in what was already a very modern newspaper premises. Signs were posted around the newsroom saying, 'Farewell to paper and pens. I can do it. You can, too!'. The two hundred and fifty reporters who worked in the air-conditioned headquarters had ergonomic work stations linked by computers to sub-editors composing the paper with full pagination; a facility enjoyed by only about half of US newspapers at that time. Recruited from some of China's best universities, the journalists represented an elite in the mainland information industry. They had access to a computerised library with about 150,000 books and periodicals, a modern gymnasium, tennis courts and a spotless medical clinic staffed by nurses in starched uniforms.

The *Guangzhou Daily* Group operated its own home-page and web site on the Internet, through which it claimed to have about 140,000 readers world-wide. Some journalists had their own e-mail addresses, but many more were Internet literate, using the net to bypass official propaganda and access international news reporting.

Yet the group faced a series of challenges in the opening and very lucrative market. State monopolies were being abolished and with them secure markets. Competition was becoming intense in China with more than 2,800 newspapers fighting for readership and advertising revenue. Hong Kong papers had not yet made inroads into the Chinese newspaper market and under the policy of 'one country, two systems' seemed unlikely to do so in the short term. But the threat to sales and advertising revenue remained. Rupert Murdoch created a dummy edition of the *North China Morning Post* before he switched to television in Hong Kong and sold the colony's leading English-language newspaper, the *South China Morning Post,* to Malaysian Chinese entrepreneur, Robert Kuok. An agreement to print and distribute copies of the *Hong Kong Standard* newspaper lapsed after a short time. Restrictions on importing foreign press continued to be enforced. Ethnic Chinese tourists arriving with newspapers under their arms at Guangzhou's palatial new tourist railway station were still being stopped, and their papers confiscated in 1997.

The New Consumerism

Hong Kong culture had, however, already jumped the border. Visitors to Guangdong province in the early 1990s could see what appeared to be large, crudely made radar dishes, mounted on almost every rooftop and pointing back towards Hong Kong. They were not bugging devices vainly hoping to glean what was left of Britain's military secrets. Rather, they were locally-designed and manufactured long distance television aerials. A subsequent banning order issued by Beijing resulted in many of them being pulled down. But improved technology allowed consumers to erect smaller, less obvious, equipment and still tune in. Guangzhou television executives admitted privately that Hong Kong television with its soapie dramas, glitzy quiz shows and above all sophisticated advertising had overwhelming appeal to a mainland public jaded by stuffy and hectoring propaganda pieces. The People's Armed Police still stood on guard with machine pistols and naked bayonets outside the studios and master control rooms of state television and radio. But their audience had already escaped.

Hong Kong television created a consumer market which exploded in Guangdong as restrictions on foreign companies were removed. Locals ate McDonalds' hamburgers, wore U2 and Giordano (Hong Kong brands) clothes and increasingly drove or were driven in Lexus and Mercedes cars. It even became fashionable to order expensive Australian red (a lucky colour) wine at restaurants, mix it with lemonade and then toast the new found success.

Guangzhou residents were becoming richer and more able to buy the tantalising consumer goods so flagrantly enjoyed for so long by the Cantonese pop stars and television soap personalities seen living in Hong Kong. According to the Guangdong Provincial Statistical Year Book, average per capita earnings increased from 1,842 yuan (US$222) in 1990 to 6,118 yuan (US$738) in 1995, a more than 300 per cent increase (GPG 1996:75). This compares to 1965, at the beginning of the Cultural Revolution when the figure was 198 yuan (US$23.9). At the end of that turbulent period, income had only risen to 258 yuan (US$31). Deng's view that 'It is good to grow rich' had resulted in a massive increase in disposable income. Literate, newspaper-reading city dwellers could be expected to earn much more than the official average. It should also be remembered that these figures take no account of unreported or even illegal earnings which could be very substantial in the freebooting, rapidly developing economic areas.

The provincial statistics showed a 30.5 per cent increase in the number of people employed by privately-owned enterprise in a single year from 1994 to 1995 (GPG 1996:138). However, the official figures did not clearly show the full extent of the shift away from state-owned enterprises to private operations. Generous investment by Hong Kong and foreign entrepreneurs had created a privately-owned industrial park which stretched across the entire Pearl River Delta region. Guangdong, unlike its rival Shanghai with its reliance on state-owned heavy industry, was being driven by private enterprise.

State enterprises, like most of those in China, were unprofitable, overstaffed and producing goods that were increasingly difficult to sell. They were in decline. For newspapers this meant that such shaky operations were increasingly unable to bulk-purchase official news-papers to be leisurely read during company time by their underworked employees. In Guangzhou city, the construction of a new urban transit system could be expected to dramatically change readers' travel habits, requiring a complete rethinking of newspaper sales.

Colonial Rule was Terminated Last Night!

For a newspaper which looked to Hong Kong for its style and inspiration, the handover promised to become the publishing event of the year. Hong Kong and Guangdong people speak a common dialect, with branches of many extended families on both sides of the border. In a province where Hong Kong investment, currency and culture dominate, the return of the former colony to China could be expected to be very big news indeed. Coverage of the event was almost breathlessly promoted:

> Recording the historical moment of Hong Kong's return to the motherland. An unprecedented event in the history of news in China! On July 1, the *Guangzhou Daily* will publish a 97-page issue. The newspaper of the day will become a 'Golden Edition' and a 'Special Edition'. A collectors' item! Please look out for further detailed announcements.
>
> (*Guangzhou Daily* June 27, 1997:1)[3]

A team of ten journalists was despatched across the border to the still British-controlled territory. Although the New China News Agency sternly warned that it retained the monopoly of 'international' news, Guangzhou journalists were determined to look for the local angles among their fellow Cantonese-speaking brethren.

The *Guangzhou Daily* marked July 1 by producing a three-edition special, with a full colour cover showing the handover ceremony. In the report, 'Newspaper sales have gone crazy', staff reporters described the response by the Guangzhou newspaper buying public:

> At 11:30 a.m., the midday issue was not yet ready for sale, but there were already long queues at retail sites. The delivery trucks could not get out the gate of the distribution department because of the crowds. In Bailing Street, there were so many people waiting, that the seller moved his sales-point to a relatively quiet spot behind Dr Sun Memorial Hall. However, he was spotted by people, and there were soon long queues there. Many people waited for hours for the midday issue after the morning issue was sold out. In the Tian He area, many sales-points did not have enough copies because paper sellers sold their copies right after they got out the gate of the *Daily*'s distribution department. At the gate, there were hundreds of people waiting to buy morning and midday issues, even when a 'one copy per person' rule was applied.
>
> The phones at our editorial and distribution departments ran hot. Readers demanded reprints to meet demand. Some people complained that price jumped from 1.5 yuan (US¢18) to five or even ten yuan each. Some places called in police to clear the confusion and keep the situation under control. Those readers who subscribed to the *Daily* are happy because their copies were delivered to their door, and they were thus saved the trouble. As this piece is going to print, many people are still waiting to buy copies, but it is hard to say whether they will be in luck.
>
> (*Guangzhou Daily* July 1, 1997:78)[4]

Pictures accompanying the report showed milling crowds and a newspaper seller with a hand-written sign saying, '*Daily* sold out'. The special edition was an advertising bonanza, packed with advertisements for real estate and luxury consumer goods. In the spirit of the new capitalist China, it even advertised 'A Guide to Hong Kong Tycoons.' 'Readers can gain knowledge about their business structures, major interests, family assets, success stories, personalities and hobbies,' it offered. The book was said to have documented Hong Kong billionaires' investment in Guangzhou.

Like the Beijing government's official *China Daily*, the *Guangzhou Daily*'s front page carried a large photograph of the handover ceremony. The photographs were taken from almost the same angle

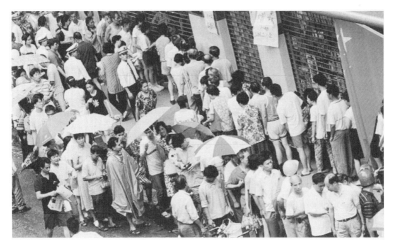

People wait to buy special handover   Source: Zhang Weiqing, *Guangzhou Daily*
edition of *Guangzhou Daily*

at almost the same time, just after midnight on July 1. But there were subtle differences. The *Guangzhou Daily*, in full colour, took in both the Chinese and British delegations, even including kilted members of the British honour guard. Its headline read, 'At Zero Hour Today Hong Kong Returned to the Motherland'. The page carried official messages; the text of Jiang Zemin's order to the People's Liberation Army to enter Hong Kong.

> This is a solemn task and heavy responsibility for you. After you enter Hong Kong, you must uphold the principles of the PLA to serve the people wholeheartedly, continue your good traditions, loyally carry out your duties, maintain high-level discipline, and administer the army through the rule of law. You must build the forces into 'an army of might' and 'an army of civility', which is politically up-to-standard, militarily strong, has a fine work style, is highly disciplined, and offers powerful protection.
>
> (*Guangzhou Daily* July 1, 1997:1)[5]

China's official international English-language newspaper, the *China Daily*, in austere black-and-white print centred on the Chinese delegation, cropping the photograph so that Governor Patten was neatly excised. 'Home at Last', it reported. The *China Daily* also

79

carried two smaller photographs: one of the countdown board at Tiananmen Square; the other of a frowning British Prime Minister, Tony Blair, and Prince Charles looking sideways at President Jiang Zemin and an apparently gloating Premier Li Peng.

Chinese newspapers were required to carry official information and the *Guangzhou Daily* was no exception here. It carried exactly the same editorial as the official *People's Daily* and the international *China Daily*. The *official* editorial praised Hong Kong's return to China in nationalistic purple prose. The bells tolling in the East would be listened to solemnly throughout the world, it said.

It is time for the Chinese nation to wash away 100 years of shame and feel proud and elated!

With the conclusion of the handover ceremony between the Chinese and British governments and the announcement of the establishment of the Hong Kong Special Administrative Region, the long-awaited dream of the Chinese nation and the long-cherished wish of generations for Hong Kong's return is fulfilled. The day will draw attention from all over the world, and be inscribed in history books forever.

At the moment when the whole nation celebrates Hong Kong's homecoming, it should be kept in the minds of all the tortuous paths that the Chinese people have gone through towards the historical day. For the day to come, millions of heroic sons and daughters of the Chinese nation struggled against colonial rule and resisted foreign aggression unyieldingly, and in wave upon wave, to defend their national dignity and maintain the integrity of the country's sovereignty.

(*Guangzhou Daily* July 1, 1997:50)[6]

The '100 years of shame' slogan could heard and seen throughout the length and breadth of China; in newspapers, on huge wall posters and on the lips of ordinary citizens supposedly making spontaneous comments to earnest CCTV reporters. In characteristic lack of understatement, the editorial said that the 'one country, two systems' policy was being widely acclaimed as a theory of broad vision and a work of great creativity in the history of civilisation.

The world can expect to see a brighter future for China. With a 5,000-year-old history of civilisation, the Chinese nation will stride ahead with pride into the new century toward the magnificent goal of modernisation. The reunification of China

洗雪百年国耻

Guangzhou street: Sign in the foreground says
'Washing Away One Hundred Years of Shame'

Source: Yoshiko Nakano

and the revitalisation of the Chinese nation will become a
glorious fact in the future.

(*Guangzhou Daily* July 1, 1997:50)[7]

But would 'the magnificent goal of modernisation' merely be defined in
economic and technological terms? *Guangzhou Daily* executive,
Madam He, was asked whether the corporate restructuring had resulted
in changes to her paper's editorial policies. She denied that this was the
case:

I don't think that there has been any change in editorial policy.
The chief editor still works for the government. This does not
make for any changes to the editorial policy. The government
requires our newspaper to be popular. Achieving political and
social effect is what it wants to see.

As far as I remember, the *South China Morning Post* devoted a
half page to reporting our newspaper, saying that we are
outstanding in walking the high-wire tightrope between production and profits. Our objectives are to be opinion-oriented and
publicity-centred. The general public is our priority and later

comes the circulation. Between the two, it is not a hard wire-walk since there are lots of writing space and we can please both sides.

It follows that much of the opening handover coverage in the 'Golden Edition' was devoted to officially-sanctioned material. There was the full text of Jiang's handover ceremony speech, provided by the ubiquitous New China News Agency, accompanied by photographs of smiling leaders being greeted by the party faithful. However, in the *Guangzhou Daily* the official articles about the leadership were bracketed by ads for herbal medicines, refrigerators, real estate, hair restorers and Nippon Paints.

What's Not News in China

On June 1, a month prior to the handover, five thousand Hong Kong people marched from Chater Gardens to the Xinhua (New China News Agency) office to protest against the Tiananmen Square massacre. Members of the radical April Fifth Action Group carried slogans condemning the 'Government of Butchers in Beijing'. The marchers unsuccessfully attempted to present a petition to the Xinhua office which was closed and protected by police. The event led Hong Kong television bulletins.

That night the main CCTV (China Central Television) evening bulletin in Beijing also led with a story from Hong Kong. It featured a children's sports day in nearby Wanchai, where students from patriotic schools waved PRC flags. The report featured a smiling Xinhua official, Zhang Junsheng, who received a garland. A Hong Kong tourist tram, decorated with SAR flags, was also shown.

Critics of the Beijing leadership, such as the Democrats whom opinion polls showed had consistently attracted the support of about 50 per cent of the Hong Kong electorate, were never quoted or indeed mentioned in the handover coverage. The demonstration staged by Democrat Party Chairman Martin Lee at the Legislative Council just after midnight was ignored by the *Guangzhou Daily*. A survey of the Xinhua database showed that none of the 121 stories carried about Hong Kong on handover day made any reference to the Democrats. Most Xinhua reports were accounts of official speeches by President Jiang Zemin, Premier Li Peng, or Chief Executive Tung Chee-hwa, congratulatory reports from foreign countries and news of celebrations throughout China. Xinhua reported, for example, on a gala gathering in Tibet occupied by the Chinese PLA:

One of the Democratic Marches that Mainland
Chinese Media Ignored

Source: Cheung Pak-chuen

Tens of thousands of people gathered in the Potala Palace, the symbol of Lhasa, for Tibetan style celebrations of the return of Hong Kong. The 1,300 year old Palace was draped with colourful Tibetan banners printed with words of welcome. 1,997 balloons and 1,997 pigeons were released as the crowd were singing the national anthem.... Hung over the streets were banners with the words, 'Celebrating the Unity of the Motherland' and 'Strengthening the National Unity'.

(Xinhua July 1, 1997)

A search through six months of Xinhua reports found no reference to the Hong Kong Democrats leader, Martin Lee. It seemed that as far as Chinese mainland media were concerned, Hong Kong's largest political party simply did not exist. In fact, it seems that mainland reporters had been advised to stay away from pro-democracy demonstrations. The *Apple Daily* claimed that mainland journalists had been under strict instructions from their Central Propaganda Department about their behaviour and whom they should report on. This was described as the Twelve Dos and Don'ts:

Do:
- Strictly follow unified arrangements for interviewing and reporting;
- Consciously abide by the laws of Hong Kong;
- Report back immediately to the organisation what is seen and seek directions;
- Conduct outdoor activities in groups;
- Prepare daily reports and summaries;
- Consciously defend the reputation of China and its journalists.

Don't:
- Express political opinions without permission;
- Release news to the outside before it is examined and approved;
- Interact or engage in activities with foreign media without permission;
- Interview opposing groups or their media;
- Interact with international organisation of unknown identities or with anti-PRC positions
- Visit night clubs, Karaoke bars or entertainment facilities of that sort.

(*Apple Daily* July 1, 1997:A19)[8]

Karaoke might have been off mainland reporters' schedules, but official functions both real and imaginary were acceptable. The *Guangzhou Daily*'s special edition included a two-page, full-colour reproduction of the reunification painting, Festive Day, which was itself notable for the omission of those who might criticise Beijing. The 4.36 metre original had taken the artist, Professor Liu Yuyi, three years to complete. Centred on the late patriarch, Deng Xiaoping, the canvas depicted SAR Chief Executive Tung Chee-hwa and President Jiang Zemin toasting each other with red wine, surrounded by whirling ballerinas and adoring flower girls. The Royal Hong Kong Police band bagpipes and French horns played accompaniment, while Miss Hong Kong, the foreign press corps, top civil servants, Chinese lion-dancers and about one hundred local business worthies applauded. A giant crystal chandelier glittered overhead. In the background, the firework-lit skylines of Shanghai and Beijing merged with that of Hong Kong Island where Lantau Island's gold Giant Buddha seemed to have levitated itself across the harbour to the top of the Peak to mark the occasion. Britain's expatriate critic, Elsie Tu, could be seen at a seat of honour at the front table. Governor Patten and the British side, and once again the Democrats, were nowhere to be seen.

The painting set a record for Chinese contemporary art later that week, when it was sold for HK$23 million. The *South China Morning Post* reported that an unsuccessful buyer broke down in tears after failing to purchase it. 'It's the best painting in the world,' said Shanghai businessman Chen Dun. 'I'd been negotiating for ten days. I was almost sure I had it. I feel very upset to lose it. I won't recover for a long time.' It was acquired instead by the property developer, the Hong Kong Parkview Group, whose founder Hwang Chou-shiuan had been convicted of insider trading earlier in the year (SCMP July 4, 1997:8).

Monkeys Scattering from a Tree Falling in the Jungle

The *Guangzhou Daily* devoted a series of articles to the departure of the British military garrison which, the newspaper repeatedly noted, had been in Hong Kong since British Imperial troops won the Opium Wars. The wars themselves had been the subject of an series of feature reports, supplemented by a review of and reports on the movie, *The Opium War*. The movie's director, Xie Jin, saw it as a truthful account, a moving story 'of people and soldiers who bravely fought against invaders' (*Guangzhou Daily* July 1, 1997:29). Yet in the movie itself, the British redcoats were depicted as merciless killers. In one scene reminiscent of John Wayne's *Remember the Alamo,* British redcoats swarmed over the Chinese defences where outnumbered defenders heroically fought against overwhelming odds.

However, the *Guangzhou Daily* reporting of the contemporary British military forces in the Orient did not reflect such nationalistic ardour. The foreign troops were portrayed as a disciplined force. The British military headquarters, the Prince of Wales Barracks, located on Victoria Harbour front was however described as a centre for military intelligence:

> Many Hong Kong Chinese worked at this centre, but they could not enter key areas, and the Chinese cleaners and typists employed were all deaf-mutes. Experts sent to this centre were said to belong to the MI5, and most could speak and write Chinese. Some had training at Hong Kong's centre for oriental languages. Some of these experts even learned to write in cursive calligraphy. The reason given was that mainland secret documents are written in this style.
>
> (*Guangzhou Daily* July 1, 1997:9)[9]

The headquarters was one of fourteen British facilities in Hong Kong turned over to the PLA, which retained its old royalist title after occupation. The small harbour for the adjacent Tamar fleet base, the last British naval base in the 'Far East', was filled in and used as the location for the Farewell Ceremony. The *Guangzhou Daily* reported that the small fleet of frigates based there had been sold to the Philippines.

> With every closure of the base and disbanding of a force, soldiers lined up for inspection, the commander gave a speech, chaplains prayed, all officers and soldiers stood in silence, and the flags for that force were lowered. During the past half year, British flags were lowered one after another. Their light was dimming as their empire was no more.
>
> (*Guangzhou Daily* July 1, 1997:9)[10]

The Royal Air Force had left Hong Kong skies forever. The RAF had sold its helicopters to Uruguay, before disbanding its Hong Kong-based 28 squadron. The RAF was reported in a positive light:

> During a typhoon in 1993, at great danger to themselves, members of the squadron saved survivors from a sinking freight ship. In 1994, their pilots saved fourteen Chinese sailors during

another typhoon and won the highest awards for bravery in rescue.

(*Guangzhou Daily* July 1, 1997:9)[11]

There even appeared to be a degree of sympathy for the colonial soldiers. In a by-lined report, Chen Weisheng described the passing of the '1,000 day' logistics regiment which had been created to wind up British military affairs in Hong Kong.

At the disbanding ceremony, the British Black Watch regiment played a military tune. A Chinese soldier lowered and folded the flag. The lowering of the regimental flag symbolises the formal disbanding of this regiment which had served around 1,000 days. The regiment is now history. This reporter met that Chinese soldier yesterday evening. He was pretty sad about the disbanding and worried about his life and employment after being discharged.

(*Guangzhou Daily* July 1, 1997:9)[12]

Here, buried in the back pages was the startling admission that at least one Chinese person was sorry to see the end of colonialism. The report by a Guangzhou-based reporter denied the claims made in the Beijing-approved editorial that all Chinese celebrated the handover.

In the spirit of the new China, the *Guangzhou Daily* completed its accounts of the departing garrison by reporting on the bargain basement sale of military surplus material. It followed up an advertisement which appeared in the *South China Morning Post*. The sale, it was said, had been the talking point of Hong Kong people. The report was headlined, 'Discounts before leaving: Fire sale as retreat is near':

Items auctioned included: two commander's limousines, bought 3 years previously.... Also, one leisure yacht and two junks, one ferry, two motor boats and two speed boats. A large quantity of tools and machines were also on sale. It seems that the British force would like to get as much money back as possible before they retreat. The funny thing is that items on sale include sheets, pillowcases and cooking equipment, which were not used up by the troops stationed in Hong Kong. The British Military obviously overestimated the duration of their stay here....

Ironically, sandbags and barbed wire which was used to control Chinese people in Hong Kong are also on sale. The glorious

British empire which once flourished its might in every corner of the world is now selling all items in a rush and has had to put ads in the classifieds before their retreat. This may be seen as a sign of that they are in straitened circumstances and in an awkward situation.

(Guangzhou Daily July 1, 1997:9)[13]

While Beijing continued to portray the British military in stereotypical and anachronistic terms, the *Guangzhou Daily*, like the Western papers it modelled itself on, sought human interest angles. In doing so, the paper to an extent balanced the familiar strident denunciations of colonialism, with softer more sympathetic stories.

Remnants of Empire

Governor Chris Patten, a figure much reviled by Beijing in the run up to the handover, also received comparatively mild treatment at the hands of the *Guangzhou Daily*. Back in 1992, when China was seeking to undermine him as Governor, mainland spokesmen had called Patten 'a sly lawyer', 'a dirty trickster', 'a clown', 'a tango dancer', 'a serpent', 'a strutting prostitute', and according to Jonathan Dimbleby, Patten's own favourite, 'a triple violator' (Dimbleby 1997:156). Five years later, the last Governor of Hong Kong was treated with more civility. He featured in the *Guangzhou Daily's* photographic coverage reviewing the Hong Kong Police, receiving the lowered British flag and sitting, with head lowered, next to Prince Charles at the farewell ceremony. Journalists Li Wanfen and Wang Zhongjie provided an 'eyewitness report' on what they saw as his 'mood of sad departure' from Government House:

> The Governor's farewell ceremony started with 'God Save the Queen', the British national anthem. The ceremony was held on the lawn in front of Government House. Governor Chris Patten, together with his wife and three daughters, attended the ceremony, giving an impression of melancholy.... Patten in a blue suit, shirt and tie, looked sad and tight-lipped from the beginning of the ceremony to the end. When the British flag was lowered from the flagpole for the last time, and as the band played *Last Post*, he could not help rubbing his nose twice. Carrying the Union Jack which had been lowered from the Government House flagpole, Chris Patten boarded his car with

88

his family, circled the lawn three times, and then left Government House.

(Guangzhou Daily July 1, 1997:6)[14]

As his black limousine disappeared in the rain, the Governor and the colonial regime he represented passed into history.

In a story headlined, 'Leaving Post Means Unemployment', a reporter, Zhang Yihua, sought the advice of two investment experts on how Mr Patten might most profitably invest his retirement bonus. Neither proposed investing in China. A Mr Cai suggested that 30 per cent of Mr Patten's money should go into high yield British Bonds and 50 per cent into British and European shares. The rest, he said, should be retained for emergency cash flows. Mr Chang advised investment in English real estate market, supplemented by blue chip shares and bonds, particularly those from South Africa which were seen as both stable and profitable. Overall, Mr Patten was best advised to complete his memoirs. 'His autobiography will bring a high rate of returns. His speaking tours will earn even more for him,' the report said (*Guangzhou Daily* July 1, 1997:12).[15]

The newspaper noted that Mr Patten, unlike nearly all previous governors, had left little to local history with no building or streets named after him. In an article, 'British Governors Left their Names and Tended to Glorify their Achievements', Hong Kong's colonial history was recorded as events occurring during governor's terms of office. The second governor, Mr Davis, conducted the first census. The seventh governor, Mr Kennedy, opened up the Peak as a residential area. The eighth governor, Mr Hennessy permitted prostitution. It was claimed that the governor who surrendered Hong Kong to Japanese forces also had no naming place (*Guangzhou Daily* July 1, 1997:13).[16]

The British monarchy also attracted some attention, although interest seems more to have been generated by its lavish lifestyle than by the railway stations, hospitals, and social welfare centres that retained their names. The Royal Yacht Britannia, which was believed to have made its last voyage to Hong Kong, had 'like her owners seen better days, though keeping its luxurious appearance'. It was noted that the yacht had served as a venue for romances conducted by Princess Margaret, Princess Ann, Prince Charles and Prince Andrew:

> The decorations and furnishings on the Royal Yacht are luxurious and classical. A line of gold leaf girdles the ship, and the mast

head is of pure gold. These things make the yacht appear luxurious and brilliant. The dining room has a big table for fifty-six people, and all the tableware carries the royal insignia. It is said that even when the yacht is buffered by strong winds, glasses on the dining table will not easily tumble. The Royal Yacht is a home at sea for members of the royal family. The antique telephones are similar to those in Buckingham Palace, which makes royal family members feel at home.

(*Guangzhou Daily* July 1, 1997:14)[17]

The British monarchy were, it seemed, like their antique telephones, merely curiosities from a rapidly receding past.

Plans

The *Guangzhou Daily* meanwhile had its eyes on the future. It planned four major projects which it believed would help propel it into greater influence in the next century.

It constructed a new remote printing centre which, it was hoped, would incorporate the best and latest foreign technology. Group executives toured western newspaper production facilities, including 'the most modern' in Australia, to collect ideas. The new centre was planned to cost more than US$100 million and cover an area of 40,000 square meters. All the funds for the project were to come from within the group itself. Trial production was scheduled to begin in July 1998. The printing centre was designed to print one million copies with forty pages each, one third of which were colour pages, in two to two and a half hours. In the printing centre, four production lines will be installed, two of which are imported from Germany and the other two from Switzerland. Each of the German production lines were to be able print 150,000 newspaper copies an hour. Together, the four lines were expected to have a printing capacity of more than 400,000 copies an hour. The printing centre was to also include a museum of printing, using photography, audio and visual displays, television, computers, film and multi-media to show the public the history of printing technological development, as well as the most advanced printing technologies and their application world-wide.

The second project aims at introducing a modern, fast, and efficient newspaper distribution system. Newspaper expansion in China has been restricted by the need to use the slow and cumbersome postal system. This was less of a problem for state enterprise papers whose sales were guaranteed to work units. But a newspaper which hoped to meet the current interests of its readers and serve the needs of advertisers could not compete under such a system. In 1997, about one third of the *Guangzhou Daily*'s staff was employed in distribution. President Li:

> We have our own circulation system network which distributes newspapers through three means – distribution centres, our own chain stores and retail sales. All of these are organised by the *Guangzhou Daily*'s distribution company. Compared with the distribution channel provided by the post office, our own system provides a better service to readers. Newspapers distributed through the post office reach readers four hours later than those distributed through our own system.

There were about sixty chain stores distributing the newspaper in the Guangzhou urban area. Another 100 stores were planned in the city, with a further hundred in the Pearl River Delta. 'Where there is a post office, there will be a *Guangzhou Daily* chain store,' Mr Li said.

The group was expanding horizontally as well as vertically. It had begun investing heavily in real estate. The third project was a high-rise development, the Newspaper Cultural Plaza, to which the newspaper's offices were expected to move by 2001. The prestigious tower building site will cover an area of 32,000 square and the tower itself will have a built area are of 200,000 square metres. The total investment was 1.5 billion yuan (US$180.9 million), all of which was once again been raised by the news group. The tower is expected to be completed in 2000. The plaza will house an office area of 50,000 square metres, a library which will be open to the public, an exhibition centre of 30,000 square metres, a business centre of 30,000 square metres and a Guangzhou Opera Hall of 20,000 square metres for musicals and drama. Outside the building, there will be open space of 20,000 square metres. The building was being constructed above a station connected to Guangzhou's new underground urban transit system which could be expected to allow fast, cheap movement by staff, customers and goods.

In a hangover from the old state enterprise days, the group provided accommodation for most of its employees. But as a symbol of its growing wealth, it was adding to staff facilities by constructing a Journalists' Country Club. 'We have our own real estate company to develop these projects. If the marketing of the apartment buildings is good, we will sell as many as possible. Otherwise, we will reserve them for our own use. The club will be of five-star hotel standard,' Mr Li said. I said to him that there would be quite a few *South China Morning Post* journalists who might be envious enough of the staff facilities to cross the border and seek work with his newspaper. He laughed. 'The *South China Morning Post* is our teacher,' he said.

Reportage Considered

Chinese reportage of the handover continued to include the official Communist party line on colonialism. Critics were routinely ignored. However, wealth derived from advertising was also allowing a larger news hole, where other views might be included. While avoiding direct criticism of Beijing policies, articles which admired colonial lifestyles, speculated about the life of the clearly decadent Royals and even praised the efficiency of the colonial occupying forces, implicitly questioned the party leadership's approved assumptions. Melodramas like *The Opium War* had already lost the battle with Hong Kong popular culture. These comparative differences could even be seen on the tightly controlled Chinese television coverage of the handover event. The pre-recorded Beijing-based CCTV bulletins were clearly leadership driven; with lengthy shots of the elderly national cadres dutifully listening as President Jiang ploughed through yet another speech exhorting the masses to new achievements. In contrast, Guangzhou television news employed tight Western style news briefs which included genuine interviews. Guangzhou TV naturally featured President Jiang. But it also interviewed and broadcast the views of Hong Kong's martial arts superstar, Jackie Chan.

Just as the Berlin Wall was shaken by faxed, telephoned and broadcast news from abroad, China's state-sanctioned news was being undermined by reports from across the border. Guangzhou journalists may not have been able to publish dissenting views, but through radio, television and increasingly the Internet, many were keenly aware of censored events, personalities and interpretations. The new consumers they wrote for were meanwhile choosing a foreign cultural package which would have sent Mao and his boiler-suited ideologues spinning.

INSIDERS' INSIGHTS

Outside the Familiar Loops

Many correspondents identify with a machismo culture, which can be found wherever stories are breaking in Asia. They cross paths in correspondents' bars, embroider their mythologies, swap stories and sometimes partners. But there are others outside the familiar loops.

Kieu Tinh had the distinction of being a non-Chinese Communist covering Beijing's final defeat of colonialism. He was in the capitalist enclave at a time when both China and Vietnam were themselves beating a retreat from Communist theories. Indeed, the only thing that seemed to remain constant was the fact that the two erstwhile Marxist states retained enmities which dated back a millennium before the arrival of the British.

Angelo Paratico might also be considered an ideological enemy of China. He wrote for a neo-fascist audience in far off Italy, a source of fashion goods now much favoured by Hong Kong capitalists and Beijing cadres alike. Both Tinh and Paratico had to choose their words and stories carefully.

Essays

The Last Communist
Kieu Tinh, Vietnam News Agency

BARRY LOWE

The ideological content of the Hong Kong handover story was, for most international journalists covering it, the story of a treasured enclave of capitalism falling into the maw of communism. Many journalists referred to this in language reminiscent of the Cold War rhetoric of the 1980s. But one reporter covering the handover stood out

– ideologically speaking – from the crowd. This was the only journalist from a communist country covering the handover. Kieu Tinh, Hong Kong bureau chief for the state-owned Vietnam News Agency, represented the shrinking world of Marxism of which his country is the last major representative outside China (the only other two remaining communist states are Laos and Cuba). But despite this shared political heritage, Vietnam and China are not close allies. Two decades ago they were at war with each other and the reconciliation process since then has been slow and tentative. Vietnam remains wary of its giant neighbour while China resents Hanoi's rival claims to South China Sea islands and oil fields. So Kieu Tinh reported the handover from the unique perspective of sympathy for the ideological orientation of Hong Kong's new masters, but as a representative of one of China's most recent enemies.

Kieu Tinh was posted to Hong Kong in 1996 where he opened his agency's first bureau in the territory. He was chosen for the post because of his fluency in Mandarin and his strong credentials as a veteran China-watcher: he had served in his agency's Beijing bureau from 1984–91. After 1991 he returned to Hanoi where he was a senior editor in the Vietnam News Agency's international section. His links with China go back even further than his reporting experience there. As a young student in the late 1970s he was sent to Beijing to study English and Mandarin at the Beijing Foreign Trade University. His stay in Beijing coincided with the China-Vietnam border war in 1979, an event that led to years of frosty relations between the two neighbours. When he returned to China in 1984 he found links were improving but still a long way from the close embrace the two countries enjoyed when China was supporting Hanoi's struggle against the US in the Vietnam War. Being a Vietnamese reporter in Beijing wasn't easy. 'There were a lot of restrictions on what I could do. But one thing that made it easier was the strong camaraderie among the journalists from socialist countries,' he recalled. 'For a while we comprised a separate bloc of foreign journalists in Beijing. But eventually we began to integrate with the Western journalists there. In fact I was the first journalist from a socialist country to join the then American-dominated Beijing Foreign Correspondents' Club.'

When he came to Hong Kong in 1996 it was a very different situation. 'Compared to my experience in Beijing, Hong Kong offered me a lot of freedom to report on a wider range of subjects and to deal with a wider range of sources. Access to officials was much easier; people were happy to answer my questions. At the Governor's press conferences I often asked questions. Chris Patten always seemed pleased to answer me. I liked his style.' While his bureau was also responsible for covering southern China and Taiwan, an overwhelming majority of his stories up to the handover concerned Hong Kong. The issues that his news agency were interested in covered a broad spectrum of political and economic themes. 'There was a strong interest in the handover in Vietnam. Hong Kong is important to us; it is our third biggest trading partner. It is also one of the biggest sources of foreign investment in Vietnam. So events in Hong Kong are of great importance to the Vietnamese economy. We'll be interested to see how China manages the "one country, two systems" policy.'

Kieu Tinh focused his reporting leading up to the handover on how Hong Kongers were reacting to the impending event. He tried to include as many people as possible in the net he cast for opinions on the handover, including members of the foreign correspondents corps, such as NHK reporters from Japan and Xinhua reporters from China. He also made several forays into the streets of Hong Kong to do vox pop interviews with people he stopped on the sidewalks. In the final week before the handover he received reinforcements from Vietnam in the form of two additional reporters. They enabled him to expand the activities of his bureau. Working in shifts, the three reporters maintained twenty-four hours a day service for their head office in Hanoi, filing stories as they broke. The extra reporters were assigned mainly to background stories. Kieu Tinh concentrated on the big events, such as the major press conferences and the ceremony at the Convention Centre. During the final week of the colony he was also required to do live reports for Vietnam Television. 'It was one of the toughest weeks of my life,' he said.

'Most people I interviewed at that time were positive about the implications of the handover. They weren't afraid of Chinese rule nor were they concerned about the PLA marching in. They believed that Hong Kong would remain a prosperous place. In Vietnam, public interest was in whether China would keep to its commitments on the Basic Law and whether Hong Kong would be allowed to preserve its identity. At the end of June, for three days running, Hong Kong dominated the front pages of Vietnamese newspapers. A lot of the stories filling those front pages came from Western news agency as well as from my bureau. The general view in Vietnam was that the Chinese leaders were too smart to let Hong Kong decline and that China sorely wanted to maintain Hong Kong's stability.' The Hong Kong handover story was disseminated in Vietnam by mass media undergoing a major transformation. According to Kieu Tinh, Vietnamese media outlets are becoming more and more concerned with facts, compared to the old days when propaganda was their main function. The Hong Kong story was, to a certain extent, a litmus test of the extent of these changes. 'I was able to report objectively on the Hong Kong handover,' he said. 'The newspapers that used my stories wanted the truth about Hong Kong and I believe I was able to give it to them.'

A View from the Right
Angelo Paratico, *Secolo d'Italia*

BARRY LOWE

Hong Kong's foreign media corps is a mixed bunch. At the top end of the pecking order are the full-time correspondents, most of them employed by major British or American newspapers and broadcasting networks, envied for their up-market apartments, frequent trips and inexhaustible expense accounts. But the majority comprise a humbler group: freelancers, stringers and part-timers who are paid by the story or by the word and often have to mix other income-earning pursuits with their journalistic endeavors. This group includes several Europeans, writing regularly – or irregularly – for a wide range of publications.

Angelo Paratico spends most of his time buying textiles for the Italian clothing distributor he works for. But for an average of one day a week he is working for *Secolo d'Italia*, a Rome-based daily with its foot firmly planted in the right shoe of Italian politics. He writes a bi-weekly column, partly analysis, partly opinion – in the manner of Italian journalism – on the issues and themes he sees as essential to his readers' understanding of Hong Kong affairs. He gleans his facts and theories from his social circles and business activities, activities that include an almost weekly trip to China where he visits the factories and offices of his company's suppliers. Most of his trips these days take him to the boom towns of Guangdong province; before they were mostly to Shanghai. He came to journalism almost by accident. He had just published a book in Italian about Confucius when a friend in Italy contacted him and asked him if he would write a few pieces for *Secolo d'Italia*. The editor of the newspaper liked his work and commissioned him to send reports on a regular basis. He has since expanded his output to include the occasional feature article for the Italian weekly news magazine *Borghese*.

As far as Italy's media representation in Hong Kong is concerned, Paratico is almost all there is. He says there is just one other Italian journalist in town – also a part-timer – who writes occasionally for another Roman newspaper, *Sola 24 Ore*. For the handover period this Italian presence was boosted by about twenty-five print journalists and TV crew-members who flew out from Italy for the occasion. 'Italians are not very interested in foreign news,' Paratico said. 'And the newspapers are little interested in publishing foreign news, especially foreign news from beyond Europe.'

The newspaper he has been writing for during the past three years is one of two political party-owned newspapers in Italy. Its owner is the staunchly conservative National Alliance. 'Not fascist, as some people like to categorise the Alliance, but certainly on the right side of politics,' is how Paratico described it. *Secolo d'Italia* was founded just after the Second World War by a group connected with Benito Mussolini's ill-fated Salon Republic of 1943–45, hence its reputation as a fascist newspaper. The tabloid-sized daily has a current circulation of about 35,000, its readership firmly grounded in the National Alliance and its support base. *Secolo d'Italia*'s emphasis is on political news. The stories Paratico writes for it run from 500 to 700 words and combine facts with comment. Here is a selection of articles – in summary – he wrote in the lead up to the handover:

March 28, 1997 – 'The Hong Kong Boom that Doesn't Wait for Anybody'
Despite apprehension over the handover Hong Kong's economic boom is continuing and will be sustained well beyond the handover.

May 10, 1997 – 'Navy of the British Queen to Stay in Hong Kong Waters'
Britain is sending a message to China that it will maintain a presence in the region – if there is an emergency over Hong Kong the British will be there.

June 11, 1997 – 'Hong Kong a Leap in the Dark'
The Tiananmen massacre is remembered, but Tung Chee-hwa says Hong Kong should look to the future and not to the past. However, Hong Kongers are passive and not used to democracy. All they want is the freedom to make money and to travel.

June 25, 1997 – 'The Queen Abandons the Hippodrome'
Hong Kong's historical development and the differences between Hong Kong and mainland Chinese society. The symbols of

colonialism are being dismantled and packed aboard the last ship of the empire.

June 29, 1997 – 'The Country Cousins Arrive in the City'
At the immigration queue at Shenzhen an old man is overheard saying: 'We don't like the British, but they're better than those bastards from Beijing.' The dirty, uneducated cousins from mainland China are moving into Hong Kong to reclaim what they assert is theirs. They don't bother knocking on the door and bang their fists on the table when they arrive.

Paratico says he tries in his reports to be objective, and not too negative, about China. However he sees a great deal of corruption during his weekly visits to the mainland. 'Overall I am optimistic about the future of Hong Kong. I don't see the Chinese takeover as a threat,' he said. As an observer of Hong Kong, he says it is not difficult to keep abreast of the news. Despite a heavy work load he manages to get to press conferences and other media events to keep in touch with current affairs in the territory. His main frustration is the Italian press industry he serves. 'The Italian press is not much good. People don't care much about news. Newspapers have political agenda and they tend to use events like the Hong Kong handover to reflect their own political ideology.'

FIVE

POMP AND
PATHOS
Through the Lens of British TV

Barry Lowe

Early in June 1997 a medium-sized office in the Hong Kong business district of Wanchai suddenly came under siege from a small army of technicians and broadcast professionals. Up till then the office in the Hong Kong Arts Centre building had been a spacious working environment for just three people, Independent Television News (ITN) Asia correspondent Mark Austin, his producer Glenda Spiro, and camera operator John Steele. More often than not the place was unoccupied, during the frequent times when the ITN news team were off in other parts of the region fulfilling their role of covering Asia for their network's news bulletin. But that changed abruptly when ITN suddenly upgraded its Far Eastern outpost into an engine house of its global news operation.

ITN was one of biggest players in the international media's coverage of the Hong Kong handover. But, as Mark Austin likes to stress, they did not just fly in at the last minute to bombard their viewers with images of the historic transition; their coverage of the handover finale was simply a high point in a sustained and comprehensive coverage that began years before the final ceremony. As Britain's second TV network, its news bulletins viewed in millions of British homes, ITN had early acknowledged that Hong Kong's loss to the empire was one of the biggest stories of the decade for its domestic audience. The network's coverage of the event was the result of detailed long-term planning. Mark Austin's role was pivotal. He would set the scene for the handover and describe its local and regional context to the British public so they understood the issues surrounding the event long before the Union Jack was finally lowered in front of Prince Charles. The ITN news staff who were flown to Hong Kong in June were there simply to provide some amplification for the loud event that would take place when the colony officially reverted to China.

ITN History

In its relatively short forty-three years of existence, ITN has made an important contribution to the way the British people understand the world and their role in it. Before ITN was launched, television news in Britain was the monopoly of the world's first publicly-owned broadcaster, the British Broadcasting Corporation. That monopoly ended under reforms to Britain's Broadcasting Act that established Independent Television (ITV) out of a partnership of four regional broadcast organisations: Granada, Associated Rediffusion, ATV and ABC Television (ITN is now owned by a consortium comprising five equal partners: Carlton Communications, the Granada Group, Daily Mail & General Trust, United News and Media, and Reuters). ITN was created as the national news division for the ITV union. Its task was to provide an alternative to the BBC's authoritative but often ponderous approach to broadcast news gathering and presenting. Its official function, as described in Section Three of the 1954 Television Act, was to provide news with 'due impartiality and accuracy'. But the task it set itself was to put more life and energy into TV news reporting, 'to combine the verve of Fleet Street with the authority of the BBC'(ITN Web Site).

In spite of minuscule early budgets (that would have been barely enough to pay the salaries of the BBC's tea-ladies) and stormy relations with the ITV board, the new news service soon began making innovations in TV news reporting that regularly prompted the BBC to change its own practices. ITN's first major contribution to news broadcasting methods was the invention of the newscaster. Early TV news, BBC-style, consisted of anonymous voiced-over footage that looked like abridged versions of cinema newsreel stories. The official BBC's position was that other visual aids, such as presenters and on-camera reporters, might detract from the integrity of the news content of the film footage. But ITN demonstrated that newscasters added personality to news bulletins and reinforced the authority of the news content by adding the presence of the journalists who reported and interpreted the day's events. An early feature of ITN bulletins was the location report which added immediacy to the story and connected the viewer to its context. ITN is also credited with inventing the vox pop, a feature of its early bulletins that has now become an essential weapon in the modern TV reporter's armoury.

The network made broadcast history in 1959 when it provided a comprehensive coverage of the British general election of that year, something the BBC had never attempted, mainly because of the logistical problems involved. Another milestone came with ITN's 1967 launch of its News at Ten bulletin, an event that saw television news colonise the late evening time slot. The News at Ten was the first substantial late evening bulletin. It also broke the mould for TV news formats, establishing the thirty-minute bulletin as the industry standard in place of the fifteen-minute program. The new half-hour format presented new logistical problems, but in overcoming these, ITV gained valuable experience in news management, experience it was able to apply to later innovations. These included the introduction of Electronic News Gathering (ENG) in 1979, the introduction of Satellite News Gathering (SNG) in 1986, the launch of the lunchtime bulletin in 1972, and the early evening news bulletin in 1976.

From a rather tentative start in 1955, ITN has become the leader in British TV news. Not only has it achieved a wide ratings margin over the BBC's TV news (its News at Ten is watched by about 6.3 million people each day), it also produces news programs for Channel Four, a more recent entry in the British TV market. Channel Four's bulletins represent a high-brow approach to TV news, with more emphasis on foreign news and in-depth analysis on news background issues. ITN's evolution was strongly influenced by its rivalry with the BBC and its determination to constantly move ahead of the BBC in style and audience approval. The two networks have inevitably remained rivals, often approaching news production from rival concepts of how newsworthy events should be interpreted and presented. There are major differences in approach, as well as more subtle variations in the way ITN and BBC package the same story. These differences are more noticeable in the coverage of a loud, sustained event like the Hong Kong handover. The BBC maintains a larger network of foreign correspondents. This network serves both the corporation's television and radio news services and thus provides a far greater depth of news gathering resources than ITN can call on. However, ITN tries to overcome this numerical advantage by making its correspondent network more focused on priority events and issues, maximising its resources according to the global location of newsworthy events.

The Hong Kong Coverage

In a matter of days, the ITN presence in Hong Kong had swelled to almost fifty. The office in Wanchai was transformed into a teeming epicentre of news production on a grand scale. Heavy metal boxes lay in every corner, their contents of cameras, microphones, mixers and edit suite components stacked high on shelves and tables. A thick tangle of multi-coloured cables snaked around the room, linking equipment and connecting video decks to satellite ports. Telephones rang constantly, the water cooler gurgled. The ITN bureau could not contain the entire team at one time; several of the ITN staffers ran their parts of the operation from nearby hotel suites. And still more of them were out on the streets, doing the business of gathering TV news. This is the sharp end of television journalism: Hong Kong's handover was the type of story that revealed the distinction between the minor players and the serious operators. And ITN was one of the most serious operators to cover this story.

'I'm not sure if it was the biggest story of my career, but it certainly was one of the biggest,' said ITN Asia correspondent Mark Austin, reflecting on the Hong Kong story after returning to the territory from a period of R-and-R he was granted once the hectic days of the handover and its aftermath had ended. Austin began his career in journalism with the *Bournemouth Evening Echo*, passing through BBC radio and television news before joining ITN in 1986. During his eleven years with ITN Austin had covered the Bosnian War, the Gulf War, the Rwanda genocide, the Afghan civil war, the Cambodian elections and post-apartheid South Africa. 'But this story (Hong Kong) had something else – it had sentimental impact,' he said, referring to the compelling interest the handover had for British audiences: the sad good-bye to a much-loved far-flung fragment of empire; a reminder of past imperial days of splendour; the last of the White Raj packing up and going home forever. British audiences related to the Hong Kong handover differently to other international audiences. It was a domestic British story – involving prominent British personalities, British prestige, a British place – as much as it was a foreign story. The story had emotional content; it represented loss and retreat and, to many, it sounded a loud note of regret.

But despite its overwhelming resonance with his audience, covering the story still presented challenges for Mark Austin. 'A lot of British people were genuinely moved about losing their last major colony. And there were British people who were directly affected: the British expats in Hong Kong, the businessmen and so on, who had to decide whether to stay or leave. But the downside of the media circus that came to Hong Kong around the time of the handover was that it produced an over-exposure. It was hard to get an original angle on the story. The handover became a show rather than an event or a breaking news story. It was all so closely stage-managed that the challenge for journalists was how to write and package it in a different way that would provide an original perspective for our viewers. For me the handover was not a two-week story about the days before and after the actual ceremony. It was a six-month story that I began reporting on at the start of the year. I was in Hong Kong throughout the period regularly producing three and a half minute feature stories for News at Ten about key issues and events related to the impending handover. I did seven or eight special reports in the run up to the ceremony. The ceremony wasn't the only story – it was just one final part. The handover provided an opportunity to tell the bigger story: what is Hong Kong and where is it going.'

A Human Perspective

Austin said ITN was already in full gear for its coverage of the handover by the time the main contingent of foreign news media arrived. Two months before the ceremony Austin supplemented his own three-member reporting team by hiring four university students as interns. Their role was to act as translators, interpreters and 'fixers' who located subjects for interviews and persuaded them to cooperate. Austin said this boosted his capacity to do people-oriented stories. 'I wanted to tell the story of Hong Kong from a human perspective, from the point of view of typical individuals involved. Not just the prominent personalities, the [Governor] Chris Pattens and the [Democrat leader] Martin Lees, but ordinary people who could tell the story of Hong Kong for us.' Among the subjects tracked down by the ITN fixers and interviewed for special reports were a university professor returning to his village in the New Territories to join his clans people in welcoming the return to Chinese sovereignty; a young student who was worried about the threat to freedom of speech and democracy that Chinese rule seemed to imply; a British colonial expatriate who recalled the Hong Kong of times past while he sipped gin and tonic served by a Chinese boatman on board his corporate junk as it motored across Hong Kong harbour. 'I wanted to find my own subjects and to avoid the clichéd stories about Hong Kong: the slum dwellers of the walled city, the people living in cage homes, the dog-meat restaurants, etc. One other thing I wanted to avoid was focusing too narrowly on the day-to-day political story running in Hong Kong. I knew this would not interest our viewers. I think the feature stories were more important because they set the scene of what was happening.' Sometimes Austin had to lobby hard for his story ideas to be approved by the news desk in London. 'Some story ideas did not get instant approval. I had to argue for them. However I was able to do the stories that I felt best represented the situation.'

Austin also found the prominent newsmakers were compelling personalities – activists like Martin Lee and another pro-democracy politician, Emily Lau. These people, said Austin, provided an opportunity to explain not only Hong Kong but, through their opposition to China, more about China. Hong Kong's story was linked to issues and changes taking place in China, issues like human rights, crime, the gap between rich and poor, and changes like the economic boom and financial reforms. Chris Patten, the colony's amiable last governor, was also a bonus for reporters covering the handover, according to Austin. 'Intelligent, articulate, accessible, he lifted the Hong Kong story – he had great appeal. But it wasn't just his personality that contributed to the story. His political reform proposals upset the [mainland] Chinese and that became a big part of the story during the past few years. His ideas changed the whole story of Hong Kong's final British years. He radically affected the story; and made it far more interesting.' Austin concedes that, like many politicians, Patten used the media. But it was a mutually beneficial relationship.

The ITN coverage was expanded in the first week of June when two additional camera crews arrived, boosting the full-time ITN staff in Hong Kong to fifteen. These additional crews enabled the bureau to cast a wider net for its background stories and to divide up the work so that one crew could be assigned to the day's breaking news stories and the other could concentrate on background and colour stories. The new team members also brought an additional editing unit so that two stories could be cut simultaneously. As the office started filling up with extra staff and equipment, more effort had to be put into coordinating operations and the deployment of resources. This involved close contact with head office in London; at the peak of the coverage one phone line in the Hong Kong office was almost constantly open to London. In mid-June a new contingent arrived, boosting the ITN team to twenty-three. This was supplemented by a further twenty new arrivals from London at the start of the last week in June. By the time handover night arrived there were forty-seven people working on the ITN coverage. They included several of the heavyweights among ITN's

Emily Lau   Source: The Frontier

on-air performers: foreign affairs correspondent Paul Davies, senior foreign affairs commentator Michael Nicholson, reporters Tim Ewart and Caroline Kerr (Kerr was at the ITN Hong Kong bureau from 1993 to 1995) and News at Ten anchor Trevor McDonald.

'Despite all those resources, we all worked under incredible pressure during that time, particularly during the last few days before the handover,' recalled Austin. 'Often we had just two hours to edit stories of up to six minutes. Pressure also came from the difficulty of deciding what to use. There was so much good news material available.' Austin said his main concern at the time was the need to simplify for his audience the often complex information available, without making his stories simplistic. He kept in mind the objective of trying to inform his viewers on the things they did not already know about Hong Kong. Austin said he relied less on official sources – such as the Government Information Services (GIS) – for news of events during the lead-up to the handover, and more on his own contacts and the story ideas he gleaned from local media sources, such as the Radio and Television Hong Kong (RTHK) morning radio current affairs program Hong Kong Today, the *South China Morning Post* and translated summaries from the Chinese press.

'It's still an interesting story. And I'm happy to be here covering that story,' said Austin. 'But the British media are currently suffering from Hong Kong fatigue. The saturation coverage of the handover has had an impact of continued public interest in the territory. Now Hong Kong is essentially part of the story about China, about how China will develop, about how its relationship with the rest of the world will change. And this is possibly the more fascinating story in the world today.' Austin felt that many of the other foreign correspondents who covered the event did so according to a predetermined agenda. The Americans, for example, often produced stories that criticised British rule. 'Many reporters came here after already deciding how they were going to tell the story,' Austin said. But he supported the journalists who had responded angrily to allegations that they were blackening Hong Kong's international image by focusing on negative aspects of the handover story. 'It was not our job to help the Hong Kong Tourist Association,' he said. 'Our job was to report on the way things were changing and they certainly were changing. Certainly there was an onus on reporters not to create the impression that Hong Kong was about to fall apart. But it is easy to find fault with the international media's coverage of the handover by looking at one or two stories – such as the stories about Emily Lau's fears of the Chinese takeover – and ignoring all the others. You have to look at the whole coverage, which in our case I think was very balanced.'

Constructing the Handover

The ITN Hong Kong bureau's output over the peak period of the Hong Kong coverage – the last few days before the handover ceremony – showed an emphasis on the key visual symbols of the event: symbols of British rule such as the Royal Yacht Britannia, Prince Charles, Government House, military bands, warships and British flags; and symbols of the implications of the impending Chinese rule such as People's Liberation Army soldiers and pro-democracy demonstrations. The two were presented as binary opposites: the British presence was framed in terms of benign sentimentality underscored by a note of sadness and regret: Britain created Hong Kong and must now abandon its favourite child. In contrast, there was an ominous undertone to references to the Chinese takeover, which represented almost entirely by just two subjects: the Chinese troops who would march into Hong Kong and the Hong Kongers who feared their arrival. The balance of the ITN coverage during the last week of the colony's existence favoured themes of British departure and was crowded with visual references to imperial rituals. British elites were represented in far greater proportion than Chinese. In essence – as Mark Austin conceded – the handover was presented as a domestic story for the home audience and not as an international story.

The ITN stories broadcast during the lead up to the handover display these salient features:

1. British spokespersons are preferred for sound bites; the exceptions are pro-democracy activists Emily Lau and Martin Lee.
2. The transition to Chinese sovereignty is framed almost exclusively in terms of the 'occupation' of the territory by Chinese troops.
3. There is more emphasis on British officials preparing to leave or observing final rituals than on preparations for the post-British era.
4. There is greater emphasis on the pro-democracy, anti-Chinese protests than on pro-Chinese demonstrations by Hong Kongers.[1]

The above features highlight a focus on the negative side of the Hong Kong handover, conforming to a tradition in news reporting that bad news, news of threat or loss, is more compelling. Although one could argue that ITN did not provide a balanced coverage of the event, a balance between Britain's loss and China's gain, between the views of opponents of Chinese rule and supporters, the ITN stories did successfully capture the emotion and drama of the event from the viewpoint of their audience: the British people who shared the sense of loss at the passing of their Far Eastern outpost. At the same time the ITN stories did include other aspects of the event, for example, pro-China sentiments were expressed by vox pop interviewees and acknowledgement of public rallies in support of the takeover. While several stories included critical comments from British (Patten, Cook, Thatcher) about the mode of deployment of the Chinese garrison, there was one comment, from Tung Chee-hwa, defending the PLA decision to arrive in armoured personnel carriers. And while the focus was on the last rituals of colonial withdrawal, there were also background stories that, in Mark Austin's words, 'told part of the bigger story of Hong Kong'. The story on the plight of the remaining Vietnamese boat people is one example. Other stories, such as the profile of the British lawyer, illustrate what Austin described as an effort to humanise the story by providing flesh and blood examples of what impact the transition was having on people who lived in Hong Kong. Furthermore, as Austin pointed out, the stories produced by ITN during the few days surrounding the handover ceremony were not representative of the network's total coverage of the issue, which included several more background stories that examined some of the broader implications of the handover. In other words, the peak period of coverage saw a closer focus on a narrow range of themes (British departure ceremonies, anti-China demonstrations, the PLA preparing to occupy Hong Kong) compared to the coverage up till the last week.

Rival Interpretations

Journalists thrive on exclusives, on original stories that no other reporter gets. But when the story is a predictable, orchestrated one that attracts a media circus, a story with the magnitude of the Hong Kong handover, journalists then pursue original angles as a way of distinguishing their coverage from that of their rivals. ITN's rival is the BBC; the two compete fiercely for the loyalty of British TV viewers. ITN is currently ahead in that race and wants to stay ahead. Mark Austin was motivated in his coverage of Hong Kong by the need to tell the story his own way, to tell it differently from others. But he made the point that competition with the BBC was not a major factor in his approach to daily breaking events; that he was more interested in developing his own approach to the whole event of Hong Kong's transition rather than in trying to make every individual story look different to the BBC's. 'We have different agendas,' Austin said. 'One difference is that the BBC do more stories than we do. But I don't really think about the different ways we approach the coverage of a particular event. I do it my way; they do it theirs. I don't care too much about comparisons.'

In fact, a look at the stories broadcast by the two networks about the day of the handover reveals few significant differences in conceptualisation and style. Austin's story, a five minute thirty-seven second package of the day's events, has essentially the same elements as the story packaged by the BBC's Matt Frei, with an equal emphasis on symbolic imagery and a script heavily repetitive of the colonial withdrawal theme. Austin's script (below) includes twenty-one phrases (in italics) expressing departure, and thickly layers the sentiment of the occasion in a string of verbal cadences. His words are tightly cued to visual references of the British withdrawal: flags being lowered, regalia

Governor Patten at Government House   Source: Hong Kong Government

being removed from Government House, Britannia sailing off. Austin's package is more loosely edited than the BBC story with pauses left between sections of the narrative so that the natural sound of bands playing and crowds cheering is retained to provide atmosphere.

> It's the *last voyage* of empire: *sailing away* from Hong Kong tonight in what are now Chinese waters the Royal Yacht Britannia, *severing the link* of a century and a half. *Leaving behind* the spectacular skyline Britain helped create out of a barren rock. Hong Kong is colonialism's greatest success story: a story that tonight *came to an end*. It was approaching the midnight hour in Hong Kong when British and Chinese leaders entered the grand hall from opposite sides to *end one era* and start another. They were followed by soldiers of the Chinese army bearing their flags who were joined by three men of the British armed forces who had come to collect theirs. The territory seized in another century and secured on borrowed time was *theirs no longer*. As the Union Jack was lowered here *for the last time* the flag of communist China was being raised. Hong Kong has returned to what the Chinese call their motherland. President Jiang Zemin is now the man in ultimate control here.

Sound Bite Prince Charles: 'China will tonight take responsibility for a place and people which greatly matter to us all. The triumphant success of Hong Kong demands and deserves to be maintained.'

President Jiang Zemin said the day would go down in the annals of history and he promised to preserve Hong Kong's autonomy and freedom, but many in the territory remain sceptical. China knows that the world will be watching to see if the promise is kept. Earlier Chris Patten's three daughters led the way as he left the colonial mansion *for the last time*. For Britain, and in particular the last governor, it was the day of the *long good-byes*. He *bade farewell* to his aide and then received the flag that had flown here for more than a century. This ceremony was only *the beginning of the end* of British rule here – there were many more tears to shed before the day was done. Mr Patten said he hopes to return to Hong Kong. But if he does, and it is unlikely the Chinese will welcome him, it will be to a different Hong Kong when British power and influence is *all but a memory*. Britain's *farewell* sunset ceremony lacked the sunset but not the emotion. A lone piper and Prince Charles battled the elements, but nothing could stop this colonial flourish. And Chris Patten delivered his own *epilogue of empire*.

Sound Bite Chris Patten: 'I am the twenty-eighth governor, the last governor. Like all the other governors and their families, my wife, my children and myself will take Hong Kong home in our hearts. Now Hong Kong people are to run Hong Kong. That is the promise and that is the unshakeable destiny.'

By now the rain had turned into a tropical downpour and the Union Jack was lowered. The emotion showed on the faces of Chris Patten and Tony Blair as, on one of the most dramatic stages in the world, Britain was saying its *final farewell*. And Hong Kong's Victoria Harbour became the backdrop as fireworks lit up the night sky above Britannia.

Reporter's Voice to Camera: 'Britain of course is well rehearsed in the last hurrahs of empire. But all this is something special. Never before has Britain handed over a colony as spectacularly successful as Hong Kong and never has it given up a colony to a communist regime.'

As they removed the relics of colonialism at the gates of Government House tonight, the Governor was already heading with Prince Charles to Britannia. At the quayside the crowds turned out to *see them off*. The Patten family boarded the Royal Yacht and conveyed all the emotions of an extraordinary day. The band of Royal Marines played on deck and slowly Britannia *moved from her moorings*. The former governor and his wife *waved their farewells* and *went on their way*. Britain had *taken its leave* of their last major colony. Mark Austin, ITN News, Hong Kong.

(CAMERA SHOTS: Britannia on Hong Kong harbour; closer shot of Britannia; Britannia; harbour front; Britannia; wider shot of Britannia; wide shot of Handover Ceremony at Convention Centre; Patten entering; Jiang entering; wide shot of both leaders ascending dais; Chinese soldiers and British soldiers marching converging together; British soldiers marching; wide shot of British and Chinese soldiers; Prince Charles and Tony Blair; flags being lowered; close shot of Charles; Chinese flag-raising; close shot of Jiang; Charles; Tung Chee-hwa with Chinese general; Charles; wide shot of ceremony; Jiang shaking hands with Charles; Patten's daughters coming out of Government House; Patten and Lavender coming out of Government House; band on Government House lawn; Patten greeting his aide; wide shot of Patten and aide; band playing; folded flag being carried by aide; tearful staff; Patten receiving flag; closer shot of Patten with flag; Patten's car driving past; Patten's car driving through gates; street parade; closer shot of street parade; marching military band; lone piper; Charles at podium; marching band; wider shot of marching band; marching band; closer shot of band; wider shot of band; Patten at podium; Blair and Lavender Patten; bandmaster shouts orders; marching soldiers turn; soldiers standing at attention; tight shot of bugler; flags going down; tight shot of Union Jack; wide shot of flags; tight shot of Union Jack; tight shot of Patten; wide shot of ceremony; soldiers marching; closer shot of soldiers marching; wide shot of soldiers marching; fireworks over harbour; fireworks over harbour; Britannia with fireworks backdrop; reporter's voice to camera; tight shot of crown being prised off gates of Government House; Patten hugging well-wishers; Charles talking to crowd; Patten waving with Charles behind him; Patten with crying daughters; Britannia at berth; Patten girls waving from deck; Patten and Lavender waving from deck; Britannia moving off.)

A BBC alternative (transcribed below) shows few stylistic differences. There are the same references to Hong Kong's economic success; the same heavy hint of suspicion about China's true intentions. Flags and other symbols of sovereignty feature heavily in the script and images. As in the ITN script the Chinese are marginalised in this interpretation of the event: only British leaders are considered worthy of a sound bite.

Under menacing monsoon skies Hong Kong woke up to its final day under British rule and to an appointment with uncertain destiny. As the city stirred into life they were preparing to welcome their new masters. Whether the flags represent shrewd courtesy or genuine patriotic fervour only they know. Then it was time to begin the carnival of retreat. Only a few hours after he arrived in Hong Kong the British Prime Minister and the last governor Chris Patten were pressing the flesh at a shopping mall. This is Britain's legacy: a free market, low tax paradise: the perfect marriage of Chinese energy and benign British administration. According to Mr Blair the handover should be an opportunity to mend relations between Britain and China.

Sound Bite Tony Blair: 'What is important, as I say, is that we try and look forward and make sure that Hong Kong becomes a bridge and not a barrier, as we said, because it's important for Britain and the people of Hong Kong and China that we use what Hong Kong has become as a basis on which we can build that stable relation in the future.'

At Government House the Pattens walked out of their home for the very last time. There were tears from the staff they leave behind. For this ceremony even the weather was British: heavy rain. The Governor who would be remembered for trying to bring democracy to the colony watched as the union flag was lowered for good. The man who had spent the last year going to leaving parties was now hosting his own farewell. As a final courtesy the band played Highland Cathedral, the Governor's favourite tune. Everything understood – no speech needed. As a parting present: a folded flag with the Governor's own emblem. And from his daughters: emotion barely contained. And one last leaving ritual for the Governor: his car circled the courtyard three times, a Chinese custom which means hope to be back. The gates of Government House were closed: end of era. Within an hour the new rulers were checking in. President Jiang Zemin: it was the first time in 156 years that a Chinese leader had set foot in Hong Kong.

Reporter's Voice to Camera: 'For everyone concerned this is history in the making. For Britain this is a last and final chapter of empire that is finally closing. For the people of Hong Kong this is the beginning of a new uncertain era: one which they face with restrained optimism. And for China itself it's the end of what they call a century of colonial shame and humiliation.'

And this evening in what used to be the old British naval base, the Prince of Wales arrived for the sundown ceremony to take his leave of the colony. From the last governor, a summing up of Britain's legacy and his personal gratitude.

Sound Bite Chris Patten: 'It has been the greatest honour and privilege of my life to share your home for five years and to have some responsibility for your future. Now Hong Kong people are to run Hong Kong: that is the promise and that is the unshakeable destiny.'

All that Britain and the rest of the world can do now is to hold China to its word.

Sound Bite Prince Charles: 'Unprecedented though this moment in history may be, we have the utmost confidence in the abilities and resilience of the Hong Kong people. Britain learnt long ago that Hong Kong people know best what is good for Hong Kong.'

As the flags come down it will be four hours before Britain is gone. The rest is up to the six and a half million people who will continue to live here. Matt Frei, BBC News, Hong Kong.

(CAMERA SHOTS: Hong Kong harbour at dawn; street scene with Chinese and Hong Kong flags; people in street; closer shot of flags; more flags; tight shot of old woman; Patten and Blair descending escalator in shopping mall; crowd in shopping mall; closer shot of crowd; head shot of Blair; crowd; Blair ascending escalator; Blair speaking; Government House; Patten descending stairs; group of Government House staff; bugler – pull out to shot of flag being lowered; dissolve to tight shot of Patten looking tearful; wider shot of Patten; band playing; tight shot of Patten smiling; Patten being handed flag; Patten's two daughters; tight shot of front of Patten's Rolls Royce; wide shot of car driving across courtyard; car driving through Government House gates; gates being closed; Air China plane on airport tarmac; Jiang Zemin waving from door of plane; Jiang meeting flag-waving children in street; reporter's voice to camera; British warship firing gun; Prince Charles getting out of car; wide shot of harbour; wide shot of crowd seated at HMS Tamar naval base; wide shot of Patten standing and walking to the podium; close shot of Patten; wide shot of crowd; Prince Charles at podium; flags of Hong Kong and Britain being lowered; wide shot of flags; close shot of Union Jack; very wide shots of flags.)

A major difference that emerges in a comparison of the two stories is in their visual construction. Although the two stories have essentially the same visual content – many of the camera shots are almost identical – the ITN version uses a different editing strategy that relies on frequent cuts between tight shots and wide shots to heighten the dramatic impact of the images. While both stories are of similar length (the BBC story is five minutes twenty-four seconds, ITN's five minutes thirty-seven seconds), the ITN version uses nearly double the number of individual shots: seventy-four to forty-two. Many of the ITN shots are juxtaposed in sequences of alternative wide views and close views, an editing technique that gives emphasis to key visual elements. The BBC version uses less abrupt transitions with sequences, consisting mainly of wide shots that focus on the panoramic aspects of event. In comparison with the ITN narrative structure, this tends to create a greater sense of distance between the viewer and the event so that the viewer has less emotional connection with the idea of Britain's loss which is an essential meaning of the event. In contrast, the ITN alternates wide and close shots to obtain a stronger emotional effect, particularly in its closing sequence which is a series of cuts between wide shots of Britannia cmbarking on its voyage and close shots of the key players – Prince Charles, Patten, the Patten daughters – waving sad good-byes. The ITN camera operator helped the editor achieve this result by providing ample static shots. The BBC package, in contrast, used more moving shots, such as the long pull out and pan from the bugler to the flag being lowered in the scene where Patten is leaving Government House. This same scene features a slow dissolve, from the flag pole to a close shot of Patten, an editing feature not used in the ITN story.

A salient difference between ITN and BBC stories was in the pace of their narration. The BBC opted for a slower pace, set by the rhythm of the camera movements and edit transitions. Zooms and pans require more time for each shot than static shots which can be strung together into sequences of very brief shots juxtaposed with shots of longer duration. The ITN story contained much more variety in the length of its individual shots, creating a faster pace which gave it a different overall appearance. The BBC's emphasis on wider, more sustained shots and a slower editing pace gave their story a sentimental feel; a wistful, regretful view of the handover event. The ITN version, with its denser image sequences, is more dramatic, highlighting the tensions between the ceremonials of departure and the reality of Britain's loss. It shows Chris Patten observing the rituals of the event with the required pomp and circumstance. But because the camera frequently gets in close, it also shows him with his stiff upper lip failing from time to time. The images, together with the way they are assembled, highlight a sense of bitterness and injured pride that is much more muted in the BBC story. The emotional response that the ITN story triggers has a harder edge to the sentimentality of the BBC story. It grounds the story in a sharper reality referring to the injury to its pride suffered by Britain in being forced to hand over territory to another power while suffering the indignity of seeing foreign troops march into that territory.

WILL THE CHINESE BE KINDER ABOUT BRITISH RULE?
The BBC

Alan Knight

As the national broadcaster of the departing sovereign power, the British Broadcasting Corporation made a comprehensive effort to cover what was seen as the effective end of Empire. About two hundred staff, including correspondents, presenters, directors, producers, camera crew, technicians and others were sent to Hong Kong to provide a comprehensive live coverage of the events.

The British Broadcasting Company had been founded in 1922, becoming by Royal Charter, the official state broadcaster in 1927. John Reith, the BBC's founding Chief Executive, had a vision of an independent British broadcaster seeking to 'educate, inform and entertain' the whole nation, free from political interference and commercial pressure. However, while the BBC might enjoy bureau-cratic independence from direct political control, it also had strong and early cultural links with the British establishment. The King, George V, was first heard on radio during a broadcast from the British Empire Exhibition of 1924. The speech was relayed on loudspeakers outside major department stores and the crowds were so large they stopped the traffic in the road. (BBC 1997)

There was an early commitment to live broadcasts of events considered to be of national importance. The first running commentary for a sporting event was the England and Wales Rugby football match at Twickenham in 1927. Other early outside broadcasts of major national events included the Soccer Cup Final, Wimbledon, the Boat Race and Trooping the Colour. The first experimental television broadcast was made in 1929.

The BBC's Empire Service, which with the eclipse of imperial pretensions, would later become the World Service, began in 1932. That same year the King gave the monarch's first Christmas Message to subjects around the world. The speech was crafted by Britain's leading Imperial fiction writer, Rudyard Kipling.

Last Service to Empire

BBC Television carried three live television crosses to Hong Kong on June 30 (London time). The governor's departure from Government House was seen in Britain just after breakfast and the formal departure presentation was shown just before lunch. In a British mixture of high apparent absurdity, the first telecast was followed by a program called 'Country Walks to Curious Places'. The handover ceremony itself was telecast mid-afternoon.

The quality of live television coverage depends directly on the number of cameras linked to the controlling studio. When covering football games, live television directors seek to marry the best action footage from these cameras with expert commentary. For the handover, the BBC, like the other live broadcasters, planned to use GIS-approved camera sites and had access to the GIS-provided live television feed. However, even such a stage-managed political event was at least in part unpredictable. Heavy rain in Hong Kong caused chaos for some networks, by shorting out circuitry and reducing choices.

The BBC World Service scheduled a 'News Hour Asia and Pacific Special' just two hours before the handover wrap up. The program began with an interview with Sir Richard Evans, British Ambassador to Beijing from 1984 to 1988. The elderly former diplomat appeared in a crumpled three-piece brown suit. He spoke with a measured, upper-class accent. The interview was interspersed with vision of a live broadcast from Beijing showing the arranged entertainment in Tiananmen Square. The questioning and the unrehearsed responses revealed some of the BBC's British national priorities. The bizarre combination of fusty commentary and live vision of dancing girls reflects the continuing volatility of live broadcasting.

Q: *Sir Richard, how does it look to you? Is it a highly choreographed affair? Wouldn't you say?*

Sir Richard: Yes. I would. But the Chinese have been past masters of choreography for several thousand years.

Q: *You were looking at the pictures earlier from, um, Hong Kong which seem to be rather more sedate. These pictures* [dancing girls in colourful ethnic costumes] *we are seeing at the moment I think are representing the greater enthusiasm that the Chinese are welcoming Hong Kong back with. Would you expect people to be lining up in China to visit Hong Kong now for the first time?*

Sir Richard: There have been very many visitors, millions in fact per year, for the past twenty years. I wouldn't expect the number to increase now. There has been more less freedom of movement into Hong Kong from the two southern provinces of Guangdong and Fujian. I think movement to Hong Kong even for business visits and holidays will be controlled from the rest of China from now on as it has been in the past. [The SAR regains border controls to limit immigration.]

Q: *Why is that?* [tentatively] *Maybe the Chinese authorities are perhaps worried about* [nervous chuckle] *the Hong Kong culture and rather more liberal atmosphere, perhaps infecting China?*

Sir Richard: Well, I think that they do have that worry, but I don't think that's the main reason they are controlling migration to Hong Kong or visits to Hong Kong. It is that if you brought ten million or fifteen million trying to get into Hong Kong, the place would be swamped. [Smiling dancing girls] And I am sure C.H. Tung would not welcome that and must have said so.

Sir Richard Evans said that the handover was a very big event in Chinese history. 'In British history books the Opium War is a footnote. In Chinese history, it is a central, and extremely humiliating event,' he said. [Dancing girls form wedge and march towards camera].

Q: *Of course recently, China has been very critical of British rule in Hong Kong. Do you think that as we are seeing the celebrations at the moment that in the fullness of time, the Chinese history books too will be rather kinder about Britain's colonial years?*

Sir Richard: In the end, but not yet. The official Chinese line is that Hong Kong, yes, has prospered and, yes, it has been stable, but this has been due to the industry and thrift and dedication to China of its Chinese people. [Dancing girls wave red silk fans. Male dancers wave umbrellas].

The interview reflected many of the weaknesses of live television coverage: there was a desperate need for live, moving pictures, whether they added to the discussion or not. Questions were often long and sometimes fumbled. The unedited responses were frequently neither entertaining nor informative. But together they filled air-time until the next news bulletin.

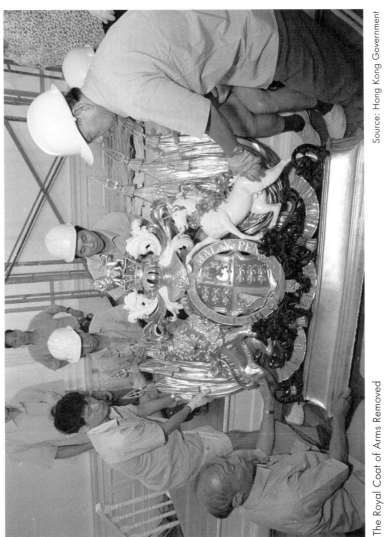

The Royal Coat of Arms Removed

BBC Television News

BBC Television News prepared three key news packages for June 30. The report presented by Matt Frei was shown on the BBC's main lunch-time domestic bulletin. While this particular report should not be considered to be representative of all BBC reports, it reflects post-imperial sensibilities which can be seen in much of the BBC's reporting of the handover.

Television news reports while brief in duration are a complex construction of scripted introductions, voice-overs and voice to cameras linked by a dazzle of carefully chosen imagery often selected from hours of raw footage.

Sound	Vision
Under menacing monsoon skies, Hong Kong woke up to its final day of British rule and to an appointment with an uncertain destiny.	Dawn over central, looking down from the Peak.

The opening shot selected to represent Hong Kong was one with particular colonial resonance. It was a perspective which would be immediately recognisable to British colonialists in Hong Kong. It was the view from the Victoria Peak, a privileged locality once exclusively populated by rich expatriates. Non-Europeans had once been prohibited from living there by the Peak Reservation Ordinance (Welsh 1993:342). This elevated view of Hong Kong was one which had also been favoured by the colonial film makers, the Government Information Services.

The dawn of the new era was seen to be threatening. The tone of the voice-over was deliberately menacing; underpinning the text's warning of a storm to come.

As the city stirred into life, they were preparing to welcome their new masters.	Street view of traditional neighbourhood decorated with PRC and SAR flags

The use of the term 'masters' suggests that Hong Kong would continue to be ruled rather than governed after reunification with China. The depiction of Hong Kong as an anachronistic market place might be something of a surprise to contemporary Hong Kong residents, many of whom work in banking, communications, brokerage and profes-sional management industries. To consider the selectivity of the representation in this BBC report, one might compare it to the description of Hong Kong made by author Robert Elegant, writing in *Pacific Destiny*:

> Hong Kong is the biggest, gaudiest, and busiest Oriental bazaar of all time – a vast chrome, glass and marble emporium that lures buyers from the entire world. Inventories and transactions are managed electronically on ultra modern computers served by self switching satellite links, but individual sales are reckoned on the wooden beads of ancient abacuses. It is mile after mile of shops, department stores, boutiques, ateliers, galleries, hawkers, and stalls supplied by a million skilled workers toiling in back street sweatshops or supervising automated, climate controlled, steel faced factories where lighting is constantly adjusted by self-servo chips.
>
> (Elegant 1990:447)

Whether the flags represent shrewd courtesy, or genuine patriotic fervour, only they know.	Head shot of elderly Chinese woman looking downwards.

The text questions whether the Chinese population is being duplicitous, by showing the national flag of the incoming sovereign power. The reporter's statement that 'only they know' what they are really thinking, begs the question; if the man from the BBC didn't know what local Chinese people have on their minds, why didn't he go and ask them? The BBC appeared to be ignoring Chinese voices. This Orientalist stereotype of inscrutability is explicitly reinforced by placing it with the image of a traditional Oriental figure.

In contrast, the British elements of the story were depicted in a modern context – politicians working the crowd at a shopping mall. Instead of anonymous and mute caricatures, the news actors are real and recognisable players, the British Prime Minister, Tony Blair, and Governor Chris Patten.

Then it was the time to begin the carnival of retreat.	Patten and Blair descend stairs to be greeted by a cheering crowd.
Only a few hours after he arrived in Hong Kong, the British Prime Minister and the last governor, Chris Patten, were pressing the flesh at a shopping mall.	Blair shaking hands.

This contrast between Chinese and British characters again has resonance with colonial documentary making; where the primitivism of the subjects is compared visually to the modernism of the authorities.

The vision of smiling uplifted faces indicated that the British politicians were certainly popular in Hong Kong. The reporter, it seemed, had little doubt about the positive results of British colonial government, which he personalised as 'the perfect marriage'.

This is Britain's legacy, a free market low-tax paradise, the perfect marriage of Chinese energy and benign British administration.	Blair and entourage depart.
According to Mr Blair the handover should be an opportunity to mend relations between Britain and China.	Blair ascends escalator, waving to cheering crowd.

The report then included a grab selected from an address delivered by Mr Blair. The material reflected the official British government position. As such, it would have been scripted in advance by the Prime Ministerial press relations staff.

(Blair actuality) What is important now is to look forward and ensure that Hong Kong becomes a bridge and not a barrier between Britain and China. It's important for Britain and for the people of Hong Kong and for China that we use what Hong Kong as the basis for a stable relationship on which we can build that stable relationship for the future.	Head shot of Blair at news conference.

The vision then switched from the present's version of the future, to Hong Kong's past; in this case, Government House. Under the colonial system, the house was more than a residence, albeit a comfortable official enclave, extensively redecorated by the Pattens with plush Chinese furniture, deep rugs and contemporary art to reflect the best of the affluent Hong Kong lifestyle. Until the handover, it had also been the nerve centre of the colonial administration. It was not merely a 'home'.

(Actuality) Military voice calls people to attention	Government House in mid vision. Royal Hong Kong Police in close vision
(Reporter) At Government House, the Pattens walked out of their home for the very last time.	Mr and Mrs Patten depart.
There were tears from the staff they left behind.	Unhappy Chinese women.

The reporter's depiction of the ceremonial relinquishment of the seat of power as leaving 'their home for the very last time' could be seen to be an attempt to strike emotional chords with the audience. He seemed to be implying that the British governor's residence in the seat of power should have been permanent.

The shot of the unhappy Chinese women was used repeatedly around the world by countless other press and television outlets. Some of Pattens' personal staff were undeniably weepy. But how representative was their view? Television, with its need for graphic images, seemed unconcerned about the answer. Meanwhile, a colonial police bugler played 'The Last Post', a tune frequently used for military funerals.

For this ceremony even the weather was British. The governor, who will be remembered for trying to bring democracy to the colony, watched as the Union flag was lowered for good.	Police bugler in rain. (Shot pulls back to show flag being lowered) Cross fade to Patten at attention

The focus of the report now moved to Patten himself. The governor, while an experienced and talented media performer, was genuinely moved by the events. The world's press, with camera angles selected and approved by the GIS, were there to record every nuance. The expert editors at the BBC crafted the imagery together to produce a tearful farewell to Empire.

The man who has spent the last year hosting leaving parties was now going to his own farewell.	Patten rubs nose.
Music (Highland Cathedral).	Band plays in rain.
In a final courtesy, the band played Highland Cathedral, the governor's favourite tune.	Patten smiles sadly.

The report editor introduced a bridging shot to allow the story to include the Patten daughters. The British satirical magazine, *Private Eye*, had dubbed them Sexy, Posh and Baby Patten, a reference to the publicity seeking pop group, the Spice Girls. The Patten daughters had long been the subject of intense and indeed fevered interest by many local journalists. One newspaper gained notoriety with a shot peering into a junior Patten's cleavage. In the caption, it was said to have made reference to ripening melons.

Even the staid BBC could not ignore these photogenic young women's perceived news-worthiness.

No speech needed	Patten presented with flag. Daughters' legs in shot.
The parting present, the folded flag with the governor's own emblem.	Shot pulls back to show daughters more fully.
And from his daughters, emotion barely contained.	Head shots of daughters weeping.

BBC coverage of the handover in general was technically excellent and invariably superbly produced. However, in spite of the mellifluous delivery, stunning images and strictly-observed television news format, 'emotion' was barely contained in BBC reportage itself. In a way, the report from the Peak merely catered to the expectations, concerns and mixed emotions of the British domestic audience.

Yet BBC World News offers a global service which explores the minutiae of news which American international services do not have the reporting networks, or perhaps experience to explore. Much of the BBC reporting of the handover betrayed its imperial heritage. Perhaps, it should be remembered as the last service to empire.

INSIDERS' INSIGHTS

Fragments of Empire

The hauling down of the Union Jack resonated around the former Empire. In Australia, journalists noted that colonialism's demise in Hong Kong coincided with a push towards their own country becoming a republic and cutting its last formal ties with Britain. Australian reporters had been based in British Hong Kong since the earliest days of the colony. Morrison of Peking, perhaps the most famous of all early China hands, started out there. Bruce Donald, who was to become Chiang Kai Shek's chief minder, edited a Hong Kong paper for a time. Their modern successor, Richard McGregor, worked for *The Australian*, Rupert Murdoch's antipodean flagship.

In contrast, many of Graham Hutchings' readers remained ardent Imperialists. His conservative newspaper sent a squad of top executives to the handover for one last chance to cocktail with the departing colonial elite. Hutchings compared his writings to theatre criticism of a ritual played out many times by Britain as it retreated back to Europe.

Essay

A Regional Perspective
Richard McGregor, *The Australian*

BARRY LOWE

One of the Australian reporters who covered the handover, Richard McGregor is, in the parlance of journalism, an Asia-hand. His career as a newsman is firmly located in Asia where he has made a long-term commitment to stay and report on the region. He is one of a breed of journalists who leave home for foreign lands and stay away, finding the task of interpreting a society from the perspective of the outsider a challenging and absorbing one. Hong Kong was his second Asian posting. He left the territory a few months after the handover to take up his third Asia assignment in Beijing.

McGregor writes for *The Australian*, Australia's only national general interest newspaper (there is also a national financial newspaper, the *Financial Review*). *The Australian*, part of Rupert Murdoch's media holdings, has a relatively small readership, which reflects the Australian preference for city-based newspapers, but its broadsheet format and emphasis on national politics make it a prestigious publication whose readers are generally at the higher end of the socio-economic scale. McGregor, who formerly worked for the government-owned Australian Broadcasting Corporation, joined *The Australian* in 1992 when he was working in Japan. It was his years in Japan that converted him into a committed observer of Asian culture and societies. He became *The Australian*'s correspondent in Japan. The Kobe earthquake was the last big story he covered there before being assigned to Hong Kong in mid-1995, two years before the handover.

'I think there were major differences in how the Australian reporters approached the story of the Hong Kong handover and how reporters from other countries, for example Americans, looked at the story. Australians saw it in regional terms: a political event that had a regional Asian context. Americans saw it as world history, a chapter in the Cold War. They tended to have definite views about what was right and wrong in the situation; Australian reporters didn't have the same missionary zeal as the Americans. The British, on the other hand, were preoccupied with notions of empire; some British reporters revealed an almost indignant tone in their reporting of the handover, indignant about what the evil Chinese were going to do with their colony.'

McGregor saw Hong Kong's transition from colony to Chinese sovereignty as a transition between two political cultures: the open political culture that Governor Chris Patten had been trying to develop and the closed political culture that Tung Chee-hwa has the task of introducing at the behest of the Chinese government. 'Patten tried to build a political culture in Hong Kong. Tung is doing the opposite: he's trying to depoliticise the territory. Hong Kong's burgeoning political life was cut off at the knees. Tung's only contribution was the addition of some Chinese theatricals to official life: like the hand-clapping in unison that the Chinese politicos go in for,' McGregor said.

McGregor was one of only a handful of Australian journalists who were in Hong Kong for the long term, who covered the handover from the perspective of a deep understanding of the territory acquired during a long term of residence. In the last weeks before the handover he witnessed the arrival of numerous countrymen and women who were sent by their outlets to report on the final days of the colony, including some colleagues from *The Australian*'s head office in Sydney. 'I worked hard on the handover story for more than a year. But the parachute journalists didn't bother me. If fact I often felt it was useful for someone fresh to come in and look at the story with a new pair of eyes. And it was good to have some back-up in the days before the handover because there was simply too much news to process for one person.'

McGregor found the night of the handover an emotion-charged event that will remain in his memory as one of the biggest stories of his career. 'It was such a unique event, and the heavy rain gave it dramatic pathos. The event was brilliantly organised. There was a lot of money spent to make sure everything went smoothly. The negotiations between the two sides over how the event would be stage-managed included some fascinating intrigue. For example, the Chinese insisted that the playing of God Save the Queen should finish ten seconds before the stroke of midnight so that the Chinese conductor had time to raise his baton to start his orchestra on the Chinese national anthem. Then was a protracted argument over the placement of the fans that would ensure that the flags billowed out instead of lying limply against the flagpoles.'

McGregor did numerous background and scene-setting stories during his coverage of the lead-up to the handover. One that amused him concerned a village in the New Territories that was given money to build a monument to the handover. 'I went out there to cover the inauguration of the monument which was clearly a monument to British oppression, ironical when you consider that the money was provided by the British government of Hong Kong. But even more ironical was when I asked to talk to the village headman – a Mr Li – they told me he was away in England seeing his son graduate from a British university.'

He was also responsible for his newspaper's coverage of China which made him somewhat reliant on China's Xinhua News Agency, whose Hong Kong office was responsible for facilitating visits and contacts by foreign journalists wanting to travel to China on reporting assignments. Xinhua was not as helpful as he would have liked. 'Xinhua had a siege mentality. Their officers were rude and nasty and obstructive. At least the Chinese Foreign Ministry staff who have taken over the role of foreign media liaison since the handover display a veneer of civility; at least they answer calls.'

On the eve of his departure to Beijing, where he will open a bureau for *The Australian*, McGregor was glad to be leaving Hong Kong. He had some critical observation about Hong Kong society: 'Hong Kong society doesn't have the levels that other societies have. In a sense Hong Kong is not a real place. Overall Hong Kong people don't have time for friendship. I'm glad I've been here but I'm glad I'm going.'

Interview

The Last Great Chapter of Imperial History

Graham Hutchings, China Correspondent, *The Daily Telegraph*

An inability to refrain from interfering in Hong Kong will demonstrate that China, despite its rapid economic growth, remains a fundamentally crude and backward country. Respect for the autonomy promised by the Joint Declaration will indicate that the new sovereign power is undergoing significant change. At the end of fifty years we would hope that 'one country two systems' will have become redundant. There will be rather 'one country one system' and that system will be Hong Kong's, with the rule of law, freedom of speech and representative government... To use a commercial expression familiar to the people of Hong Kong, we are looking for the biggest reverse takeover in history.

'Will the East be Red?'
The Daily Telegraph Editorial July 1, 1997

The Daily Telegraph's Graham Hutchings was a China scholar with an ambition to work as a journalist because he said it gave him 'the opportunity to be more exposed to China'. Twelve years ago, he wrote to a number of British newspapers and pleaded, 'You need to improve your China coverage and I am the man to help you do it'. He was hired by the Daily Telegraph, *so that he could employ his fluent Mandarin to report from Beijing. He first came to Hong Kong in 1983 and began work here a decade later.*

Knight: *What was the most important angle in the handover story for you?*

128

Hutchings: The object was to present for a British audience a story which was about the transition in the last major British colony. It had been in the making for thirteen years but which firstly was unusual because the territory concerned wasn't going to be independent. Secondly, it was going to be transferred to a country which operated on very different principles from those which had applied before the transition. It was a story of some drama, magnitude and some menace.

Nearly every news organisation has a limited news hole in which stories are placed. With the handover, most of that space was taken by coverage of structured events. Was there much room for anything else?

Hutchings: No. The aftermath was a bit weak. It was a question of tracking the speeches that followed, trying to get the flavour of the new regime and of course relying on people on the streets telling you what they thought about it. In a way, it was a one or two shot story.

What was the role of the Government Information Services?

Hutchings: Well, they were the gatekeepers of all the major events. I had known them for some years before this happened. It might have been more difficult for people who had just arrived. This was not a spontaneous news story. The script was written thirteen years before it happened. There wasn't going to be any blood. There probably weren't going to be any unexpected developments. So in a way, you were doing a bit of theatre criticism, a review of some sort of performance rather than trying to rush around and keep pace or keep a step ahead of a moving story.

Were some journalists expecting violence?

Hutchings: The congregation of so many media people could have generated something. There might have been somebody in the community who would use the occasion to do something they might not otherwise. In the story itself, it [violence] wasn't likely. The fact that this place was under the international gaze and probably would never be so again, made that a possibility, but no more than that.

Were the parachute journalists disappointed?

Hutchings: I imagine so. It had the ingredients for them for a dramatic and sexy story. It must have been somewhat tame, particularly as many of them were battle-hardened reporters who had seen many more exciting events than the transition to Chinese rule in Hong Kong. Parachutists understand that this goes with the job.

There are good and bad ones. For them, this [story] probably wasn't a very good one.

I am personally a little uncomfortable with this style of journalism. I am a little old-fashioned in a way because I believe a journalist performs best if he is at home in the culture of the place he's reporting. But I admire many of my colleagues who do this work. They do the job and seem able to switch off and enjoy themselves when they have done so. Whether readers enjoy it as much is for them to say.

Do parachutists have any advantage over resident correspondents?

Hutchings: They are perhaps more in touch with their audiences and editors. They know what is required. They do have another advantage related to the story, I think. If they are good journalists, they can see with a clarity which is sometimes given to people who approach a story from the outside. The issues can get lost by a local person looking for the nuances and subtleties. The down side is you get prejudices and stereotypes as well. Journalists should, up to a point, jump the hurdles of language and culture.

You are a China specialist. How would you feel about being parachuted into another region next week?

Hutchings: I wouldn't like it all. I would probably have a headache.

Why did so much of your newspaper's reporting of the handover concern itself with the ritual of end of empire?

Hutchings: *Telegraph* readers seem to be interested in that. It's a paper read by large and small 'c' conservatives and is a paper associated with an imperial tradition. Therefore the unravelling of empire, the nostalgia, the sadness of it, the uncertainty of what will follow add the feeling that a chapter was about to close, [and it] was important to get over. Personally I feel sensitive to those issues and feel a certain amount of emotion about it myself. I felt very much at home writing about it.

(Knight)

CHAPTER
SIX

JAPANESE RADIO VOICES
Parachuter's Paradox

Yoshiko Nakano

It was 4:05 p.m. on the last colonial day in Hong Kong. As British rule dwindled to less than eight remaining hours, NHK Radio 1's handover special went on the air carrying its first voice from Hong Kong:.

> (Light jazz in the background)
> Hello, this is Yoshihiko Tsubokura in Hong Kong. You're listening to 'Asia as a Whole: "Ni hao" Hong Kong, Handover Special'. Hong Kong will be returned from Britain to China at midnight of June 30, or 1 a.m. Japan time. How is Hong Kong going to change? We will report it along with conversations on lifestyle and culture of Hong Kong. In the next thirty hours – until tomorrow night – we will bring you programs from time to time from this studio in NHK Hong Kong Bureau.
>
> (NHK Radio 1 1997a)[1]

Over the next thirty hours, Japan's public radio NHK carried forty-two more voices from Hong Kong for a total of over five hours of live news analysis and talk show format. NHK's temporary radio studio was in a high-rise in the Central business district. It was actually a tiny video editing room which was also used to store newspapers. The removal of an editing machine left just enough space for two microphones on a small table and four collapsible chairs for a host and guests.

'We were broadcasting from Hong Kong, but we weren't broadcasting from the [Convention] Centre where the Ceremony was taking place,' said Yoshio Ueda, a senior program director who orchestrated NHK radio's handover coverage. 'We weren't broadcasting from where the People's

Liberation Army troops were moving in. Our studio was a place for broadcast operations, and not where things were happening. What else could we see from the bureau? Fireworks? No, we couldn't even see the fireworks. We went live, but it was "live coverage" only to that extent.'

Ueda was fully aware that his team, which flew in six days before the handover, was removed from the centre stage. His team was not an army of foreign correspondents, but a production crew – three producers, two presenters and a technician. In Tokyo, their programs mostly covered domestic issues, and they were not used to processing information either in English or in Chinese. For breaking news, they relied on dispatches from NHK's corespondents who based themselves in the Press Centre. In short, the radio operation had rather limited access to information.

Because of this limited access, Ueda designed programs that focused on people and context rather than news itself. 'Our main goal is to report how people in Hong Kong feel about the handover, and what the future holds for Hong Kong,' Ueda said a few days prior to the handover. To bring Cantonese and English voices on the air, he prepared pre-packaged reports, and planned live interviews by reporters. He sent out two English-speaking freelance reporters – including myself – and armed us with Cantonese-Japanese interpreters. To broadcast the speeches of Prince Charles and President Jiang Zemin

Program director Ueda (on the right) in editorial meeting   Source: Kazuaki Hanada

live, Ueda made arrangements for simultaneous translation. In contrast to the broadcast speeches, translation was not an option for talk shows and commentaries, as the translators' stiff voices could not track conversations which were characterised by a fast paced rapport. One consequence of this was that all studio guests – three Hong Kong Chinese and four Japanese – had to be Japanese speakers.

Many visiting journalists also operated with the constraints of limited access, a lack of timely information and the difficulty in dealing with local languages, and still managed to produce long hours of live programming. This chapter looks at the operation of NHK Radio 1, and examines how the producers coped with these constraints, in order to broadcast voices from Hong Kong.

Hong Kong Hype

On the handover eve, there were twice as many Japanese journalists as British or mainland Chinese journalists in Hong Kong. Over 1,300 Japanese journalists from forty-five organisations applied for press accreditation, while there were only 688 applications from Britain and 610 from mainland China. The size of the Japanese press corps was second only to Hong Kong's local media.

Why did the handover attract so many Japanese journalists? For many Japanese, Hong Kong was one of the most familiar foreign lands. In 1996, according to the Hong Kong Government (1997), 2.4 million Japanese visited Hong Kong, making it the No.1 Japanese tourist destination. For Japanese tourists, Hong Kong has been a giant bargain shopping mall. In addition, Hong Kong is a business centre for more than 3,000 Japanese companies including about forty-five banks licensed to operate in Hong Kong. The beloved territory was about to be handed over to a China which many Japanese regarded as authoritarian and closed. They were also vaguely uncomfortable as China's growing wealth reshaped the region. In a poll conducted by the Japanese Prime Minister's Office (1997), when Japanese people were asked whether they felt sympathetic to China, 50.2 per cent of respondents gave negative answers. Hong Kong-based writer, Ichiro Yoshida, satirised the fact that the Japanese press corps were flooding into Hong Kong to see what was going to happen to 'the beauty' in the arms of 'the beast'. In addition, the handover coincided with a gradual shift in Japanese interest from the United States to Asia. As a result, Asian coverage led to a higher audience share and larger circulation.

133

Japan's massive coverage of Hong Kong extended back at least to the beginning of 1997. For a New Year's Day Special, NHK TV 1 broadcast a live feature program from Victoria Harbour, and invited 'Happy Together' movie director Wong Kar Wai to produce a short video that captured the mood in 1997. For its first issue of 1997, the *Asahi Shimbun*'s weekly, *AERA* magazine, published a bright red cover with movie star Jackie Chan and a seventeen-page special on the 'Hong Kong Countdown'. The articles ranged from the bubble economy in the property market to stories on the Peninsula Hotel.[2] Countless TV entertainment shows sent singers and actors to Hong Kong for travelogues that introduced sharks-fin soup, factory outlets, and fortune tellers.

Handover coverage became a contest of who could tell the best stories about Hong Kong's determination, struggle and anxiety, and who could capture the most spectacular fireworks. By June 23, NHK had set up an open TV studio on the roof of the Fleet Arcade overlooking the Hong Kong Convention and Exhibition Centre, which was to be the site of the historic handover ceremony. NHK's satellite TV channels, which are roughly the equivalent of cable channels in other countries, broadcast a fifteen-hour marathon coverage of the handover, linking studios in Hong Kong and Tokyo. Fuji TV had booked their transmission satellite more than a year before the handover, and set up their mini broadcast centre in a luxury hotel in Wanchai. *Asahi Shimbun* commissioned the Hong Kong University Social Science Research Centre to conduct opinion polls of over 1,000 Hong Kong people for its 'thirty more days to the handover coverage', and also ran a thirty-six-part series entitled, 'Hong Kong Stories' that profiled numerous Hong Kong residents. Japan was saturated with stories from Hong Kong. 'When we have this much information,' NHK's senior analyst Kazuo Kobayashi commented during a radio handover program, 'we don't have time to reflect on it. We are busy just reading it' (NHK Radio 1 1997b).[3]

NHK

Nihon Hoso Kyokai (or Japan Broadcasting Corporation) was one of the major players during the handover. It sent over eighty staff – including five TV anchors – from Tokyo and other Asian bureaux. They represented the various broadcast mediums of NHK: terrestrial TV, satellite TV, AM radio, and international shortwave radio. NHK is arguably the most trusted news broadcast source in Japan. When a 7.2 Richter-scale earthquake hit the city of Kobe on January 17, 1995, 70 per cent of the people who were affected tuned into NHK TV or radio. NHK Radio calls itself *Anshin Radio*, or reliable radio, the radio that people can count on during times of natural disaster such as earthquakes and typhoons.

NHK is the only public network in Japan, and maintains that 'we are independent of both government and corporate sponsorship, being supported almost entirely by our audience' (NHK 1997:2). NHK collects a *receiving fee* from 35.8 million TV and radio households in Japan: ¥1,395 (US$12.2) for those with terrestrial TV, and ¥2,340 (US$20.5) for those with satellite dishes. Its annual budget for fiscal year 1997 amounted to ¥610.99 billion (US$5.34 billion).[4] In short, NHK is a giant, elitist, and well-financed organisation, which is often compared to the BBC. For any expert, an appearance on NHK's programs is a sign of recognition, and makes one's parents proud.

Despite the prestige that it enjoys in Japan, because of the language barrier, NHK is relatively unknown overseas. The majority of its programs are broadcast in Japanese, and do not directly reach living rooms outside of Japan. While NHK produces English TV news for audiences in North America and Europe, and broadcasts news on short-wave radio in twenty-two languages, the audience is still rather limited.

NHK's news does not reach an overseas audience easily. When it does reach overseas, it is often through foreign correspondents based in Tokyo. For example, on June 30, NHK's *Close-up Gendai*, a thirty-minute news analysis program, broadcast an exclusive interview with the Chinese Vice-Premier and Foreign Minister Qian Qichen. In the program titled 'Hong Kong Handover: Can Prosperity and Freedom be Protected?', Foreign Minister Qian explained the Chinese stance on 'one country, two systems', freedom of speech and assembly in Hong Kong, and the future of Taiwan, which were the three questions most media were asking. When asked about the Chinese prospects regarding reunification of Taiwan, Minister Qian replied:

(Voice-over in Japanese)
Seiji-teki na jittai dewa naku, Taiwan ga jikkō suru seido to shite mitomeru no desu... Seiji taisei ga kotonaru to iukoto wa tōitsu shinai riyū ni wa narimasen... Taisei ga chigattemo hitotsu no kunitoshite, tōitsu dekiruno desu.

(NHK TV June 30, 1997)[5]

(Translation)
[China] doesn't recognise [Taiwan] as a political entity, but [China] recognises a system that Taiwan practices... Having

different political systems is not a reason for us not to unify... Even with different systems, it's possible to be united as one country.

This quotation was picked up by a Taiwan *China Times* reporter in Tokyo, and produced the following headline on July 1, 'Mr Qian does not recognise Taiwan as a political entity':

Vice-premier of China, Mr Qian, was exclusively interviewed by NHK and he stated that China does not intend to take over Taiwan but instead wants to unify the whole China through 'one country, two systems'. Taiwan can maintain the present army, but China does not recognise Taiwan as a political entity.

(*China Times* July 1, 1997: 4)[6]

Although this was one of only a few TV interviews with Chinese leaders regarding the handover, it was largely unrecognised outside of Japan, and reached Taiwan only indirectly.

Radio Operation

Radio 1 is one of two AM stations at NHK, and reaches several million people throughout Japan. 'Radio 1 is like a magazine that covers everything for everybody,' Yoshio Ueda, the program director, explained. The handover special was a part of their on-going project to broadcast local perspectives from Asia. For Ueda, this was his second live broadcast project out of Hong Kong. In the summer of 1996, he directed a ninety-minute special that focused on cultural gaps between Japanese managers and Hong Kong workers. The program questioned Japanese ways of doing things through an examination of frustrations and surprises raised by the Hong Kong workers in Japanese corporations. The series continued from Taiwan and Malaysia. In 1997, Radio 1 launched another series of live broadcasts from Asian countries. 'Reports from Asia are often one-dimensional, because the air time is so limited,' Ueda said. 'So we thought, "Why don't we devote a day to a country, and introduce each country as a whole?"' The series 'Asia as a Whole' featured the culture and the lifestyle for five to seven hours from the host country. On April 29, Ueda's team broadcast from Hanoi, Vietnam; on June 30 and July 1 from Hong Kong – the handover special; on September 15 from Ulan Bator, Mongolia; and on November 3 from Shanghai, China. They framed the handover special as another chance to introduce Hong Kong perspectives.

At NHK Radio 1, the preparation for the special began in February, 1997. 'There won't be much news,' Ueda said prior to the handover. 'On the handover day, I guess things will happen just as planned.' Then, he pointed to the thirteen year lead time since the Sino-British Joint Declaration in 1984: 'The handover isn't some accident, and people are mentally prepared.' Ueda allocated straight news to be read in Tokyo. He then began to weave the past and the future prospects of Hong Kong into the coverage of planned festivities. He built the schedule around the live coverage of the Handover Ceremony, and calculated how much historical context the Japanese audience would need before the Ceremony, and how many hours he would need after the Ceremony to report reactions. A few days before the broadcast, Ueda said:

> I think many [Japanese] people probably don't know why Hong Kong is going back to China anyway. So, we decided to go over the history of Hong Kong. We also want to report what it is like for the local people to live through the handover, and how Sino-British negotiations proceeded. To spell these things out to a large number of people, I gather we needed several hours before the Ceremony.
>
> Once the Ceremony is over, it takes some time for the handover to sink in before we can report local people's reactions, and consequently what will happen. So I thought we would need more than a day to give an overview. But at the same time, I thought that we won't have enough information to broadcast constantly for more than twenty-four hours from Hong Kong.

Ueda's solution was to produce three feature programs, and spread shorter pieces in news programs. By fifty days before the handover, he had decided to broadcast live from Hong Kong for over five hours in a twenty-nine hour period between 5:00 p.m. on June 30 and 11:00 p.m. on July 1.

For preparation, Ueda read more than ten books on Hong Kong written in Japanese, news stories in a Japanese-language news database Nikkei Telecom, and the Hong Kong-based Japanese-language monthly *Hong Kong Tsushin*. 'I can only read Japanese,' said Ueda with an uncomfortable smile. To fill the gap, Ueda visited Hong Kong in May and set up a four-person research team in Hong Kong – two Japanese, including myself, who would be reporters on the handover day, a former *Sing Tao Daily* reporter, and a university sophomore. Ueda recruited the reporters from a pool of contributors to radio programs in Asia. We gathered materials and conducted interviews.

The two Hong Kongers were our link to the local community, acting as interpreters and guides for the two months leading up to the handover. Three additional interpreters joined us for the live coverage, and translated Cantonese vox pop (or reactions from ordinary people) into Japanese. With this team, Ueda gathered seventeen pre-taped interviews and nine live vox pops.

In addition, Ueda invited seven guests to the studio: the main commentator from Tokyo, three local Chinese who commented in Japanese, and three Japanese who resided in Hong Kong. An economist, Professor Toshio Watanabe of the Tokyo Institute of Technology, appeared on six programs, and commented on the future of the Asian economy, Hong Kong history, and politics. For local perspectives, Ueda looked for female voices that would be distinguishable from the voices of the host and Professor Watanabe. Ueda asked the research team in Hong Kong to find Chinese women who could express their opinions fluently in Japanese. These female guests were going to be a part of conversational volleyball for a few hours each, and since simultaneous translation was simply not an option, this limited the possible range of guests.

According to Hong Kong Government statistics, only 1.2 per cent (or approximately 75,600) of Hong Kong residents speak Japanese. This number includes 21,500 Japanese temporary residents, which left 54,100 non-Japanese. After many phone calls, two people agreed to be on the program. One was Professor Chee Ming Choo at the Chinese University of Hong Kong who specialises in the Japanese economy and Japanese investment in Asia. The other was Ms Maggie Kwan, a young Japanese language teacher at Hong Kong University. Ueda assigned Professor Chee to the live coverage of the Handover Ceremony, and Ms Kwan to two talk shows. In addition, Mr Ma Tin Wing, Deputy Managing Editor of *Hong Kong Commercial Daily*, and another Japanese speaker agreed to be studio guests for a segment on freedom of the press. The Japanese-speaking population, who are a minority in Hong Kong, had a strong presence in the broadcast.

The following is a description of live programs and reports that NHK Radio 1 broadcast from Hong Kong on July 1. The subjects ranged from the handover's implications to the outlook for the Asian economies, to shopping for brand-name goods, to unlicensed food hawkers on Temple Street, reflecting the magazine-like nature of Radio 1. The hours noted are Japan standard time. The on-air time in parentheses includes only live broadcasts from Hong Kong, and it does not include handover-related coverage from Beijing, Taipei, London, and Tokyo:

138

NHK Radio 1 Handover Special Rundown

1. *Opening (Historical review)*
   June 30, 17:05 – 17:55 JST (55 minutes)
   Theme: From early eighteenth century to post-handover Hong Kong
   Guests: Toshio Watanabe, Tokyo Institute of Technology
   Maggie Kwan, Hong Kong University
   4 live reports
   - Protest/celebration in Legislative Council area
   - Government House
   - Tour boat from Japan – 3 vox pop
   - Tsim Sha Tsui district
   2 pre-taped reports
   - Heavy reliance on food from China – vox pop
   - Kai Tak Airport

2. *Radio Evening Edition*
   June 30, 18:00 JST (10 minutes)
   Theme: Tourism and shopping after the handover
   - Interview with a Hong Kong Tourist Association official
   - Interview with a Japanese department store PR person
   Live report: from a Japanese department store, Causeway Bay

3. 19:00 Evening News
   June 30, 19:00 JST (5½ minutes)
   News wrap-up: arrival of Chinese officials, British ceremonies, correspondent's report from Beijing, Taiwan's official statement
   Guests: Toshio Watanabe, Tokyo Institute of Technology

4. *Hong Kong Q & A*
   June 30, 20:05 – 21:30 JST (85 minutes)
   Theme: Things that will and will not change after the handover
   Questions from the listeners
   - Currency
   - Shopping
   - Mandarin vs. Cantonese
   - Movies and music
   - Property market price – vox pop
   - Identity of Hong Kong people

Guests: Toshio Watanabe, Tokyo Institute of Technology
Maggie Kwan, Hong Kong University
Ichiro Yoshida, *Hong Kong Tsushin* Monthly
4 live reports:
- Shops that accept RMB (Chinese currency)
- Pre-taped interview with a jewellery shop manager
- Food vendors on Temple Street – vox pop
- Stamp shop owner on Royal stamp speculation
- Reactions from a shopping district, Times Square
1 pre-taped report:
- Interview with a linguist on Cantonese vs. Mandarin

5. *NHK Journal*
June 30, 22:00 JST (15½ minutes)
News wrap-up: 500 PLA soldiers crossed the border, pouring rain, celebrations
Live report from Victoria Park – vox pop
2 pre-packaged vox pop
Guests: Toshio Watanabe, Tokyo Institute of Technology

6. *The Handover Ceremony*
June 30 – July 1, 24:10 – 01:45 JST (95 minutes)
Live coverage of the Ceremony
6 pre-packaged interviews (Celebrity Agnes Chan and 5 other Hong Kong people)
Guests: Toshio Watanabe, Tokyo Institute of Technology
Chee Ming Choo, Chinese University of Hong Kong
Live report from an expats' home party, 2 vox pops

7. *Good Morning Radio*
July 1, 6:00 JST (6 minutes)
Guest: Toshio Watanabe, Tokyo Institute of Technology

7:00 JST (16 minutes)
Theme: Freedom of the press
Guests: Ma Tin Wing, *Hong Kong Commercial Daily*
Tetsuo Miki, *Hong Kong Post*
2 live reports: Newspaper stand
Local Chinese café – vox pop

8:00 JST (6 minutes)
2 live reports: People waiting for a train to China – vox pop
Food market in Wanchai

8. *Radio Evening Edition*

    July 1, 18:00 – 18:50 JST (11½ minutes)

    News wrap-up: 4,000 PLA soldiers advanced into Hong Kong, pouring rain, Jiang Zemin's speech, 1,500 democracy advocates marched, *South China Morning Post* publishes Jiang Zemin's speech in Chinese

    Theme: Reactions of young generation in Hong Kong

    Live report: Mongkok

    Guest: Mariko Watanabe, Institute of Developing Economies

9. *NHK Journal*

    July 1, 22:00 – 23:00 JST (12 minutes)

    News wrap-up: To what extent would China keep the promise to protect democratisation and freedom of speech?

    6 pre-packaged vox pops (3 Hong Kongers, 1 Swiss businessman, 1 Filipina domestic worker, and 1 British businessman)

    Live report: Fireworks

    Correspondent's report: 1,500 democracy advocates marched, Tung Chee-hwa's domestic agenda

    (Correspondents' report from Beijing, Taipei, London and Tokyo [18 minutes])

The coverage was a two-day crash course on Hong Kong and the handover. The only live event was the ceremony. Radio was not suitable to cover the British Farewell Ceremony or the new SAR official's Inauguration Ceremony.

While there were various voices of anonymous citizens such as a property agent, a vegetable vendor, and a Filipina domestic worker, there was a notable omission. Martin Lee's voice and name were missing from the broadcasts. Although the reports frequently mentioned democracy advocates as a group, and reported the march on the afternoon of July 1 that was organised by a faction of the Democratic Party, the Hong Kong Alliance in Support of Patriotic Democratic Movements in China, they did not cover Lee's speech at the Legislative Council building. Unlike many English-language media and Japanese newspapers that chose Lee's voice as a symbol of democratic hope, Ueda produced programs that explored issues in Hong Kong through more than thirty voices of local residents.

Conflicting Identities

Instead of Martin Lee, the Japanese media had their own Hong Kong icon and one out of necessity who could address the audience in

Japanese – a 1970s pop star turned celebrity, Agnes Chan. For many Japanese, Agnes Chan represented a Hong Kong that was ready to face challenges. As a teenager, she moved to Japan, learned to sing in Japanese with an accent, and became a pop star. She later earned a doctorate from Stanford University, and often acted as a cultural critic. On the handover eve, she was featured in a forty-five minute oldies music show on NHK TV, sang in a pre-handover concert at Happy Valley Racecourse in Hong Kong, and reported the historical countdown from a local Chinese café for TV Asahi. On July 1, she appeared for an hour on NHK's satellite channel as a part of their wall-to-wall coverage. On NHK Radio, her pre-packaged interview ran for over two and a half minutes while the world awaited the entrance of Prince Charles and Jiang Zemin and the commencement of the Handover Ceremony:

> **Host:** Now, many people are awaiting the Hong Kong handover with various thoughts. We asked several people for their comments. I'd like you to listen to them. The first one is from somebody you know very well, Hong Kong-born personality, Ms Agnes Chan.

> **Chan:** (in Japanese) I'm really excited. After it returns to China, is [Hong Kong] going to change or not going to change? I'll watch closely and try to do what I can. When I first heard [about the handover], I was stunned. We like what we're used to, so we panicked. Some went overseas, and many of my friends moved overseas. But as the time went by, some said, 'Well, maybe it's okay,' and came back [to Hong Kong]. In the meantime, I got married, and then came the Tiananmen Incident, and people panicked again. Then, the democracy movement began in Hong Kong, and thus changed people's consciousness in many ways. People in Hong Kong have various thoughts. I think this handover is a part of a big historical trend that can't be reversed by an individual. I think this is the way it should be. I'm now convinced that this is a good thing.

> (NHK Radio 1 1997c)[7]

Chan gave a personal account of the Sino-British Joint Declaration, the Tiananmen Incident, and the handover, all done in Japanese in her familiar voice. She linked the historical context with the emotions that Ueda was trying to communicate to the audience. Her comments were followed by studio discussion, and then a set of four taped vox pops in

142

Cantonese with Japanese voice-over. Opinions ranged from great expectation to some concerns for freedom of expression:

Host: Now, please listen to what four Hong Kong people have told us (when we asked) how they feel about the handover and what they think about life after the handover.

Female 1 (Cantonese with Japanese voice-over): I'm 50 years old. I moved here twenty-one years ago from Shanghai. As a Chinese, I have great expectations. I think the economy will be better because Hong Kong and China will be together and the economic sphere will expand. I think, politically, 'one country, two systems' will work and things will continue to be the way they are.

Male 1 (Cantonese with Japanese voice-over): I'm 20 years old. I think politics and the economy will stay the same for the next few years. But I don't know what will happen after that. I haven't done anything special to prepare [myself for possible changes], and I'm not planning to do anything special.

Female 2 (Cantonese with Japanese voice-over): I was born in Hong Kong and have been here for thirty years. I'm happy because we'll join fellow Chinese people. But I've had a free lifestyle until now, and I'm concerned that it may become a bit difficult to say things about politics.

Female 3 (Cantonese with Japanese voice-over): I'm 23 years old. I'm looking forward to the handover. I was born in Hong Kong and haven't lived with the [mainland] Chinese people. After the Tiananmen Square Incident occurred, our family talked about moving to another country around 1990, but now we plan to stay in Hong Kong. I hope to share Hong Kong's vibrancy and good things about Hong Kong with the [mainland] Chinese people.

(NHK Radio 1 1997c)

The four interviews were taped during Ueda's research trip in late May. They represent a complex mix of emotions. Each interview segment was followed by brief discussion by the two studio guests, Professor Watanabe and Professor Chee:

Host (live): I hear many people who say that they thought about emigrating to another country, but they now calmly await the handover. Professor Watanabe, what did you think?

143

Watanabe (live): Listening to these comments, I thought they tell us that, for the people of Hong Kong, the handover to China touches their delicate emotions. They have lived in colonial Hong Kong, and didn't have their motherland. Some people were saying that they were happy to see Hong Kong return to its motherland. But most people in Hong Kong fled from the People's Republic of China after it was established and crossed the border. Reunification with China evokes anxiety for the future, so most people seem to have mixed emotions. The interviews tell us that people are happy and anxious at the same time.

(NHK Radio 1 1997c)

The people in colonial Hong Kong often lived with conflicting identities. The same people who identified as British subjects are also Chinese citizens, and yet often distanced themselves from the people in mainland China. The taped interview portrayed people with multiple identities.

Compare these vox pops with the ones from the *Guangzhou Daily* which uniformly addressed pride and joy. A *Daily* reporter at Kai Tak Airport describes a Chinese-American family who flew in from Los Angeles as:

A boy passenger wore a T-shirt bearing the Chinese characters 'Celebrate the Return, Wash Away National Shame'. His grandfather said: 'As overseas Chinese, we are so proud that we have seen this day !'

(*Guangzhou Daily*: July 1, 1997:8)[8]

At Kowloon train station, a passenger from Guangzhou raved about a stronger China:

A certain Mr Zhang excitedly said: 'I returned to the mainland from Hong Kong to set up a plant, and have personally felt the changes in China and its growing strength and wealth following the reforms. It would not have been easy for Hong Kong to return if China was still weak and poor. So I dropped my business there to come back to Hong Kong to witness this historic moment'

(*Guangzhou Daily*: July 1, 1997:8)

Although these voices were presented as vox pops, they echoed the Chinese Communist party lines.

By contrast, the BBC TV's vox pops communicated nostalgia. The BBC broadcast a piece on the last colonial regatta by the Royal Yacht

Club which was the only institution to retain the word 'Royal'. An elderly British couple on a yacht commented on the final day in the colony:

Husband: Sadness. And not a little doubt about the future.

Wife: I think we will be not necessarily third class citizens. But we are visitors, but not owners anymore.

(BBC: June 30, 1997)[9]

Unlike the Chinese and British press, NHK Radio was a third party to the handover, and presented more complex and conflicting emotions from the streets of Hong Kong. In addition, the void of visual spectacles left room to examine the issues through pre-recorded interviews. Mr Raymond Ng, who managed an advertising agency, expressed in Japanese his concerns over corruption and nepotism:

Ng: I think many Hong Kong citizens are not interested in politics. As long as we can live freely, and travel overseas freely, we'd rather think about making money. Until now, Hong Kong has been ruled by the British Government, and our lifestyle and ways of thinking are completely different from [people living under the Chinese] Central Government. So we definitely have some concerns. Of course, we are concerned about politics. After [Hong Kong] returns to China, can we live as freely as before, and conduct business as freely? I think this is the biggest concern of the Hong Kong people. And, for example, for my business, I have some concern that Chinese bureaucrats, or some powerful figures will come to Hong Kong, or their sons and daughters will come to Hong Kong, and ignore Hong Kong's law and, for example, bribe people. But because this person is a daughter or son of so-and-so, we can't arrest him. In a free market [economy], people compete with each other, but if these people use their power, it won't be free competition.

(NHK Radio 1 1997c)

Mr Ng gave one of the most candid interviews expressing his fear regarding corruption after the handover. After Ng's segment, Professor Chee, speaking in Japanese, followed him by saying that corruption ranks high among post-handover concerns in various surveys conducted in Hong Kong, and suggested one solution:

Chee: (live in Japanese) The question is how we should overcome this [issue of corruption]. I think this is probably not

145

an issue which Hong Kong can solve by itself. Of course, Hong Kong's governmental bodies such as the ICAC [Independent Commission Against Corruption] will establish more offices to regulate corruption. But at the same time, this [problem] should be controlled within China. Actually, people in China are very unhappy about corruption. In that sense, it is important [for China] to establish a policy that reduces corruption.

(NHK Radio 1 1997c)

Later in the program, Hong Kong-based British playwright Dino Mahoney and his mother who flew in for the handover shared their thoughts in a live interview from his home party:

Nakano: (live in English) The sun is finally setting on June 30. What are your thoughts?

Mahoney: It's a very symbolic time. It's an artificial time. I mean the date really doesn't mean anything. It's not a part of usual sensible period. But we are feeling that maybe it's the end of the British Empire. There is a feeling of kind of nostalgia, and feeling of relief.

Nakano: What do you mean?

Mahoney: I think some people would feel that the British Empire has finally ended, and some people would feel that it's good that it ended because we feel guilty about having an empire.

(NHK Radio 1 1997c)

In this report which I filed using a cellular phone, Mr Mahoney's mother commented, 'I feel that it is only fair that it is given back to China. Because after all, it was taken from them, and it has to go back where it belongs.' I translated these comments consecutively on the air.

NHK Radio topped these voices with commentary that was relatively confident about the future. The main analyst, Professor Watanabe who specialises in the economy of Greater China, gave an optimistic opinion on the implementation of 'one country, two systems', and he basically repeated the following comments over five programs:

Watanabe: Economically speaking, as I said earlier, Hong Kong is an extremely important place for the modernisation of the Chinese economy. I think [Hong Kong and China] agree that if Hong Kong's prosperity is harmed, there is no future for China.

146

So I think it will be fine economically. Politically speaking, I think there are difficult issues, but I think China will respect Hong Kong's freedom, political freedom. The reason is that, for China, there is an extremely important agenda awaiting which is the reunification of China and Taiwan. If China intrudes in Hong Kong's affairs, and clearly curtails political freedom, reunification of Taiwan will be more and more unrealistic. Therefore, I think there are many small technical difficulties, but ['one country, two systems'] will be basically respected.

(NHK Radio 1 1997d)[10]

The Ceremony

While the reporting of unofficial voices was a strength of NHK Radio coverage, live broadcast of official events was not. Ueda's operation was removed from the Convention Centre where the Ceremony was taking place, and cut off from the sources for breaking news. NHK's correspondents were filing their news from the Press Centre in Wanchai, which in turn transmitted the news dispatches directly to Tokyo. As Ueda put it, the studio was not 'where things were happening'. When a presenter in Hong Kong wanted to confirm how many People's Liberation Army soldiers were to cross the border and at what time, the news editor in Hong Kong asked staff in Tokyo to fax the news manuscripts to the Hong Kong studio. Ueda noted that this set-up was not unusual, and was often used for earthquake coverage:

> When a natural disaster occurs, we rush to the scene. Depending on the size of the disaster, large areas could be affected. We say we are reporting from where things are happening, but it is just one spot of the large affected areas. We know what is happening there, but not in other places. We send people to various spots, and they file their news to Tokyo [News Center]. And because there are so many of them filing stories, we often ask staff in Tokyo to send the script back to where we broadcast.

In the small 'studio', a few miles away from the Convention Centre, the presenter and his two guests broadcast the Ceremony live looking at three TV monitors and referring to Japanese notes based on press releases by the Government Information Services (GIS) and on information from various other sources. 'We didn't know exactly what was going to happen,' Ueda said reflecting on the live broadcast. 'We

147

didn't have a detailed schedule of the Ceremony until the last minute. In fact, well, we didn't have one even after the Ceremony began. We were really nervous, because midnight of June 30 was the critical moment.'

Ueda distributed to his staff the broadcast schedule which contained the following description of the Handover Ceremony:

NHK Radio's Broadcast Schedule for the Handover Ceremony

23'37" – 23'40"	Principals enter
23'40" – 23'53"	British and Chinese honour guard salute (5 minutes each)
23'53" – 23'58"	Speech by Prince Charles [simultaneous translation]
23'58" – 23'59"	Union Jack and Hong Kong flag lowered (British national anthem)
23'59" – 24'00"	[Time for adjustments]
24'00" – 24'02"	Chinese and SAR flags raised (Chinese national anthem)
24'02" – 24'07"	Speech by Chinese President Jiang Zemin [simultaneous translation]

'It's really sketchy,' Ueda said referring to this section of his broadcast schedule. It was indeed sketchy as a basis for live programming. But the GIS press release was no more detailed. It offered only one piece of additional information – the configuration of the British and the Chinese flag parties:

Schedule of Handover Ceremony provided by the Government Information Services

1. Audience enters Grand Hall
2. Military bands take position
    British and Chinese delegations and HK representatives take seat
3. Honour guard formation
4. Principals enter
5. Honour guard salute
6. Speech by Prince of Wales
7. ■ 3 British military and 3 Chinese military carrying PRC flags move onto stage. Chinese flag party presents PRC flag to Chinese principals, British flag party salutes British principles [sic].

- 3 RHK Police and 3 SAR Police carrying SAR flag move onto stage. SAR flag party presents SAR flag to Chinese principals, HK flag party salutes British principles [sic.]
- Chinese and SAR flag clipped on

8. British national anthem
   - Union and Hong Kong lowered [sic.]
9. Chinese national anthem
   - Chinese and SAR flags raised
10. Speech by Chinese senior leader
11. Departure

The GIS press release did not even have a time schedule attached to each entry.

An additional constraint was that nobody in the radio team had been inside the new wing of the Convention Centre, nor had anyone seen rehearsals of the Handover Ceremony. In other words, the presenter was not much more familiar with the ceremony than people watching TV in their living rooms around the world. Ueda explained:

> We broadcast as we were watching an official feed, as many other [radio] stations or TV stations did. If we had seen the Convention Centre before, when Charles came walking, we could've figured out whether he was in a lobby or the Hall by looking at the walls. But we had never been inside of the building. So when we saw Charles on the screen, we didn't know where he was.
>
> According to the time schedule that we had, it was not yet time for Charles' entrance. But we saw him on screen. Then we panicked, 'Is he inside the Hall already? It's obviously inside of a building, but is he in a lobby or the Hall?'

In the broadcast, the NHK presenter at least made it clear that he was reporting off the television images. But other journalists, including wire services, conduct this kind of indirect reporting without any attribution, prompting the President of Hong Kong Foreign Correspondents' Club, Diane Stormont, to say, 'it's a dangerous trend'.[11]

The NHK radio team also did not know what the 'Honour guard salute' was. And they confused the honour guard with the flag parties which consisted of twelve police and military men variously carrying the Union Jack, Hong Kong flag, Chinese flag, and Hong Kong SAR flag. According to Ueda's schedule, both British and Chinese honour guards were to perform consecutively for five minutes each:

Chinese Flag Party   Source: Hong Kong Government

> The entrance of the 'honour guard' was also nerve-wracking. Our
> understanding was that parties would come in separately. So I
> thought the British would come in first, and then the Chinese. But
> they walked in together. So we wondered, 'Maybe they're not the
> "honour guard." Or are they?'

The presenter, who was smooth throughout the evening, hedged as the
parties proceeded to the stage. And instead of calling them 'military
and police personnel', he said: 'Now in the Hall, uh British in sailor's
suits and uh Chinese ... uh ... people came up to the stage. Looks like
they are carrying the Chinese flag.' In fact, they were not an honour
guard, but they were the flag parties. The honour guard and the band of
each country performed for five minutes each, and then the flag parties
entered the hall together as planned.

NHK Radio carried Charles's speech with simultaneous interpreta-
tion. When the clock struck midnight on June 30, the presenter,
Kazuaki Hanada, gave NHK Radio's version of Hong Kong history.
With a carefully prepared script, he regained his control of the event:

> It is now midnight. Midnight on June 30. Hong Kong is in a new
> era. The Hong Kong Special Administrative Region of People's

Republic of China has been established. As the band playing the Chinese anthem, the red Hong Kong SAR flag which bears a white bauhinia flower with five stars on the petals, and China's five-star national flag are being gradually raised.

It has been 155 years since Hong Kong Island was ceded to Britain from the [Chinese] government under the Nanking Treaty signed after the Opium War in 1842. During the course, Japan occupied [Hong Kong] for three years and eight months during World War II. In 1982, negotiations regarding the future of Hong Kong between Britain and China began. China proposed 'one country, two systems', a concept which was unprecedented in the world, in which socialism and capitalism co-exist in one country, and asked for compromise. In December, 1984, then British Prime Minister Thatcher and then Chinese Premier Zhao Ziyang signed the Sino-British Joint Declaration, and today in 1997 [Hong Kong's] sovereignty was returned to China. In the Joint Declaration, China and Britain agreed that Hong Kong will maintain current capitalism, and possess a high degree of autonomy in areas except diplomacy and defence, as a Special Administrative Region of China.

(NHK Radio 1 1997c)

Live Coverage and Isolation

Live coverage by visiting journalists is full of paradoxes. To reach millions of people, the journalists must be isolated from the event which they are covering, and isolated from the community which they are reporting from. Rosie Dimanno (1998) of the *Toronto Star* covered the Olympic Games in Nagano, in her words, 'with no media accreditation, no hotel room and no clue.' She had flown into Japan with fear of being 'shut out' from the normal reporting activities. But she bathed publicly and ate rice and grilled sardines for breakfast at an inn, and saw a more human side of Nagano:

> It's the media throng – as I recognize now, from half a dozen Olympics past – who are actually 'shut in' by their assignment and their privilege. We go to a local saloon, in a foreign country, and think we're absorbing the culture, soaking up the atmosphere, even as we operate in a narrow tunnel of exposure.

NHK Radio could have broadcast the Handover Ceremony live from Tokyo, or for that matter London or Beijing. After all, the handover was an event for a television spectacle, and not for a radio narrative. But because Ueda was aware of the paradoxes, he put together a sensible examination of fear of corruption, freedom of speech, and conflicting identities. 'I think we succeeded in reporting a variety of local voices,' Ueda said.

Any regrets? 'This is my third trip to Hong Kong. And yet again, I didn't have time to go up to Victoria Peak.'

INSIDERS' INSIGHTS

Imposed and Self-Imposed Limitations

In 'free' societies, the news can be constrained by journalists themselves. Even in democratic countries, audience size can be considered more important that the weight of information presented. ABC correspondent Jim Laurie sought to report a complex event involving Asia for US network television, a competitive world where ratings were king. In the interview that follows, Laurie considers the conflict between providing information and keeping the viewers entertained and the sponsors happy.

Hong Kong journalists also face unseen economic influences on the news. However, as their union leader Carol Lai suggests, the sponsor in Beijing may be more concerned about keeping the population uninformed by imposing a form of economic censorship. But whether through indifference or intervention, news from Hong Kong may still drop off the international agenda.

Interviews

Whither Hong Kong? – In the Minds of Many Americans, So What!

Jim Laurie, Senior Correspondent, ABC TV

Jim Laurie has been covering the 'Asia' beat since 1970 when he arrived as a freelancer to cover the Vietnam War. He has spent twenty years working as a television reporter.

Laurie: Television is at its best when it's covering famines, wars, events that are highly visual. It is at its worst when its covering complex events, in those areas that require a longer attention span. Economics, finance are areas where television doesn't work very well.

Knight: *During the handover didn't we see issues being obscured by images?*

Laurie: I think the handover was a set-piece television event. Because of these set-piece things – bagpipes, fireworks, ceremonies in the Convention Centre – it's fair to say that issues in Hong Kong were obscured. It was only in the months leading up to and after the handover that at least television networks that I am familiar with could begin to look at the issues. At the ABC we began doing so as early as 1996. If you looked just at the events of that day, you would not have seen a very good explanation of the issues.

But much of ABC coverage immediately around the handover consisted of live reports, did it not?

Laurie: That's right. We had about four and a half hours of live programming. But it was largely focused on the ceremony. There were inserts and occasional live interviews.

There were occasional correspondent reports from various live locations, but they were more in terms of 'this is what it looks like' and what people were saying. You didn't get into core issues about China's intent or any of the major issues that affect Hong Kong; whether the Democrats, local politics, corruption, the free press or the economy. These issues were not addressed in those four hours.

Yet you had some serious interviewees such as the US Secretary of State, Madeleine Albright.

Laurie: I can certainly relay some of the complaints of the US Consulate here. They did complain to us about having her interview delayed by approximately twenty minutes because of ABC's desire to cover what was colour [good pictures as opposed to good substance]. Just as television is great covering the Macy's Thanksgiving day parade or the Rose Bowl in California, it's great covering bagpipes, marching bands and fireworks. The problem was also that there was a great question in the minds of the average American as to whether Hong Kong meant anything to them. Whither Hong Kong? In the minds of many Americans, so what! So perhaps that was part of the rationale for emphasising the ceremonial over the substance. I can also say that there were a lot of pre-packaged reports that were put together for use during the live coverage and most of these reports were not used. They were background reports which talked of economics and politics. They were sacrificed because of the event itself.

But doesn't live television at least offer the opportunity to grill the key people involved.

Laurie: Except that two of the people most crucial to this handover, Patten and Tung Chee-hwa, were not available to anybody for live interviews during that day. They both claimed their schedules were too busy. They had both been available for pre-packaged interviews the weekend before the handover, but none were available on the day. It goes without saying that none of the Chinese leadership made themselves available for interviews. Each one of these individuals was asked.

We have talked about the triumph of style over substance in live reporting. But also isn't there a question of perspective? Live television appears to many viewers to be an accurate and immediate account of events, yet isn't it really sometimes just an ad hoc account of the sliver of reality surrounding the broadcast site?

Laurie: I have been in that situation dozens of times myself in Baghdad, Bosnia, in China and elsewhere and the trend is sadly to use the technology because it is there. Because you can go live, you do go live. I remember in 1991, during the coup in Moscow and then the so called parliamentary attempted coup against Boris Yeltsin. We and CNN were going live. We did not know what was going on inside the White House which we could have got to, had we not been chained to camera positions. I don't think that many correspondents are very good when they are doing live television. They would be much better to take time to think, not have to be extemporaneous, to write something, craft it and be out there to see and talk and come back, digest and then get on with it. There is very little digestion of information possible when you are going live all the time. What we now have at the BBC and CNN, we have more of this around the clock revolving news. I don't think all news is better news. It is simply more news and often worse news in terms of content.

(Knight)

Self-Censorship in Hong Kong Media

Carol Pui-yee Lai, Chairperson, Hong Kong Journalists Association

The Hong Kong Journalists Association is a trade union. It monitors freedom of expression, lobbies for legal reform, and publishes an annual report. Its 1997 report says, 'It is self-censorship, rather than

155

direct intervention, that will more likely undermine freedom of expression in the future' (HKJA 1997b). The chairperson, Carol Lai, says self-censorship began several years before the handover, and it happens mainly due to the pressure from editorial or management level. Prior to heading the Hong Kong Journalists Association, Lai was a reporter for several Hong Kong newspapers including Oriental Daily News, South China Morning Post, Hong Kong Economic Journal, *and* Ming Pao.

Nakano: *Can you share some of the concerns that were raised by your members during the handover coverage?*

Lai: In early July, a lot of criticism was reported to the SAR government, because they had very bad handling of the press. The first meeting between Mr Tung [Chee-hwa] and the head of the People's Liberation Army was a very closed one. They only invited Xinhua and CCTV people. Then the pictures and footage were later despatched to the local media.

People were very furious about this. They weren't happy because under the British colonial rule, local media people enjoyed press freedom, and they were given a chance to report especially those official occasions.

One journalist said that when he went to cover the PLA moving in across the border, CCTV had good positions, everybody else was in rather distant positions. Was it brought to your attention?

Lai: I haven't heard much about that. Some colleagues reported to us by saying that very often CCTV had enjoyed privilege over the local media. When there was a cordoned off area for the press, CCTV people usually didn't need to go inside. They just walked around outside of the corded area. In fact, the local media weren't very happy about that.

When, do you think, self-censorship began in Hong Kong?

Lai: Many people ask about self-censorship, and in fact it's difficult to say. When we talk about it, we cannot just look at local media in 1997. In fact, many local media including newspapers, TV stations and radio stations have already been adjusting their reporting for quite some time, because Hong Kong people knew about the July 1 [handover] date since 1984.

In the past, we had the so called Kuomintang papers that were funded by the Taiwanese Kuomintang. In fact, many papers carried dates according to the nationalist Taiwan calendar. But eventually they dropped this in the last five years. And the last one dropped it in 1996. So right now they are clean – without any visible linkage with Taiwan. In fact, pro-Taiwanese papers have either closed or retreated back to Taiwan in the past five years.

Some middle-of-the-road newspapers are more sympathetic to Beijing authority in terms of their editorial decisions. For instance, after 1989, most of the Hong Kong newspapers, including Chinese and English language ones, used the term 'June 4 Massacre.' It reflected the papers' attitude toward that incident. Maybe two or three years ago, people started to drop that term. Even in the *South China Morning Post*, one reporter told me that he insisted on writing 'June 4 Massacre', but it was edited by his sub-editor.

At what level, do you think, has self-censorship been practised?

Lai: I think most of the reporters, especially front-line reporters, didn't join the field to self-censor their own stories. People joined the field to get something done. I'm not saying that reporters don't alter their own stories. But I think most of the pressure is coming from the top – from editorial level, or management level. Of course, sometimes [pressure] is not direct, but indirect.

Reporters also have pressure from their sources of information: from Hong Kong SAR officials, from Chinese officials, and even from [Hong Kong] politicians. In our [annual] report, we mention carrot-and-stick tactics. This is some kind of general tactics used by the Chinese authority – if you are good and 'friendly', then you can have a carrot. They are going to invite you for briefing. They are going to invite you to China. But if you are 'unfriendly' and criticise Chinese policy, perhaps they will penalise you by blacklisting you. In fact, *Apple Daily* and *Next* magazine reporters suffer a lot, because until now they haven't been able to get official accreditation to go to the mainland to cover news. Recently the Foreign Ministry of China had a briefing in Hong Kong, and *Apple Daily* reporters wanted to go and cover it, but they were refused.

So the point is most of the reporters don't want to self-censor their own stories, but in reality, they receive lots of pressure from the larger environment and from their newsroom. So they need to adjust themselves very often. Sometimes, they need to tone down certain stories, sometimes they just have to compromise. But I still believe that most of them want to get things done.[1]

(Nakano)

157

CHAPTER
SEVEN

THE EAST WIND IS BLOWING

Alan Knight and Yoshiko Nakano

> There are a lot of things the media do not understand in the West.... Just because in Hong Kong, Asia is not taking Western democracy wholesale, they think it is wrong.
>
> Robert Chua, television entrepreneur (1997)

Western foreign correspondents' privileged dominance of international news is almost over. The safari-suited reporter who interpreted Asian affairs, banged out his stories on ancient typewriters before filing them down crackling telephone lines, now exists more in the minds of romance novelists rather than in the electronic reality of the late twentieth century. The slicked down and suited television anchors who dropped into Hong Kong for handover week fulfilled expectations of audience demand for what were seen as roving reporters. Yet many were unqualified and simply unable to act as news gatherers. Many instead served as news actors appearing before a colourful backdrop devised by the Hong Kong Government Information Services. In any case, some news directors seemed more interested in the lavish spectacle than the substance of the events. Those Western journalists who sought the deeper story found access to official sources strictly rationed, and opportunities to ask questions restricted.

Out of Press Releases

The handover was a series of staged events. And press release reality prevailed. Many respected news organisations based their reports of the handover on handouts from the Government Information Services and other political sources.

Consider the coverage of Governor Patten's departure from Government House, the colonial administrative nerve centre which some reporters chose to style simply as his 'home'. The report for the BBC's main lunchtime domestic bulletin was loaded with a long-standing affection for an empire passing. Although BBC staunchly defends its independence from government directives, when it comes to international news, it emerges as the distinctive voice of Britain. In the case of the handover, an event of emotional significance to both the British people and the government, such ethical differences maybe imperceptible to non-British person watching the World Service.

When the BBC reported on the last governor leaving Britain's last major imperial outpost, the script came from an immaculate colonial source. The final shots from the departure sequence revolved around an event heralded by a press release from the Government Information Services. The release, titled 'Brief on Government House Departure Ceremony', had been issued the day before. The expected departure was precisely timed (4:20 p.m.) and included musical accompaniment (Auld Lang Syne). The press release noted:

> Mr. Patten will also follow the tradition of doing three rounds in his car in the grounds of Government House to signify that he will return.
>
> (GIS June 29, 1997)[1]

However, Governor Patten on this occasion did not follow the script, the BBC did.

Sound	Vision
And one last leaving ritual for the governor.	Union Jack flag on limousine bonnet.
His car circled the courtyard three times, a Chinese custom which means	Patten looks through rain-streaked car window as vehicle appears to circle the drive.
'hope to be back.'	Limousine leaves gates. Shot taken from outside looking in.
The gates of Government House were closed. End of era.	Gates close. Shot taken from inside looking out.
	(BBC June 30, 1997)

Patten's Car Did *Not* Circle the Courtyard Three Times

Source: Hong Kong Government

Even the *New York Times* also reported the Governor's departure as:

> Slowly, the long black car flying the governor's ensign from the hood circled the courtyard before Government House three times, a Chinese ritual performed by all previous governors to signal "we shall return".

(New York Times July 1, 1997)[2]

America's Cable Network News' live coverage also mirrored the press release. It sought to milk the departure for its emotive potential. CNN's fawning commentary, provided by presenter, May Lee, could be only loosely described as reporting:

> **Lee:** I would like to bring in Caroline Courtauld. She is a very close friend of the Pattens. Caroline, what is Mr Patten thinking right now? What kind of emotions are going on? We have seen his daughters and they were very emotional.

> **Courtauld:** I am sure that when he was handed the Union Jack by his ADC there with the strains of God Save the Queen, I am sure he would have longed to fall through the floor. He has grown to love the people of Hong Kong. Although he's had a very

difficult time from a political point of view, in other senses he has had a very interesting time, as he often says.

Lee: Tell me about Governor Patten behind the scenes. What was he like when he was in the spotlight?

Courtauld: I think he's an incredibly caring man, a very spiritual man and I think that, without that spirituality, he would have found the strain of the relationship with China impossible. He's a very close family man with a wonderful wife and a supportive family.

(CNN June 30, 1997)

As the live picture showed the Governor in his Rolls Royce, Lee and Courtauld commented on the ritual:

Lee: Now the Governor's car is circling around the driveway three times which is traditional. And he will be heading to Tamar to watch the Farewell Ceremony there. What is the tradition behind –

Courtauld: Three times around the drive? I think it is to ensure that the Governor will come back.

Lee: So we are saying 'So long', but maybe I will be back.

Courtauld: Exactly.

(CNN June 30, 1997)

Sadly for journalists who failed to use their eyes to check press releases against real events, the governor's car did *not* circle the court yard three times on this occasion. Other organisations which echoed the mistake included the *South China Morning Post*, *Ming Pao*, *Wen Wei Po*, *Guangzhou Daily*, the *Straits Times*, and *The Australian*.[3] However, *Apple Daily* and *Time* magazine had a different version of the story. *Time* magazine reported:

> But when his black Rolls-Royce arrived to take him and wife Lavender away for the last time, he surprised onlookers by failing to go around the circular drive in front of Government House three times – a colonial ritual signifying, "I shall return." Without informing his staff, Patten ordered the driver to make only one-and-a-half circuits. Loathed by Beijing for the democratic reforms he instituted, Patten had no illusions about returning to this symbol of colonial power.
>
> (*Time* July 14, 1997)[4]

Perhaps Patten was signifying that he would not be back.

Ripples

News no longer moves in one direction, back to the Western metropolis on linear cables. Instead, journalists across the world are increasingly bound together in a seamless web of information that covers almost everyone and everything, from the glass towers of Hong Kong to the jungles of Cambodia. Satellite television, interactive news services, improved telephone and fax services and the Internet do not acknowledge border checkpoints, allowing tidal flows of information. The handover prompted a series of web sites on the Internet, featuring both hard and soft news. In contrast to the sanitised but glossy *China Daily* site, China critics such as cartoonist Larry Feign provided regular updates of their views of developments.[5] Legislator Emily Lau, whose Legislative Council seat was abolished by Beijing, kept up her strident attacks and distributed her press releases and speeches on the net. Meanwhile the lives of ordinary Hong Kong people were documented by the American public television service, PBS, on its web site: *Hong Kong 97: Lives in Transition.* Alan Knight used a lap-top computer to produce *Dateline Hong Kong* (1997b), which recorded the views of local and international journalists on the transition of sovereignty.

The Internet has also changed the way media handlers were reaching their targets. As veteran journalist V.G. Kulkarni observed, reporters might have been thousands of miles away from Hong Kong, but still had access to the government version of events. Had editors been aware of the digitised press release service, they in turn might have been able to check the work of many of their far-flung reporters against the original script.

News consumers can sit at home and use the Internet to learn about events in distant locations; reading local papers, accessing government and business databases and even communicating directly with those actually involved. Of course, this is not the same as a live television cross to an eyewitness report of PLA tanks rolling across the Chinese border. But perhaps computer-collected information may prove to be more comprehensive and, in the long run, more useful.

Foreign reporters are becoming an anachronism. On the spot reporters who merely recycle official press releases may indeed be foreshadowing their own redundancies. They may in future owe their existence to news organisations which wanted to maintain an illusion that they were providing original reports from distant places.

Western reporters no longer have a monopoly on international event reporting. Their reports get back to the places they report on. Western assumptions no longer go unchallenged. Robert Chua, the Chief Executive of CE TV, an Asia-based satellite television station, produces 'positive' television documentaries sold to Chinese state television. He claimed that pro-Western reporting by foreign correspondents would damage Hong Kong's business interests. While Patten's departure was portrayed as sad, Beijing's arrival was depicted as a threat:

> When I travel around the world, being a Chinese issue, it [the handover] should be a celebration for us. But not one single person has ever congratulated me to say, 'Congratulations, Hong Kong will be back to China. It will be a big nation, 1.2 billion.' Not one person congratulates us. People always ask, 'What is going on? Will Hong Kong be OK?' Always there are these negative questions being asked all the time. I feel very concerned about this. There is a lot of negative bias in the media reporting.
>
> (Chua 1997)

Chua blamed foreign journalist reports, rather than Beijing's actions, for a perceived fall in confidence in Hong Kong's future. He saw correspondents as irresponsible and biased.

Bias, of course, lies in the eyes of the beholder and foreign correspondents may be in danger of being unfairly castigated for a robust approach to reporting, if not for their insensitivities to non-Western cultures. Working journalists' lack of self-analysis can mean that many assume that value systems which they learn in Western cultures are universal. When foreign correspondents with such views arrive in Asia, this ignorance of 'other' media procedures can be interpreted as cultural arrogance. The collision between differing journalism value systems can result in what Singapore's Senior Minister, Lee Kuan Yew has called 'friction'.[6] Western correspondents' identification with their national interests and with what many Asians identify as the old colonial powers has made them easy targets for increasingly well-connected and articulate Asian critics. Robert Chua explained:

> Everybody wants freedom. The media is misusing the freedom they are getting. They are not reporting truthfully. What we need is a well-balanced picture. But we are not getting that. We should inform the media in the West and ask them to ask more questions to find out what we have here. Let them talk to the people in the streets.
>
> I just asked a taxi driver and he said, 'No problem'. The majority are happy with what is going on.

I have been to China since April 1979. I have seen China change and I am very confident that China will give us the freedom it has promised and Hong Kong will be part of 'one country, two systems'. I have seen China change over the years. Now in Shanghai, they have talk shows and people are allowed to express themselves on the radio, complaining about various things in government, facilities and so on. They are changing. So they are wrong when they say China has no freedom at all.

(Chua 1997)

Chua was able to ignore China's selective reporting of handover events. Clearly the work of the *Guangzhou Daily* and other Chinese media showed that freedoms were expanding within China. But Beijing's continuing attempts to impose censorship on mainland media might indicate that, irrespective of Chua's entrepreneurial optimism, open questioning of key state policies is still not possible.

The 'Socialist' Ideal

Despite its drive for economic rationalisation, China remains a country under the control of a Communist Party which encourages a planned economy. The government still seeks to maintain tight control of information received by the population. Radio and television stations are state controlled; their executives belong to the relevant government Propaganda Department, bulletins are still being censored on air, and armed guards with machine pistols and drawn bayonets are still on sentry duty outside studios and master control rooms. Newspapers, particularly those in the wealthy provinces or those which report business rather than strictly political affairs, are able to exercise a higher degree of independence. But in 1997, they were almost all still state-owned and bound to the idea of socialist journalism.

Under this journalistic philosophy, newspapers are integrated with the policies of the party and government. Articulating this theory in 1901, V.I. Lenin said that the press should disseminate ideas for political education, and enlist political allies, acting as a collective propagandist, agitator, and a collective organiser. Lenin likened newspapers to the scaffolding around a building under construction: a scaffolding which not only marked the contours of the work and which facilitated communication, but also one which allowed the builders to distribute the work and view the results. Lenin saw newspapers playing a critical role in the development and training of the 'revolutionary' party itself. Communist journalists would become more than a voice of the communist state; they would be perceived as an arm of the ruling party. While the communist building might be crumbling, Lenin's enfolding scaffolding has remained largely in place throughout China.

On 28 November 1989, Jiang Zemin, who had just become Party Secretary, declared that the media should operate as 'the mouthpiece of the party' as well as 'of the people'. He claimed that some Chinese journalists' support for the pro-democracy movement was linked to bourgeois liberalisation, a product of a deviation from Marxism, which he said had created confusion among the masses. Chinese journalists were subsequently required to educate the people in the spirit of patriotism, socialism, collectivism, and self confidence in the struggle, to overcome difficulties on China's road of reconstruction and reform. According to Jiang, journalism was an important part of the party's work, and had to keep close contact with the masses and fight persistently against bourgeois liberalisation (Lehrke 1993:213).

Gunter Lehrke, a former Deputy Secretary-General of the Singapore-based Asia Media Information Research Centre, claimed this enforced politicisation caused disillusionment among mainland journalists and created disaffection among audiences:

> Demotivation and political suppression of those involved in program production are taken as tools to 'improve' the output. The officials obviously give credence to the continuous repetition of slogans that brainwash and form the new socialist individual, neglecting the desire of the audience. However, the people seem to know better and listen to foreign broadcasts. Today even farmers in remote rural areas buy short-wave receivers in order to get more reliable information. In the southern province of Guangdong, peasants purchase satellite dishes to get access to foreign TV. The future beneficiaries of such systems are already identified; commercial channels and their international media tycoons.
>
> (Lehrke 1993:218)

It could be seen that an open media in Hong Kong constituted both a threat to those who sought to 'brainwash', and a promise of a more affluent lifestyle. The heavily-guarded border had proved porous to Western ideas.

In the closing days of British colonialism, Cantonese-speaking Hong Kong-based reporters regularly crossed the China border to record incidents otherwise ignored by the mainland media. Their stories about

Chinese Delegation

Source: Hong Kong Government

strikes, industrial accidents, and police corruption provided new insights for viewers receiving broadcasts in Guangdong. They also attracted growing criticism from Chinese officials acutely embarrassed by evidence of widespread laissez-faire exploitation in what the official Chinese media still promoted as a workers' state. Hong Kong, while still a British Crown colony, was unquestionably the most consistent base for 'libertarian' journalism in East Asia. Hong Kong journalists making the transition to Beijing control were keenly aware of what it could mean for their work. Before the handover, there was concern that China might be more ready than Britain to enforce moribund but still repressive colonial legislation which was never erased from the Hong Kong statute books (HKJA 1993). Hong Kong Journalists Association activist, Mak Y.T. (1996), said journalists were under pressure to conform:

> While the clandestine nature of self-censorship means that it is difficult to pin down actual examples, there has at the same time been little evidence to suggest that the situation has improved. Television documentaries vilified by the Chinese government have been bought and then never broadcast, popular but critical TV programs have been axed, and critical newspaper columns and cartoons suddenly dropped. There are many reasons for self-censorship. Proprietors might wish to maintain good relations with the Chinese government to ensure post-1997 survival and a stake in the huge China market. Front-line journalists may exercise self-censorship to maintain a harmonious relationship with their contacts.... Given the close relations between China and Hong Kong, Beijing is unlikely to allow Hong Kong a free hand if the political situation on the mainland becomes more tense. The media tends to become the first casualty in any such situation.

The Association's concerns were heightened by the creation of a new journalists' union, the Hong Kong Federation of Journalists, which drew its membership from the executives of Beijing-funded papers in Hong Kong. In contrast to the Association's campaigns for freedom of speech, the Federation saw 'better relations with the motherland' as its primary role.

Winds of Change

Fears about the future of press freedoms appeared to be confirmed when the colony's leading English language newspaper, the *South China Morning Post*, appointed a high level Communist Party official to its staff. Feng Xiliang, then 75, was employed as a consultant in April 1997. A founding editor of the official *China Daily*, he was known to have powerful connections with China's ruling elite. Although he had lived in the United States in recent years, he was still a member of one of the most senior organs of the Beijing government, the Chinese People's Political Consultative Conference.

There was a time when the *South China Morning Post* was the pillar of the British establishment in Hong Kong.[7] But times have changed as the Empire was eclipsed by Chinese economic power. Rupert Murdoch divested himself of the information-rich *Post* and its Western intellectual baggage to concentrate on the entertainment-oriented Star [satellite] Television as it sought to harvest the rapidly-growing China advertising market. Newsman Murdoch sold out to a Malaysian-based Chinese businessman, Robert Kuok: a sugar magnate said to be the second biggest of all foreign investors in China.

Such investments can make media proprietors particularly vulnerable to political pressure. Self-made Hong Kong multi-millionaire, Jimmy Lai, was forced to divest himself of his shares in the Giordano clothing chain after his newspapers said rude things about the Chinese Premier, Li Peng. Kuok would have much more to lose than the comparatively diminutive Lai, if one of his minor subsidiaries offended a Chinese government known to wreak commercial retaliation against foreign critics.

Fears that the *Post* subsequently went soft on China were difficult to substantiate. Nevertheless, by 1997, aides to the outgoing Governor, Chris Patten, were claiming that the *Post* had gone over to 'the enemy camp'. One aide quipped that the only time that Patten had got a sympathetic press from the *Post* that year was after some unknown person had tried to poison one of his terriers. The dog survived. Patten was again relegated to the back pages.

Enter Feng Xiliang.

'I am working there as a consultant to strengthen links with China. I act only as an advisor to give an opinion to the editor and management,' he said.

Would Feng be looking at articles at the *Post* before they were printed? 'I have no role in day-to-day things such as reporting. I am not intending to comment on work unless I am asked to. I am going to be more involved in setting up links.' Feng's former colleagues spoke highly of him. An academic who met him in 1963, when Feng was an editor of the *Peking Review*, described him thus:

He was a very dapper (the word fits very well) man of great charm who to my youthful eyes appeared to be more of a language and journalism, than hard-core agitprop type. He dressed as sharp as one could get away with in those days and had slicked-down hair and more often than not the touch of a smile instead of the grim revolutionary look. His English was excellent.

Feng was described as a Chinese liberal who was said to have become somewhat disillusioned after the Tiananmen Square massacre. By that time, he had already attended a number of journalism conferences at the U.S. East-West Center and acquired a taste for life in Hawaii. He left China to become a Mass Media Fellow at the Center in 1991. 'He's one of the good guys,' a former Center colleague said effusively. But a liberal in China is something else again in the West; in Feng's case a person who has served on the national propaganda committee, a key part of the top Communist Party establishment which enforces directives requiring that Chinese journalists toe the party line. Even in effective retirement, he was made a member of the People's Consultative Committee, a repository for old and trusted senior cadres.

When questioned about this, Feng said his role at the Consultative Committee would soon be completed. He was distressed by the negative reaction to his appointment at the *Post*.

'They are calling me a censor. I am not. I don't have the power. It is in the hands of the editor and the proprietor to manage editorial policy.'

'They don't need more people to strengthen their hands'.

'I have no power. There's so much talk, I begin to wonder why I am doing it,' Feng said.[8]

The editor of the *Post*, Jonathan Fenby denied that there had been undue pressure to moderate the news (See Appendices – 'Interview'). However, he said that more than 60 per cent of the newspaper's readership were Chinese people and stories should reflect their interests. Fenby described Feng as a 'consultant', but did not elucidate on his duties.

A former *China Daily* journalist thought he had the answer to that question. Feng would be able to provide invaluable insights for the *Post* as it prepared to cover mainland affairs from within China. Would this result in better coverage? 'Not necessarily', he said. Would Feng's appointment be a form of insurance for the *Post*? 'More like a gamble', was the reply.

'Negative' Coverage and Tourism

The dispute which erupted in Hong Kong over how the handover should be covered laid bare the fault line in conflicting journalistic philosophies. It revealed a confluence of self-interest linking communist officials seeking a stable transition and business leaders determined to secure continuing profits. It reflected the central paradox of the Special Administrative Region itself: a government of freebooting capitalists appointed, approved and perhaps directed by the greatest of the communist governments.

Free reporting was characterised as being bad for free enterprise. Hong Kong expatriate public relations agency owner, Ted Thomas, claimed that prior to the handover itself, many foreign correspondents stressed divisions in Hong Kong and hoped for a disaster story. This was bad for business, Thomas said:

> These guys are coming here for a story and [think] if it's not bad news it's not news. They don't want to hear there has been a peaceful handover, that the place will continue to succeed and prosper. What newsmen are looking for is rioting in the streets, the PLA marching down the road with fixed bayonets.[9]
>
> (Quoted in Knight 1997b)

Thomas claimed that such reports would discourage tourism, correctly predicting a slump after Beijing took control. He sought to enlist local journalists whom he planned to send around the world telling the 'truth' about Hong Kong. His attempts to change international perceptions failed. According to Hong Kong Tourist Association statistics, the total number of visitors in 1997 was 10.4 million compared to 11.7 million in 1996 – a drop of 11.1 per cent. Japanese visitors showed the sharpest decline. The Tourist Association explained:

> From Japan alone, arrivals fell by 42.5 per cent, due primarily to the huge surge in arrivals from Japan in 1996, which created an unusually high base, as well as the worsening economic situation in Japan throughout 1997.
>
> (Hong Kong Tourist Association 1998)

In less than four months after the handover, Hong Kong came under the spotlight in Japan due to an exposé of overpricing for Japanese tourists. On October 11, 1997, the *Mainichi Shimbun*, which reached four million readers, revealed that hotel rooms in Tsim Sha Tsui area cost Japanese guests up to HK$2,350 (US$305) while non-Japanese paid only HK$750 (US$97).[10] Although some had long suspected this practice, it created media scrutiny and haunted Tung Chee-hwa during his first trip to Japan as the SAR Chief Executive. During his press conference in Tokyo, he was repeatedly asked to clarify his stance:

Reporter: Both Japanese newspapers as well as television news have presented the evidence to show that higher rate charge.

Tung: Well, I have not seen that, although the first time the question was raised in Hong Kong it was raised by your newspaper reporter. But today I met the leaders of tourist industry in Japan and they themselves confirmed to me there is no such fixed practices by the Hong Kong hotel industry against Japanese

Chief Executive Tung Chee-hwa   Source: Hong Kong Government

tourists and this confirmation comes from your own tourist people. As I say, individual cases there might be, but we certainly would take these things very seriously because we would like you to continue to come to Hong Kong.

(Government Information Centre 1997)

Tung suggested that he had more confidence in the leaders of the tourist industry in Japan than he did in journalists. According to the *South China Morning Post* (October 18, 1997), a Hong Kong tourism official urged journalists to stop reporting stories which damaged the tourism industry: Hong Kong Hotels Association chairman Thomas Axmacher asked the media 'not to try to do more damage by reporting on this issue' and to 'put this to rest'.[11]

Cheerleaders?

Those who saw journalists as servants of a business to be exploited in practice espoused the persistent Leninist notions of a 'responsible' press. They clashed with those who believed that journalists' first responsibility was to their readers, rather than to the state and its subordinate business interests. Western foreign correspondents reacted to such attacks with cynicism and anger, nettling Asian sensitivities. Keith Richburg, as President of the Foreign Correspondents' Club in 1997, responded strongly and swiftly to the calls for restrained reporting. 'It's not our job to be cheerleaders,' he said:

It would be an inaccurate story to say that Tung Chee-hwa was elected or selected by four hundred people to be Chief Executive in a ceremony which was supported by most Hong Kong people, if you are going to ignore the fact that some of the most prominent people in Hong Kong politics were outside demonstrating in the streets. That is part of the story. Now I know that they would rather we ignore that part of the story. The people we talk to, Martin Lee and Emily Lau, were elected with the largest majority of the popular votes of any politicians running here. They to me represent the voice of the Hong Kong people, more than some of these clowns on these committees who have not been elected to anything. I don't know why it is that people think we as media should ignore people who poll 70 per cent of the popular vote any time they stand up and run for office.[12]

(Quoted in Knight 1997b)

Richburg explicitly affirmed a libertarian philosophy of journalism, where journalists were required to question and criticise rather than support the state. Profits and public interest were not necessarily identical:

> The story of Hong Kong's continued economic vibrancy is not necessarily a story. We have reported that. It is in every story. You just don't repeat that over and over and over again because that is not news. Continuity is not news. News is what is conflict. News is where there is disagreement.
>
> When Chris Patten put out his proposals for democratic change, we went off and found some reaction from Xinhua and Beijing to criticise those proposals. That is what news is. News is where someone puts up something and someone else on the other side says where they have problems with it.
>
> If one hundred planes land safely at Kai Tak airport and the passengers get off and get their luggage and go home, we don't report that. If one plane, one day, has a mishap, say a tyre blows out and skids off the runway, that will be a front page story with a photo. Now the airport controllers may say that is unfair, 'How come you report this one incident when the day before you had a hundred land safely?'
>
> My reply is, 'You expect them to land safely. News is when one skids off the runway'.
>
> (Quoted in Knight 1997b)

But there were few political plane crashes to report. Many foreign correspondents, based in Hong Kong, remained wary of the new government's intentions after the handover. Yet as the event receded, and business appeared to go on as usual, their organisations found Hong Kong less newsworthy. Reuters moved its office to Singapore, citing lower rents and lower employment costs. Individual reporters moved to Beijing to cover Chinese affairs, while others moved to Bangkok to more closely monitor the ASEAN countries. As decision-making moved behind closed doors, there was little open conflict to report.

Western Paradigms

Journalism is a flawed craft, harried by those who would censor and dissemble, and hemmed by the political and cultural assumptions which reporters inevitably carry with them. Western foreign correspondents learn industry practices and priorities within a professional culture

173

which tolerates if not encourages criticism of governments, corporations and prominent personalities. They usually endorse the first article of the code of professional conduct for the International Federation of Journalists which states that 'Respect for the truth and for the right of the public to the truth is the first duty of the journalist'. However, the Western pursuit of the 'truth' can be delayed and diverted by the business interests of media ownership and government interventions, not to mention defamation, contempt of court and security legislation. As local media organisations are absorbed into transnational media entertainment corporations, commercial considerations can also be seen to influence international news coverage.

Hong Kong journalists still hope that they will not topple into the philosophical chasm that divides the one country with two systems. In the last half of 1997, their media appeared to operate much as it always had. There were no arrests or newspaper closures. But the threat remained. Hong Kong editors still had to be cautious of the prickly sensitivities of those in control in Beijing. Y. Joseph Lian was the Chief Editor of the *Hong Kong Economic Journal*, a newspaper which had been subjected to economic pressure in 1992 after it carried articles critical of communist-controlled 'Red Chip' companies. Lian said the Beijing leadership was the product of a culture which found Western modes of journalism difficult to understand if not tolerate.

Lian: Their background is as guerrilla fighters hailing from Yenan and other places. Whereas we grew up in a free and open society. How do we bridge the gap? It is very difficult for them to accept the style of the press in free countries. They have this mentality of seeing everyone as enemies.

Knight: We already know that some issues like the independence of Tibet or Taiwan will be particularly sensitive. How can Hong Kong journalists skirt around these?

Lian: We can talk about abstract principles and I think on that score there will be no room for negotiations. China will not permit journalists to advocate independence for its territories. On the other hand, I think there is practically nothing that you cannot discuss honestly and openly in the [Hong Kong] press. Of course, you have to pay a price. As I said, they may withdraw some economic benefits. If you say 'no problem', then you can do things your way.[13]

(Quoted in Knight 1997b)

Lian said that Hong Kong journalists should be prepared for economic retaliation against critical reporting. While some critics would be silenced, others should continue to engage in 'brinksmanship', he said.

Conclusion

During the handover, cultural and political assumptions created ideological prisms through which reporters from different countries reported the same stage-managed events. Many reporters acted as conduits for a confection of events which had been scripted by the Government Information Services. The theme to these presentations had been agreed some time before, in private negotiations between the representatives of Britain and China. As a result of this, the London *Daily Telegraph* correspondent, Graham Hutchings, saw reportage which resembled theatre review.

State censorship narrowed Chinese mainland reporting, especially in selective accounts of the political arena. In Britain, which enjoys a relatively free press, BBC reporting was skewed by nostalgia, created in part by an apparently unconscious identification with the lost empire. Japan's NHK Radio was constrained by language differences which effectively excluded much of the informed local talent. Yet the void of visual spectacles created the room to examine complex issues and emotions with pre-taped interviews. The demands of live broadcasting magnified the problems of coverage, resulting in exaggerations and mistakes. The ability to instantly transmit developments in this global event allowed media manipulators to construct theatrical tableaux to meet program needs. The fierce competition between journalists left little time for reflection, often allowing the spectacular images to obscure the issues.

Western journalists frequently assume ethical superiority over their colleagues who are subjected to, and indeed part of, systems of state censorship. But as mainland Chinese journalists increasingly adopt Western styles of reporting, bases for distinctions between state-sanctioned reports and those of Westerners who refrain from critical or informed journalism become blurred. In the context of a constructed event like the handover, such reports can become indistinguishable. More news does not necessarily mean better news. Wall-to-wall coverage can overwhelm choices which might otherwise allow the public to make informed judgement.

Hong Kong entered its post-colonial era an enigma; a bastion of freebooting capitalism ruled with the blessings of the last great Stalinist state. A city-state managed by a captain of industry, abetted by a British style civil service, backed by former communist agitators and yet opposed by liberal democrats. Local journalists were in theory able to write and say what they liked. Yet they faced the prospect of economic censorship, if not jail or expulsion. To foreign correspondents, who saw Asian news through colonial eyes, Hong Kong was no longer a story.

APPENDICES

INTERVIEW

Judge Us on What We Publish!

Jonathan Fenby, Editor, *South China Morning Post*

Jonathan Fenby has been editor of the South China Morning Post *and the* Sunday Morning Post *since 1995. A former editor of the* Observer, *Fenby first came to Hong Kong in 1965, while on leave from covering the Vietnam War. He says he began his career as a journalist employed as a 'tea boy' at Reuters news agency. Fenby added that the* South China Morning Post *must adjust to the post-colonial realities. This is an edited text of an interview conducted at the* South China Morning Post *office at Quarry Bay in Hong Kong on 10 June 1997.*

Fenby: There was a time when a lot of people would look at the *Post* to see what the British government thought or what the big British interests here were thinking. The readership of the paper at present is between 60 and 65 per cent Chinese. Another 10 per cent would be non-Chinese Asians. So three quarters of the readership are Asian people living in Hong Kong. That's a long way from the conventional view from outside which would be that because of the history of the paper and because we are in English language, we are therefore an expatriate newspaper.

If you looked at the paper fifteen years ago, you would find the automatic assumption that really quite minor events in Britain were the natural area of interest for the readership. Whereas you would not find that to be the case today. Over the last couple of years we have developed a much more Asian coverage both in the news and in the features, analysis and business sections. That's not a political decision, as such. It's a reflection of what we think our readers are interested in.

The *Post* seeks to reflect the different layers of Hong Kong. We report the law courts, crime, big traffic accidents, land slips, whatever it may be and so on. That is reporting Hong Kong as the town newspaper of Hong Kong. We are then reporting Hong Kong as a political centre. We are reporting Hong Kong as a business and finance centre. We are trying to reflect the Hong Kong–China relationship; hence the China page. We are reporting Hong Kong as the Asian centre and as an international centre.

That's obviously different from fifteen years ago when the paper saw itself as primarily reporting Hong Kong as a British colony.

Knight: *Will reporting these things be more difficult [in future]?*

Fenby: I can't see any reason why it should.

Yet there is quite a difference between the way Western journalists operate and say Xinhua?

Fenby: We are the *Post*. I don't think anyone is suggesting that Xinhua be the yardstick for the way the media operate in the SAR.

But surely the difficulty is working out what the yardstick is going to be?

Fenby: I have no idea.

There's been a lot of talk about Hong Kong papers needing to be more responsible to the government, in the way they are in Singapore. Has there been any of that sort of pressure on the Post?

Fenby: None at all.

Has Tung Chee-hwa's office had any talks with the Post?

Fenby: Not that I have seen. As in most parts of the world, the editor of a newspaper would meet people in government and yet this is seen by some people as extremely sinister. There's been no contact about what we should do and how we should do it. When I first arrived here, I received a couple of calls from Government House suggesting how stories might be handled in some ways. Although they deny it, I was so surprised that I took a note of it. On one Saturday night they were actually suggesting I should move a story off the front page because it might embarrass the governor. The reality is, everywhere that I have worked, those in charge of media relations are the spin doctors. Their job is to ring up newspapers, and try to influence them in one way or another. In England some of the calls I have had; from cabinet ministers trying to put us off running a story embarrassing to them. So I am not shocked if spin doctors here, whether in government or in commerce, should try to influence us. I can honestly say that no-one from Tung Chee-hwa's office has got into that game, as far as I am concerned.

... You are assuming that people in Beijing want the Hong Kong media to operate like the media in China. Nobody has ever proved that. Of course Hong Kong commercially-operated media and media in China, which are part of the state apparatus, are completely different. You have to believe and trust that this will be so. You have to think that the SAR will have to preserve the Hong Kong media system. That is part of the two systems in the one country. That will be one of the fascinating things to see what happens.

Will there be a need for journalists to be more sensitive or careful [than before the handover]?

Fenby: ... We are going to be in uncharted waters.... The free press, the independent press, should continue and we should do everything to ensure it does continue. When you have Anson Chan [the Chief Secretary] saying publicly and on several occasions that is actually a statement about the future, nobody takes a blind bit of notice of it.

Mr Feng has been appointed [as a consultant] to your own paper. He has extensive contacts in China and is well regarded by many in the west. What sort of advice has he been giving you about coverage?

Fenby: That is not his role. I am the editor of the paper.

Is it fair to ask what his role would be?

Fenby: His role is to be a consultant and a consultant is there because we may want to do things in China where a consultant may help you to achieve, to get done. Just like a lot of companies in Hong Kong have consultants who help them with their activities in China, help them to expand. You can have a point of view of denial of saying that July the first does not really exist and just pretend China does not exist and it will go away. Or you could take the attitude I would take that it's happening and China is there. It's a huge story and part of our role at the *Post* should be to be reporting on China as fully as possible, given our readership that exists with the thousands of journalists who will be here over the next few weeks. It is in the interests of information in general and this paper in particular to be able to expand its coverage of China and if you want a consultant to help you do that, it seems a logical way to go.

... The difficulty is that people see all this because it has to be a sinister story to make it a story. It all fits very neatly together. As a journalist, I can entirely understand this. The trouble is that it does not actually accord with reality.

Where then do you see the Post *in five years time?*

Fenby: To answer that you have to say where you see Hong Kong. Newspapers always interrelate with the society in which they operate. Obviously what happens to Hong Kong and what happens to the *Post* are linked together. I would like to see the *Post* remaining as an independent, objective newspaper in Hong Kong as part of China.

Do you think Hong Kong will remain as important as it has been for the English language media?

Fenby: Probably. There is such a strong media base here to begin with. It is commercially strong, giving it apolitical roots here. I think that will continue. I think the independence and strength of the media here does contribute something to the overall success of Hong Kong. There is a free flow of information, a free flow of ideas. I hope that is something that people, even though they sometimes may be irritated by the media here may recognise.

People who would say they are the defenders of freedom of the press can't resist taking a baseless pot shot at a newspaper which is actually doing what they say they are reporting. There is something quite unhealthy in this.

(Knight)

VOX POP FROM THE *GUANGZHOU DAILY*

Countdown for Colonialism

The *Guangzhou Daily*'s team of reporters fanned out across Hong Kong to record the last hours of the old regime. Their reporting, like much of that in the Chinese press when not reproducing official speeches, used anonymous sources which in Western journalism might be characterised as 'vox pops'. In 'The 24 Hours Before the Handover', they produced on-the-spot reports from Hong Kong. The text conveys the reporters' obvious excitement at reporting a major event outside mainland China:

> Yesterday, June 30, 1997, was the last day for Hong Kong under British colonial rule. As you read our reports today, Hong Kong – the Pearl of the Orient – will have already returned to the embrace of the motherland.
>
> At this moment of great historic significance, we, as Chinese reporters, are so excited, emotional and proud to witness this historical change in Hong Kong. Yesterday, our reporters all worked non-stop, spreading out around Hong Kong island, Kowloon and the New Territories. We tried our best, with our pens and cameras, to record eyewitness accounts during the last 24 hours of colonial rule, so that we could share them with our readers.

0:00 hours
Possession Street, Hong Kong.

> This is a street only about 100 metres long.... On January 25, 1841, the British warship appeared in Hong Kong waters, and British soldiers were flagrantly sent to land at Possession Street. The next day, the British marines hoisted the Union Jack in a flag-raising ceremony and officially declared the occupation of Hong Kong. To commemorate this 'outstanding' military action, this

street was given the English name of Possession Street. Britain then began its one and half centuries of colonial rule over Hong Kong.

A 70 year-old man surnamed Zhang said that he moved from Guangzhou to Hong Kong during the war against the Japanese. To see with his own eyes the return of Hong Kong to the motherland during his lifetime was his greatest wish he had. He was most proud about being at the original landing place of the British soldiers to witness the return of Hong Kong.

6:30 a.m.

Kai Tak Airport, Hong Kong

This reporter went to the airport to receive the first group of visitors during the last 24 hours before the return.

Flight 811 Cathay Pacific from Los Angles safely touched down at Hong Kong airport. A boy passenger wore a T-shirt bearing the Chinese characters 'Celebrate the Return, Wash Away National Shame'. His grandfather said: 'As overseas Chinese, we are so proud that we have seen this day!'

At 10:25 a.m., this reporter went to Kowloon station to meet a trainload of passengers from Guangzhou. A certain Mr Zhang excitedly said: 'I returned to the mainland from Hong Kong to set up a plant, and have personally felt the changes in China and its growing strength and wealth following the reforms. It would not have been easy for Hong Kong to return if China was still weak and poor. So I dropped my business there to come back to Hong Kong to witness this historic moment'.

10:00 a.m.

City Hall, Central.

On the shore of the Victoria Harbour, a newly-wed couple walked down the steps of the City Hall.... The registry staff worked overtime to complete the procedures for 212 couples who wanted to get married on the last day under British rule.

Couples gave a variety of reasons for this choice.... Being registered on June 29, taking photos on June 30, and having a big banquet for families and friends on July 1, so that their marriage ceremony extended through the handover gave people a deeper feeling of significance.

There was also a foreign couple who got married on this last day. They were British, and said that regardless of what their own ancestors had done, they wanted to wish Hong Kong a better future.

12:00 noon

The Government offices and Legislative Council building: Hong Kong people look forward to witnessing history.

This reporter had interviews with some Hong Kong personalities at various sites of celebration activities.

Li Ka-shing: Hong Kong is where China meets the West. Hong Kong understands the cultural differences between China and the West, and it also has an advantageous geographic position and is rich in management skills. It has thus realised outstanding achievements. After its return to China, with strong backing from the motherland, Hong Kong will achieve more. I believe Hong Kong investments in the mainland will increase at a pace which supplies the world and win praises.

Tsang Hin-chi: Being able to witness the return of Hong Kong to the motherland, I feel very lucky. Why has Hong Kong been able to return to the embrace of the motherland so smoothly? The fundamental factor is that the motherland is strong. To have gotten Hong Kong back from the hands of Britain without this factor, would have been unthinkable.

11:58 p.m.

Star Ferry clock tower: We witness history together.

The moment which we Chinese people had longed for several generations had finally arrived.... A group of students from the Chinese University of Hong Kong hugged each other and waved their coloured balloons. They said to this reporter: 'We are happy, very happy!'.... The We family's 9 year-old son said: 'Teachers at school taught us that Hong Kong has been occupied by the British for more than 100 years. Now they are giving Hong Kong back to China. In future, schools will be able to raise the five-star Chinese national flag'.... This reporter asked a policeman whether he felt anything special. He replied that they had been previously Royal Hong Kong Police, but now they were SAR police. The duties are the same, namely to serve the Hong Kong people.

12:00 mid-night

Britannia: The final conclusion.

A full stop was forever put to British colonial rule over Hong Kong, as clock bells rang at zero hour.

At this time, the new wing of the Hong Kong Convention Centre was full of lights. The Handover Ceremony was in process. In the meantime, the Royal Yacht Britannia which will carry away Prince Charles and the last governor, Mr Patten, is quietly waiting for its masters to end colonial rule in Hong Kong and sail for the open seas. It would sail away from the Pearl of the Orient in South China and disappear into the dark seas. At the same time, the British military radio, which started broadcasting in 1972, has fallen silent forever.

Compared with the triumphant British troops who landed in Hong Kong 156 years ago, the last governor of Hong Kong must have had mixed feelings. From 4:00 p.m. yesterday afternoon, Mr Patten had attended at least four flag-lowering ceremonies. The Union Jack would never again be raised in Hong Kong as the flag of a colonial master.

Colonial rule was terminated last night! This historic moment was fixed thirteen years previously in 1984 and today it has finally arrived. Hong Kong is now entering a new era.

(Guangzhou Daily: July 1, 1997: 8)[1]

The combined reports contained little official rhetoric, but also failed to deviate from the official line of rejoicing at Hong Kong's return to the embrace of the motherland. There were no critics among those selected for reportage, nor apparently were any of the 3,000 demonstrators seen near the Legislative Council just after midnight. Yet there was little bitterness apparent. It seemed the reporters, like the newly-wed Britons, wanted to look to the future. They chose to report a Royal Hong Kong policeman who saw no difference between working for the colonial government and for the new SAR. His reported concept that the police should serve the people rather than the state-owed more to Western notions of responsible government than to mainland dictums.

(Knight)

ITN BULLETINS

From 22 June to 1 July 1997

A brief description of the visual and verbal information content in a representative selection of eighteen stories prepared by the ITN reporters in Hong Kong between June 23 and July 1 reveals this emphasis on symbolic references to Britain's reluctant leave-taking. As several of these stories were filed for different ITN bulletins (midday, early evening and late) on the same day, they often contain repeated material:

June 22   British lawyer cruising on junk says in sound bite that the Chinese have never been good administrators in their 4,000 years of history.

June 23   Britannia arriving; Britannia's captain talking about the ship in sound bite; staff packing at the British garrison commander's home; PLA soldiers assembling in Shenzhen; a pro-China dragon dance in Hong Kong street; Chinese flags in Hong Kong streets.

June 23   Lights and decorations on harbour-front buildings; Britannia arriving; PLA soldiers assembling in Shenzhen; Emily Lau in sound bite warning of impending Chinese crackdown; pro-China dragon dance; Chinese flags in Hong Kong streets.

June 24   High society dinner dance with British expatriates and local elites mingling.

June 24   PLA soldiers in Shenzhen preparing to enter Hong Kong; soldiers taking English lessons, singing and drilling.

June 25   Chris Patten visits Chinese temple in Hong Kong; Patten complains in sound bite about China's plan to send in troops in armoured personnel carriers on the morning of the handover.

June 25   Pro-democracy (anti-China) protesters rally as police divers make a security check of the route that the Chinese

185

delegation will follow on handover day; a pro-China rally is also held amid a sea of red flags.

June 25   A largely British crowd assembles in a stadium to watch a tattoo by the British garrison band.

June 26   This story explores the plight of the Vietnamese boat people still left in Hong Kong and how they will fare once the Chinese take over. The script refers to the irony of the plight: refugees from one communist regime, now at the mercy of another.

June 26   The Royal Yacht Britannia arrives with Prince Charles; the British foreign minister Robin Cook meets Hong Kong chief executive Tung Chee-hwa; Cook, in a sound bite, complains about China's decision to send troops across the border in armoured personnel carriers on July 1; a British warship HMS Chatham fires a twenty-one gun salute.

June 28   The last garden party at Government House is held to celebrate the Queen's birthday; Prince Charles arrives on board Britannia; Robin Cook meets Tung Chee-hwa; Margaret Thatcher in a sound bite complains about China's decision to send troops to Hong Kong in armoured personnel carriers, referring to the Tiananmen Square massacre; a military band performs on the quayside where Britannia is moored.

June 29   Prince Charles hands out Queen's birthday honours at Government House; Chris Patten and family attend mass; Patten broadcasts on Hong Kong radio, rejects the claim that Hong Kongers only want money not democracy; Tung Chee-hwa meets Australian foreign minister Alexander Downer; local couples getting married in a Hong Kong park; Patten's dogs are sent off to France.

June 29   A military band plays at the quayside near Britannia; China's foreign minister arrives; the Patten family attend mass; Patten broadcast on Hong Kong radio; Prince Charles hands out Queen's birthday honours at Government House; crowns are removed from government building facades; Patten's dogs are sent to France; Britannia at quayside.

June 30   Dawn over Hong Kong harbour; PLA soldiers in Shenzhen wait to cross the border; British navy ships make final patrol of Hong Kong waters; pro-democracy supporters getting ready for anti-China rally; pro-democracy leader Emily Lau warns in sound bite that China will crack down once the foreign media have gone; Chinese flags fly over Kowloon street market; vox pops with local people in the market, who express confidence in Hong Kong after the handover.

June 30   Pro-democracy supporters prepare for midnight demonstration; PLA soldiers assembling at the border; PLA soldiers in trucks and buses driving across the border; PLA soldiers arrive at the Prince of Wales barracks in Hong Kong; pro-democracy protesters gather; Emily Lau in sound bite warns of Chinese crackdown.

June 30   Pro-democracy demonstration outside the Legislative Council building; sound bites from Emily Lau and Martin Lee expressing fears of Chinese crackdown; Tung Chee-hwa is sworn in as Chief Executive; vox pops of locals who express confidence in the future under Chinese rule; Britannia lies at dockside.

July 1   Pro-democracy demonstration on the morning after the handover; sound bites from Emily Lau and Martin Lee expressing fear of China.

July 1   Pro-democracy demonstration the morning after the handover.

July 1   Empty champagne bottles at harbour side the morning after the handover; vox pops of local people who express confidence in the future under Chinese rule; pro-democracy demonstrations; Emily Lau sound bite expressing fear of Chinese rule.

OFFICIAL ANNOUNCEMENTS FOR THE PRESS

1997 Handover Events Core Feed Program

The Hong Kong Broadcast Consortium

28 June (Sat)

Hong Kong Time	Events	Location	TV Producer
19:00 – 19:30	Queen's Birthday Reception	Government House	RTHK

29 June (Sun)

Hong Kong Time	Events	Location	TV Producer
11:15 – 12:45	Investiture (1)	Government House	RTHK
16:30 – 17:30	Investiture (2)	Government House	RTHK

30 June (Mon)

Hong Kong Time	Events	Location	TV Producer
16:15 – 16:35	Governor's Departure	Government House	RTHK
18:15 – 19:27	Farewell Ceremony	East Tamar	RTHK
20:15 – 20:45	A Salute to the Hong Kong Handover	Victoria Harbour	RTHK
20:45 – 22:45	Banquet	Hong Kong Convention and Exhibition Centre Hall 2	RTHK
20:00 – 03:00	Reunification Spectacular at Happy Valley	Happy Valley Racecourse	ATV
21:00 – 03:00	Hong Kong Extravaganza '97	Cultural Centre	TVB

23:30 – 00:10	Handover Ceremony	Hong Kong Convention and Exhibition Centre Grand Hall	RTHK

1 July (Tue)

00:10 – 00:45	Final Departure	East Tamar	RTHK
To be confirmed	Entry of People's Liberation Army	Border	RTHK
01:30 – 02:15	The Ceremony for the Establishment of the Hong Kong Special Administrative Region (HKSAR) of the People Republic of China (PRC) and the Inauguration of the Government of the Hong Kong Special Administrative Region	Hong Kong Convention and Exhibition Centre Hall 3	RTHK
02:45	Provisional Legislative Council Sitting	Hong Kong Convention and Exhibition Centre	RTHK
10:00 – 11:30	A Ceremony to Celebrate the Establishment of the Hong Kong Special Administrative Region	Hong Kong Convention and Exhibition Centre Hall 3	RTHK
11:30 – 12:00	Presentation Ceremony of CPG's gift to SARG	Hong Kong Convention and Exhibition Centre Waterfront	RTHK
16:00 – 17:00	SARG Reception	Hong Kong Convention and Exhibition Centre Grand Hall	RTHK
18:30 – 20:30	1st July Reunification Gala	Hong Kong Coliseum	RTHK
20:30 – 22:00	Hong Kong '97 Spectacular	Victoria Harbour	RTHK

189

2 July (Wed)

15:00 – 17:00	Parade in Celebration of the Return of Hong Kong '97	East Tamar	RTHK

(The Hong Kong Broadcast Consortium 1997)

World's Media Welcomed to Hong Kong

Press Release by Government Information Services

15 June 1997

Representatives of the world's media have been welcomed to Hong Kong as they begin to arrive to report on the historic Handover and related events.

The Director of the Handover Ceremony Co-ordination Office, Mr Stephen Lam, and the Director of Information Services, Mr Thomas Chan, extended the warm welcome at the opening today (Sunday) of the Press and Broadcast Centre (PBC) in the Hong Kong Convention and Exhibition Centre.

The 9,000 square metre media centre – the biggest yet established in Hong Kong – will be home to thousands of media staff reporting on the events during the Handover period.

In his opening remarks, Mr Chan said the occasion marked an important milestone for the Information Services Department. 'It's the first time in our history Hong Kong is providing a media centre on this scale and complexity to media organisations from all over the world.'

'I know some of my colleagues have lost a lot of sleep over it, trying to ensure that everything will run smoothly to facilitate our media friends from all over the world in reporting on the Handover Ceremony. That moment has arrived and now we are welcoming our first PBC residents,' he said.

Mr Chan said the PBC would not have been completed on time without the valuable contribution of the contractors, Venue Creative Services Limited and Charter Broadcast, and their numerous sub-contractors.

The Director of the Handover Ceremony Co-ordination Office, Mr Lam, said that in organising the Handover Ceremony many important facilities had to be established, and this had been quite an experience.

'I am delighted to see the first of the major strategic facilities coming on stream and one that will serve the media of the world over the next few weeks,' he said.

Mr Lam said it was important to have the support of the media in using the centre for television and radio coverage of the historic ceremonies and for up to date reports of the various events by the world's press.

The Press and Broadcast Centre takes up the entire seventh floor of the Hong Kong Convention and Exhibition Centre. It includes some 150 booths for use by the electronic media, more than 80 booths for the print media and a free-seating area for more than 600 journalists.

Just over 8,000 media representatives from 770 organisations are in the process of being accredited. Of these some 2,800 are from Hong Kong. The other major media interests come from Japan (1,300), the United States (1,000), the United Kingdom (700) and China (600).

The Information Services Department will man an information and reception counter around the clock during the operation of the PBC, while the Hong Kong Tourist Association and the Hong Kong Trade Development Council will also have their own information counters.

Facilities in the media centre include two large video walls, which will show the host broadcast feed of the Handover and related events as well as daily programme rundowns and schedules, a photo processing facility, a business centre, cafeteria, telecommunications service centre and a post office.

Resident broadcasters will have access to 18 feeds from different venue locations around Hong Kong. The PBC is also operating a bookable studio for interviews or presentations, two editing suites and a tape library with record and playback facilities.

In all, some 400 kilometres of video and audio cables have been used to link the broadcast booths to the master control centre and over 40 tonnes of television equipment have been installed in the technical nerve centre to ensure the signals get to the broadcasters and uplinked to satellite for global distribution.

(Government Information Services 1997)

Notes for Media Sessions

by Government Information Services

General

1. A session on pooling arrangements for Handover and related main official events, i.e. Farewell, Handover, Inauguration and Celebration.

2. Detailed media arrangements such as assembly place and time, transport, will be announced next week.
3. Media arrangements for other events, such as PLA's arrival at border and Britannia's departure, will be announced separately.

Principles

1. Wherever possible, to ensure that at least one seat will be given to each of the accredited media organisations.
2. Where this is not possible, to ensure that at least one seat is given to each of countries.
3. As agreed among the host parties, up to half of the seats will go to media organisations from Hong Kong, UK and China. The remaining will be allocated to the rest of the world on a pro rata basis according to the number of media organisations having registered with us.

Unilaterals

1. A number of unilateral positions have been booked by TV and radio broadcasters for live broadcast of the events.
2. Each position will accommodate three persons.

Names

1. Names of representatives nominated for the events will have to be sent to us by fax 2519XXXX before the end of the following day. Failure to submit the names to us before the deadline will mean that the organisations have decided to give up the seats and no event passes will be issued to these organisations.
2. Representatives nominated must come from the accredited media pool.

Event Passes

1. An event pass will be issued to each of the nominated media representatives.
2. Event passes for Farewell Ceremony at Tamar will be issued at the ISD's Event Pass Counter at Atrium 2 of HKCEC Extension between 9 a.m. and 12 noon on June 30.

3. Event passes for other events at the HKCEC Extension will be issued at ISD's Event Pass Counter at Atrium 2 of HKCEC Extension before the events, normally this means at least two hours before the events.
4. Media representatives covering an event must carry both the accreditation badge and the event pass in order to gain access into venues.
5. All event passes are not transferable.
6. For the Farewell Ceremony at Tamar, pre-issued event passes will not be replaced at the media check-in counters at City Hall.

Contents of the Press Kit

1. Carrying Bag (sponsored by DHL)
2. Ring Binder of materials including background facts, feature articles, CVs etc.
3. Press and Broadcast Centre (PBC) Guide (sponsored by Hang Seng Bank)
4. Sino-British Joint Declaration
5. Basic Law
6. Souvenir Watch
7. Polo Shirt (sponsored by Golden Emblem Investment)
8. Baseball Cap (sponsored by Northwest Airlines)
9. Belt Pouch containing six rolls of film and lens cleansing kit (sponsored by Kodak)
10. Hong Kong Tourist Association information folder containing general information on tourism, discount coupon book, CD-Rom carrying 250 images of Hong Kong and a map of Wanchai dining guide.
11. Notice-card for photo-journalists to get a free vest from Fuji Service Centre at the PBC.
12. Notice-card for photo-journalists to get a free vest and obtain free repair/rental service from Nikon Service Centre at Hutchison House.
13. Hong Kong Annual Report 1997
14. Programme of Activities organised by the Association of Celebration of Reunification of Hong Kong with China.
15. Programme of Official and Non-official Events during Handover Period
16. Briefing & Visits for the Media
17. *The Hong Kong Advantage*, Oxford University Press (sponsored by DHL)

KEY SPEECHES

Governor Chris Patten's Speech at the Farewell Ceremony

30 June 1997

Your Royal Highness, Prime Minister, Distinguished Guests, People of Hong Kong:

For Hong Kong as a whole, today is cause for celebration not sorrow. But here and there, perhaps there will be a touch of personal sadness as is true of any departure, a point to which I shall return.

History is not just a matter of dates. What makes history is what comes before and what comes after the dates that we all remember. The story of this great city is about the years before this night, and the years of success that will surely follow it.

Of course, Hong Kong's story is not solely that of the century and a half of British responsibility, though it is the conclusion of that chapter that we mark tonight.

This chapter began with events that, from today's vantage point, at the end of the following century, none of us here would wish or seek to condone. But we might note that most of those who live in Hong Kong now do so because of events in our own century which would today have few defenders. All that is a reminder that sometimes we should remember the past the better to forget it.

What we celebrate this evening is the restless energy, the hard work, the audacity of the men and women who have written Hong Kong's success story. Mostly Chinese men and Chinese women. They were only ordinary in the sense that most of them came here with nothing. They are extraordinary in what they have achieved against the odds.

As British administration ends, we are, I believe, entitled to say that our own nation's contribution here was to provide the scaffolding that enabled the people of Hong Kong to ascend. The rule of law. Clean and light-handed government. The values of a free society. The beginnings of representative government and democratic accountability. This is a

Chinese city, a very Chinese city, with British characteristics. No dependent territory has been left more prosperous, none with such a rich texture and fabric of civil society, professions, churches, newspapers, charities, civil servants of the highest probity and the most steadfast commitment to the public good.

I have no doubt that, with people here holding on to these values which they cherish, Hong Kong's star will continue to climb. Hong Kong's values are decent values. They are universal values. They are the values of the future in Asia as elsewhere, a future in which the happiest and the richest communities, and the most confident and the most stable too, will be those that best combine political liberty and economic freedom as we do here today.

All of us here tonight, and I am sure all my fellow countrymen and women watching these events from afar, wish the Chief Executive of the Special Administrative Region and his excellent team the very best of luck as they embark on their journey. C.H. Tung and his wife, Betty, will serve Hong Kong with dedication, strength and enthusiasm. Everyone here, and people outside Hong Kong as well, will be willing them to succeed in the challenging years that lie ahead.

I said that tonight's celebration will be tinged for some with sadness.

So it will be for my family and myself and for others who like us will soon depart from this shore. I am the 28th governor. The last governor. Like all the other governors and their families, my wife, my children and myself will take Hong Kong home in our hearts. You have been kind to us. You have made us welcome. It has been the greatest honour and privilege of my life to share your home for five years, and to have some responsibility for your future. Now Hong Kong people are to run Hong Kong. That is the promise. And that is the unshakeable destiny.

(Government Information Services 1997)

Speech by the Prince of Wales at the Handover Ceremony

30 June 1997

President Jiang Zemin, Premier Li Peng, Distinguished Guests, Ladies and Gentlemen:

This important and special ceremony marks a moment of both change and continuity in Hong Kong's history.

It marks, first of all, the restoration of Hong Kong to the People's Republic of China, under the terms of the Sino-British Joint Declaration of 1984, after more than 150 years of British administration.

This ceremony also celebrates continuity because, by that same treaty and the many subsequent agreements which have been made to implement its provisions, the Hong Kong Special Administrative Region will have its own government, and retain its own society, its own economy and its own way of life.

I should like to pay tribute this evening to those who turned the concept of 'one country, two systems' into the Joint Declaration, and to the dedication and commitment of those who have worked so hard over the last thirteen years to negotiate the details of the Joint Declaration's implementation.

But most of all I should like to pay tribute to the people of Hong Kong themselves for all that they have achieved in the last century and a half. The triumphant success of Hong Kong demands – and deserves – to be maintained.

Hong Kong has shown the world how dynamism and stability can be defining characteristics of a successful society. These have together created a great economy which is the envy of the world. Hong Kong has shown the world how East and West can live and work together. As a flourishing commercial and cultural cross-roads, it has brought us together and enriched all our lives.

Thirteen years ago the Governments of the United Kingdom and the People's Republic of China recognised in the Joint Declaration that these special elements which had created the crucial conditions for Hong Kong's success should continue. They agreed that, in order to maintain that success, Hong Kong should have its own separate trading and financial systems, should enjoy autonomy and an elected legislature, should maintain its laws and liberties, and should be run by the people of Hong Kong and be accountable to them.

Those special elements have served Hong Kong well over the past two decades. Hong Kong has coped with the challenges of great economic, social and political transition with almost none of the disturbance and dislocation which in other parts of the world have so often accompanied change on such a scale.

The United Kingdom has been proud and privileged to have had responsibility for the people of Hong Kong, to have provided a framework of opportunity in which Hong Kong has so conspicuously succeeded, and to have been part of the success which the people of Hong Kong have made of their own opportunities.

In a few moments, the United Kingdom's responsibilities will pass to the People's Republic of China. Hong Kong will thereby be restored to China and, within the framework of 'one country, two systems', it will continue to have a strong identity of its own and be an important international partner for many countries in the world.

Ladies and Gentlemen, China will tonight take responsibility for a place and a people which matter greatly to us all. The solemn pledges made before the world in the 1984 Joint Declaration guarantee the continuity of Hong Kong's way of life. For its part the United Kingdom will maintain its unwavering support for the Joint Declaration. Our commitment and our strong links to Hong Kong will continue, and will, I am confident, flourish, as Hong Kong and its people themselves continue to flourish.

Distinguished Guests, Ladies and Gentlemen, I should like on behalf of Her Majesty the Queen and of the entire British people to express our thanks, admiration, affection, and good wishes to all the people of Hong Kong, who have been such staunch and special friends over so many generations. We shall not forget you, and we shall watch with the closest interest as you embark on this new era of your remarkable history.

(Government Information Services 1997)

Speech by President Jiang Zemin at the Handover Ceremony

1 July 1997

Following is the official translation of the speech by President Jiang Zemin of the People's Republic of China.

Your Royal Highness Prince Charles, Prime Minister Tony Blair, Distinguished Guests, Ladies and Gentlemen:

The national flag of the People's Republic of China and the regional flag of the Hong Kong Special Administrative Region of the People's Republic of China have now solemnly risen over this land. At this moment, people of all countries in the world are casting their eyes on Hong Kong. In accordance with the Sino-British Joint Declaration on the question of Hong Kong, the two governments have held on schedule the handover ceremony to mark China's resumption of the exercise of sovereignty over Hong Kong and the official establishment of the Hong Kong Special Administrative Region of the People's Republic of China. This is both a festival for the Chinese nation and a victory for the universal cause of peace and justice.

Thus, July 1, 1997 will go down in the annals of history as a day that merits eternal memory. The return of Hong Kong to the motherland after going through a century of vicissitudes indicates that from now on, the Hong Kong compatriots have become true masters of this

Chinese land and that Hong Kong has now entered a new era of development.

History will remember Mr Deng Xiaoping for his creative concept of 'one country, two systems'. It is precisely along the course envisaged by this great concept that we have successfully resolved the Hong Kong question through diplomatic negotiations and finally achieved Hong Kong's return to the motherland.

On this solemn occasion, I wish to express thanks to all the personages in both China and Britain who have contributed to the settlement of the Hong Kong question and to all those in the world who have cared for and supported Hong Kong's return to the motherland.

On this solemn occasion, I wish to extend my cordial greetings and best wishes to the six million or more Hong Kong compatriots who have now returned to the embrace of the motherland.

After the return of Hong Kong, the Chinese Government will unswervingly implement the basic policies of 'one country, two systems', 'Hong Kong people administering Hong Kong' and 'a high degree of autonomy' and keep the previous socio-economic system and way of life of Hong Kong unchanged and its laws basically unchanged.

After the return of Hong Kong, the Central People's Government shall be responsible for the foreign affairs relating to Hong Kong and the defence of Hong Kong. The Hong Kong Special Administrative Region shall be vested, in accordance with the Basic Law, with executive power, legislative power and independent judicial power, including that of final adjudication. The Hong Kong residents shall enjoy various rights and freedoms according to law. The Hong Kong Special Administrative Region shall gradually develop a democratic system that suits Hong Kong's reality.

After the return, Hong Kong will retain its status of a free port, continue to function as an international financial, trade and shipping centre and maintain its economic and cultural ties with other countries, regions and relevant international organisations. The legitimate economic interests of all countries and regions in Hong Kong will be protected by law.

I hope that all the countries and regions that have investment and trade interests here will continue to work for the prosperity and stability of Hong Kong.

Hong Kong compatriots have a glorious patriotic tradition. Hong Kong's prosperity today, in the final analysis, has been built by Hong Kong compatriots. It is also inseparable from the development and support of the mainland. I am confident that with the strong backing of the entire Chinese people, the Government of the Hong Kong Special Administrative Region and Hong Kong compatriots will be able to manage Hong Kong well, build it up and maintain its long-term prosperity and stability, thereby ensuring Hong Kong a splendid future.

Thank you.

(Government Information Services 1997)

Inaugural Speech by Tung Chee-hwa, Chief Executive of the Hong Kong Special Administrative Region of the People's Republic of China

1 July 1997

President Jiang, Premier Li, My Fellow Countrymen, and Friends:

This is a momentous and historic day: July first, nineteen ninety-seven. After one hundred and fifty-six years of separation, Hong Kong and China are whole again. This is a solemn, stately, and proud moment. We are here today to announce to the world, in our language, that Hong Kong has entered a new era.

In recent history, China, as a nation, and we, as a people, have been through days of glory and times of despair. We have lived through days of hope, prosperity and glory. We have lived through days of despair, humiliation and hopelessness. The lesson is clear: the most precious possession of any nation or any people is the ability to chart one's own future, to be master of one's own destiny. Indeed, over the past century and a half, many compatriots, driven by lofty ideals and steadfast conviction, have devoted themselves to the advancement of our people and safeguarding the territorial integrity of our nation. Their enormous sacrifice and tireless efforts have brought us to where we are today. Never have we, as a nation, had such prosperity and potential to achieve greatness as we do today. Nor have we achieved greater recognition and dignity in the international community as we do today; as Hong Kong is finally re-united with China in a smooth and peaceful manner.

Today, we, as a nation, are fortunate to be in a position which our predecessors could only dream about. As a Chinese living in Hong Kong, and on behalf of all the people of Hong Kong, I would like to express our profound respect and gratitude to all the men and women who have made such sacrifices and given us what would otherwise have been impossible to attain.

The resumption of sovereignty over Hong Kong under 'one country, two systems' is an ingenious and novel concept. The eyes of the world are on us, as Hong Kong accepts the great honour, and the challenge, of charting new waters which will make history. We are confident that we will rise to the challenge and build a brighter and better future. Our confidence is well founded. Our conviction is based on the intellect and vision of a great patriot and statesman; on the solemn commitment of a great nation; and on the wisdom, industry and versatility of the Hong Kong people, a legacy from our heritage and culture. Above all, we, as one nation and one people, will implement the 'one country, two systems' concept; it is entirely within our prerogative to make it work.

Through a solemn act of law, the Central People's Government has granted Hong Kong a high degree of autonomy, unparalleled anywhere in the world. We value this empowerment, and we will exercise our powers prudently and responsibly. We are embarking on a new era. With the respect and trust from the entire nation, we will be that much more equipped to sail forward with confidence and with conviction. We will play a part in facilitating the re-unification of the entire nation, and bringing a better life to all in the nation.

For the first time in history, we, the people of Hong Kong, will be master of our own destiny. The Special Administrative Region Government is fully committed to preserving the Hong Kong way of life, maintaining Hong Kong's free and open economic system, upholding the rule of law, and building a more democratic society. We will be compassionate to those in need, and we will maintain Hong Kong as a vibrant and international city.

The nation and the people have entrusted to me the responsibility as Chief Executive of the Hong Kong Special Administrative Region of the People's Republic of China. As I stand here at this historic moment, a moment of great honour and pride, I am mindful of the enormous responsibilities which lie ahead. Throughout my life, I have experienced the joy and satisfaction of success and the pain and frustration of failure. I understand the hopes and aspirations of Hong Kong people. I am fully aware of the power in unity of purpose and direction. I will resolutely uphold the principles of autonomy as set forth under the Basic Law. I will carry out my duties with honesty, sincerity and determination. I will lead the 6.5 million people of Hong Kong, along with our indomitable spirit, towards the future. As part of China, we will move forward as one inseparable nation with two distinct systems.

I firmly believe, as a Special Administrative Region of China, the future of Hong Kong will be more glorious and more successful.

(Government Information Services 1997)

Speech by the Chief Executive Tung Chee-hwa at the Ceremony to Celebrate the Establishment of the Hong Kong Special Administrative Region of the People's Republic of China

1 July 1997

A Future of Excellence and Prosperity for All

President Jiang, Distinguished State Leaders, Honoured Guests, Fellow Hong Kong Citizens and Friends,

Today is a momentous day for China. Today is a joyous day for all Chinese people. First of July, nineteen ninety-seven, marks the return of Hong Kong to China after a long separation. It marks the establishment of the Hong Kong Special Administrative Region of the People's Republic of China. In the midnight hours behind us, China officially resumed sovereignty over Hong Kong; the Hong Kong Special Administrative Region was sworn in by the Central People's Government. In peace and solemnity, Hong Kong opens a new chapter in its history.

As Hong Kong proudly strides into the new era with a new identity, our thoughts and remembrance go, with great reverence, to the late Mr Deng Xiaoping. There was a time in the early 1980s when Hong Kong people became increasingly concerned about the uncertainties surrounding 1997. Despite rapid economic growth, the mood in Hong Kong remained apprehensive due to the lack of a clear direction on the future. Mr Deng stepped forward decisively and created a blueprint for Hong Kong after 1997, under the imaginative concept of 'one country, two systems' and taking into account the fundamental interests of China and the Chinese people as a whole. The concept, widely accepted by all parties concerned, resolved the uncertainties over Hong Kong's future.

Today, I am particularly pleased that Madam Zhuo Lin can be here to take part in activities to mark Hong Kong's reunification with China. We express our respect and warm welcome to Madam Zhuo Lin.

We should express our gratitude to President Jiang Zemin and the entire leadership in China. During the sometimes turbulent transitional period, they have worked tirelessly to smoothen the path leading up to the handover, lay the ground for a better Hong Kong, and ensure a smooth and successful transition. This is a remarkable achievement.

We can now move forward, on the basis of the solid foundation of past successes and under the guidance of the Basic Law, to lead Hong Kong to a new height. The Basic Law provides the constitutional framework for the Hong Kong Special Administrative Region. It has documented and institutionalised the 'high degree of autonomy' conferred upon us. It clearly prescribes the social, economic and political systems in Hong Kong which are different from those in the Mainland. It reaffirms the implementation of a different system within one country. It protects the rights and lifestyle of Hong Kong people and delineates our obligations.

Hong Kong is at present the freest and the most vibrant economy in the world. Free enterprise and free trade; prudent financial management and low taxation; the rule of law, an executive-led government and an efficient civil service have been a part of our tradition. All these factors which underlie our success have been guaranteed in the Basic Law.

Leaders in China have said time and again that the prosperity and stability of Hong Kong will contribute to the modernisation of our country. Furthermore, the successful implementation of 'one country, two systems', 'a high degree of autonomy' and 'Hong Kong people administering Hong Kong' is the first step towards the ultimate re-unification of China.

Citizens of Hong Kong, this is our mission. There is before us a heavy responsibility and a long way to go.

Our country has given us a high degree of autonomy, and her full support. Now is the time for us to apply our intelligence and work arduously for a better future.

Like most people in Hong Kong, I am not a passer-by. Our home, our career, and our hope are here in Hong Kong. We have deep feelings for Hong Kong and a sense of mission to build a better Hong Kong. Today, I wish to share with you my thoughts on the future development of the economy, education, housing and care for the elderly, issues which are of great concern to the people.

Hong Kong can be proud of its achievement over the past thirty years. There is no question about this. Nevertheless, we have to be alert to the challenges which lie ahead. We face keen competition in trade and services, and our competitiveness is threatened by persistently high inflation. We have to resolve a series of social problems arising from a growing and ageing population, meet the pressing demand for more and better housing, and deal with employment dislocation due to re-structuring of the economy. All these require urgent attention and careful handling. Beneath the surface of prosperity, there are insidious threats which are taxing our courage and determination.

Our foremost task is to enhance Hong Kong's economic vitality and sustain economic growth. Only through the creation of wealth can we improve the living of the people of Hong Kong, and continue to contribute to our country. It is the responsibility of the Special Administrative Region Government to create a good business environment, plan for and train the necessary manpower, and uphold the principles of free trade, fair competition and non-interference in the market. We will strive to enhance Hong Kong's position as an international financial centre and a cosmopolitan city. We will promote the services sector and facilitate the development of value-added and high technology industries. The world is entering an information era. We must adopt positive measures to encourage investment in the information industry and infrastructure, and nurture expertise in this area. Only then can Hong Kong remain at the forefront of the new age with vigour and vibrancy.

Education is the key to the future of Hong Kong. It provides a level playing field for all, and the human resources required for further economic development. Our education system must cater for Hong Kong's needs, contribute to the country, and adopt an international outlook. It should encourage diversification and combine the strengths of the east and the west. We shall draw up a comprehensive plan to improve the quality of education, and inject sufficient resources to achieve this goal.

The thrust of our policy will be to improve primary and secondary education. To start with, we must have quality teachers and principals with a strong sense of mission. We have to raise the professional qualification of teachers. In the foreseeable future, new teachers for primary and secondary schools should all have a university degree and teacher's training. We will extend full-day schooling to all primary schools and abolish floating classes in secondary schools as soon as possible. We will raise the standard of language training; formulate a comprehensive policy on the application of information technology in education; improve the system of examinations and school management; promote diversification in the school system. We will encourage tertiary institutions to develop areas of excellence. We will further review the academic system in terms of the length of and the interface between the various stages of education, so as to ensure that our education system meets the long-term interests of Hong Kong.

We have to foster among our youngsters a sense of responsibility towards the family, the community, the country and the world; and to develop in them the strength of character, the spirit of enterprise, and

203

the versatility to cope with vagaries in life. We will encourage our young people to have all-round development covering ethics, the intellect, the physique, social skills and aesthetics. To achieve this goal, the school, the family and the community must work together and share the responsibility.

Owning one's home is an aspiration shared by the people of Hong Kong. It is crucial for nurturing a sense of belonging and maintaining social stability. Housing cost also has a strong bearing on the economic vitality of Hong Kong. The crux of the housing problem is inadequate supply, causing prices to soar and creating opportunities for speculators.

The fact of the matter is: Hong Kong has enough land to meet our housing needs. With unfaltering determination, it should be possible to resolve the housing problem. We will draw up a ten-year housing plan: to speed up reclamation and land formation; extend the mass transit system and infrastructure development; and increase the efficiency of housing production through a comprehensive review of the existing organisation and working procedures. We will substantially increase the production of home ownership flats, actively implement the sale of public rental flats to sitting tenants, and address the needs of the 'sandwich class'. We will increase overall housing supply at a target of not less than 85,000 flats a year. The aim is to achieve a home ownership rate of 70 per cent in ten years. We will also speed up urban redevelopment, clear all temporary housing areas and cottage areas, rehouse the dwellers of bed space apartments; and reduce the average waiting time for public rental housing to three years.

Rampant speculation in the property market in recent months has seriously affected our competitiveness and people's livelihood. We will devise a range of anti-speculation measures and monitor the market closely. We will take resolute action when it becomes necessary to do so.

Our senior citizens have contributed to Hong Kong's success. They deserve respect and care from the community. The Special Administrative Region Government will develop a comprehensive policy to take care of the various needs of our senior citizens and provide them with a sense of security, a sense of belonging and a sense of worthiness. We will set up a 'Commission for the Elderly' with wide community representation to formulate policies and co-ordinate the delivery of services.

We will set up the Mandatory Provident Fund Scheme as soon as possible. We will also carry out an in-depth review of the Comprehensive Social Security Assistance Scheme which aims to assist the needy among our senior citizens and improve their living. We will encourage families to live with their elderly members through

204

adjustment to the public housing allocation policies; provide supporting services to carers of the elderly; and increase the supply of housing and residential services for senior citizens. We will also improve primary health care and strengthen services for the chronically ill. Furthermore, we will promote the physical and mental well-being of senior citizens and encourage them to do voluntary work, so that they can continue to contribute to the community.

Reunification with China opens up new opportunities for Hong Kong. Successful implementation of 'one country, two systems' requires us to develop a better understanding of our country, cultivate a congenial relationship with the Mainland, embrace a distinctive set of values; safeguard the rule of law; protect our freedoms; promote democracy; and establish a common long-term purpose.

The interests of Hong Kong and the Motherland are intricately linked and intertwined. Due to our long separation, there is a general lack of understanding about China among the people of Hong Kong. The reunification has created a new environment and better conditions for us to understand our country and our people, and to love our country and our people. Only then can we firmly establish our roots and make 'one country, two systems' a success. We must strengthen the understanding and relationship between Hong Kong and the Mainland, through mutual trust, mutual economic benefits, cultural interaction, and mutual respect for each other's way of life. We know Hong Kong and the Mainland will move forward together, hand in hand.

Every society has to have its own values to provide a common purpose and a sense of unity. Most of the people of Hong Kong are Chinese, some are not. For a long time, Hong Kong has embraced the eastern and western cultures. We will continue to encourage diversity in our society, but we must also reaffirm and respect the fine traditional Chinese values, including filial piety, love for the family, modesty and integrity, and the desire for continuous improvement. We value plurality, but discourage open confrontation; we strive for liberty but not at the expense of the rule of law; we respect minority views but also shoulder collective responsibilities. I hope these values will provide the foundation for unity in our society.

Maintaining and developing the legal system and the rule of law in Hong Kong is immensely important. We will continue to ensure that the executive, legislative and judicial branches of the Government will operate independently. We will keep up our efforts against corruption and maintain a clean society. We will ensure equality before the law and provide an attractive environment for investors and the people of Hong Kong.

We will preserve the existing freedoms and lifestyle, and ensure that the people of Hong Kong will continue to enjoy the freedoms of speech, assembly, association, the press and other freedoms guaranteed by the International Covenant on Civil and Political Rights.

Democracy is the hallmark of a new era for Hong Kong. The Special Administrative Region Government will resolutely move forward to a more democratic form of government in accordance with the provisions in the Basic Law. We will provide opportunities for every stratum of the society and legitimate political organisations, and people with different shades of opinion, to participate in the political process. The Special Administrative Region Government will adopt an open attitude and be accountable to the public.

Hong Kong has an outstanding and honest civil service. They will have a crucial role to play under 'one country, two systems'. Together, we will serve the community and work for a better Hong Kong.

For the first time in the history of Hong Kong, we now have the opportunity to chart our own destiny. Under 'one country, two systems', we will move forward with conviction, prudence and determination. We will work together for a better future. Our vision of Hong Kong is:

- a society proud of its national identity and cultural heritage;
- a stable, equitable, free, democratic, compassionate society with a clear sense of direction;
- an affluent society with improved quality of life for all;
- a decent society with a level playing field and fair competition under the rule of law;
- a window for exchanges between China and the rest of the world;
- a renowned international financial, trading, transportation and communication centre;
- a world class cultural, education and scientific research centre

Distinguished guests, my fellow citizens of Hong Kong:

In two years, the People's Republic of China will be celebrating its fiftieth birthday. In three years, the world will be greeting the beginning of a new millennium. And I know, in two years, Hong Kong will achieve greater successes and a better life for all, as we move into the next Century. Our nation will be proud of us.

I invite you to join me in wishing China thriving prosperity; I invite you to join me in wishing Hong Kong continuous success.

(Government Information Services 1997)

NOTES

The book provides snapshots of the coverage of the handover day. As a result, the titles and positions of those quoted and referred to are those held on that day.

Preface

1. *Guangzhou Daily* (1997) 'The battle of the century for Chinese and foreign media', p. 62, July 1.
2. V.G. Kulkarni, interview with Alan Knight.

Chapter One: The Pearl of the Orient

1. Reluctance to report on *burakumin* and Koreans may, in recent years, have been influenced by a sensitivity to identifying people as belonging to a disadvantaged community.
2. Yash Ghai, interview with Alan Knight on February 27, 1997.
3. V.G. Kulkarni, interview with Alan Knight.
4. Eric Falt, interview with Alan Knight on May 25, 1993 in Phnom Penh, Cambodia.
5. Eric Falt, interview with Alan Knight on May 25, 1993 in Phnom Penh, Cambodia.
6. Mark Austin, interview with Alan Knight.

The Tourists of History

1. Diane Stormont, interview with Alan Knight, June 19, 1998.

Will Hong Kong People Wear Mao Suits?

1. Ichiro Yoshida, interview with Yoshiko Nakano, December 5, 1997. This is an edited text of an interview conducted in Japanese.

Chapter Two: Channelling the Flood

1. Phillip Robertson, interview with Yoshiko Nakano on December 5, 1997.

Propaganda Came First and the Troops Second

1. *Apple Daily* (1997) 'Jiang Zemin announces regulations for the army and bids the three forces to abide by them', July 1 A4.

Chapter Three: Setting the Stage for a Democratic Hero

1. Lau Sai-leung, interview with Yoshiko Nakano, January 23, 1998.
2. *South China Sunday Morning Post Magazine* (1995) 'Martyr Lee', September 15.
3. *New York Times* (1997) 'China resumes control of Hong Kong, ending 156 years of British rule', July 1.
4. *Washington Post* (1997) 'Activists vow to press fight for freedom', A13, July 1.
5. *The Times* (1997) 'Millions mute as curtain falls on final act', p. 4, July 1.
6. *Asahi Shimbun* International Satellite Edition (1997) Chikyū 97nen, shuzai no genba de: Hong Kong henkan, usureyuku nisei-do (World 1997: reporter's eye; Hong Kong Handover, diminishing two systems), p. 7, December 27.
7. *South China Morning Post* (1997) '3,000 rally to democracy, freedom call', p. 2, July 1. *Hong Kong Economic Times* (1997) '48 hours around the handover, Martin Lee: We shall return', A8, July 2.
8. *Straits Times* (1997) 'Isolated protests as clock ticks away', p. 7, July 1.
9. *Washington Post* (1997) 'One man's anti-communist crusade: opposition leader vows to continue campaigning for democracy', June 30.
10. *South China Morning Post* (1997) 'Success part of symbolic gesture', p. 2, July 1. *Hong Kong Economic Times* (1997) '48 hours around the handover, Martin Lee: We shall return', A8, July 2. *Oriental Daily News* (1997) 'Martin Lee: support reunification, long live democracy', A4, July 1. *Express News* (1997) 'Ousted legislators declare from the balcony', A9, July 1. *Time* magazine Asia edition (1997) 'Playing by new rules', p. 28, July 14.
11. *Time* magazine Asia edition (1997) 'The 25 most influential people in the new Hong Kong', p. 33, June 23.
12. *South China Morning Post* (1997) 'Anchors aweigh in the great ratings war', p. 23, June 30.
13. For example, on June 4, 1997, when the Alliance held the eighth candle-light vigil for the Tiananmen Square victims, the whole ceremony was conducted in Cantonese. A reporter, however, did not have to understand

Cantonese to cover it. The Alliance strategists prepared an English translation of Szeto Wah's Memorial Speech, the Declaration, and the lyrics of two songs of protest. Computer printouts of these English texts were ready for reporters to pick up as they left Victoria Park.

14. *Washington Post* (1997) 'Activists vow to press fight for freedom', A13, July 1.
15. *Time* magazine Asia edition (1997) 'Playing by new rules', p. 29, July 14. *The Times* (1997) 'Millions mute as curtain falls on final act', p. 4, July 4.
16. Reuters News Service (1997) 'Handover Stories, China: Chinese arrive in downpour to garrison HK', Web Site, http://hk97.webhk.com, July 1.
17. *Newsweek* International Pacific Edition (1997) 'The flags of midnight', p. 18, July 14.
18. *Bangkok Post* (1997) 'Democrats pull off balcony rally: Party leader promises freedom fight to go on', p. 5, July 1.
19. Jonathan Mirsky, interview with Alan Knight.
20. *Time* Magazine Asia edition (1997) 'Playing by new rules', p. 29, July 14. *Newsweek* (1997) 'The flags of midnight', p. 18, July 14. *The Times* (1997) 'Final farewell to Hong Kong', p. 2, July 1. *Washington Post* (1997) 'Activists vow to press fight for freedom', A13, 1 July. *Los Angeles Times* (1997) 'Activists quickly test tolerance for dissent', Web Site, http://www.latimes.com., July 1. Reuters, 'China: Chinese troops arrive in downpour to Garrison HK', Web Site, http://hk97.webhk.com. *Bangkok Post* (1997) 'Democrats pull off balcony rally: Party leader promises freedom fight to go on', p. 5, July 1. *New York Times* (1997) 'China resumes control of Hong Kong, ending 156 years of British rule', July 1. Associated Press (1997) 'Triumph, pathos as an era ends and Hong Kong becomes China', July 1. *South China Morning Post* (1997) '3,000 rally to democracy, freedom call', p. 2, July 1.
21. Kathy Wilhelm, interview with Yoshiko Nakano, June 17, 1998.
22. *South China Morning Post* (1997) 'We pledge to the voice of the people', Web Site, http://www.scmp.com., July 1.
23. Democratic Party of Hong Kong: July First Manifesto (1997), Web Site, http://www.martinlee.org.hk/July1Declaration.html
24. *China News* (1997) 'Shut out by new sovereign outgoing lawmakers plan protest', p. 5, July 1.
25. *Apple Daily* (1997) 'Martin Lee attracts foreign power', A11, June 30.
26. *The Times* (1997) 'Millions mute as curtain falls on final act', p. 4, July 1. *Washington Post* (1997) 'One man's anti-communist crusade: opposition leader vows to continue campaigning for democracy', June 30. *Yomiuri Shimbun* Tokyo morning edition (1997) 'Minshu-ha ga demo, Chûgoku-ki moyasu (Democrats demonstrate, burned the Chinese national flag)', p. 7, July 1.
27. *Hong Kong Economic Times* (1997) '48 hours around the Handover, Martin Lee: We shall return', A8, July 2.
28. *Hong Kong Economic Times* (1997) '48 hours around the Handover, Martin Lee: We shall return', A8, July 2.

The Party at the Barricade

1. Kathy Wilhelm, interview with Yoshiko Nakano on June 17, 1998.

One Magazine, Two Editions

1. *Newsweek* International (1997a) 'From the editor-in-chief', p. 4 in Special Commemorative Edition, Hong Kong, The City of Survivors: What does the future hold?, May–July.
2. *Newsweek* International (1997a) 'Why the world watches', p. 7 in Special Commemorative Edition, Hong Kong, The City of Survivors: What does the future hold?, May–July.
3. *Newsweek* (1997b) 'Why the world watches', p. 35 in Special Report, China Takes Over, Can Hong Kong Survive?, May 19.
4. *Newsweek* International Pacific Edition (1997c) 'Changing of the guard' in Pictures of the Year, p. 22, December 22.

Chapter Four: Washing Away One Hundred Years of Shame

1. He, interview with Alan Knight on June 16, 1997 in Guangzhou, China.
2. Li Yunjiang, interview with Alan Knight on June 16, 1997 in Guangzhou, China.
3. *Guangzhou Daily* (1997) Advertisement, p. 1, June 27.
4. *Guangzhou Daily* Midday edition (1997) 'Excellent sales: *Guangzhou Daily* a sought after paper', p. 78, July 1.
5. *Guangzhou Daily* (1997) 'Jiang Zemin orders the PLA to enter HK', p. 1, July 1.
6. *Guangzhou Daily* Midday edition (1997) 'A great centennial event for the Chinese nation', p. 50, July 1.
7. *Guangzhou Daily* Midday edition (1997) 'A great centennial event for the Chinese nation', p. 50, July 1.
8. *Apple Daily* (1997) 'Different tactics for reporting the handover: Lots of "Don'ts" for mainland reporters', A19, July 1.
9. *Guangzhou Daily* (1997) 'Account of the British military retreat from Hong Kong', p. 9, July 1.
10. *Guangzhou Daily* (1997) 'Account of the British military retreat from Hong Kong', p. 9, July 1.
11. *Guangzhou Daily* (1997) 'Royal Air Force disappears from the Hong Kong sky', p. 9, July 1.
12. *Guangzhou Daily* (1997) 'The thousand-day regiment fell like a tree and monkeys living on it all dispersed', p. 9, July 1.
13. *Guangzhou Daily* (1997) 'Moving sale', p. 9, July 1.
14. *Guangzhou Daily* (1997) 'The last governor bids his farewell to Government House', p. 6, July 1.
15. *Guangzhou Daily* (1997) 'Financial advisors made suggestions to Mr Patten', p. 12, July 1.

16. *Guangzhou Daily* (1997) 'British governors left their names in Hong Kong and glorified their achievements', p. 13, July 1.
17. *Guangzhou Daily* (1997) 'The sunset journey for Britannia', p. 14, July 1.

Chapter Five: Pomp and Pathos

1. See Appendices (p. 185) for a brief description of ITN Bulletins from 22 June to 1 July.

Chapter Six: Japanese Radio Voices

1. NHK Radio 1 (1997a) 'Marugoto Asia: "Ni hao" Hong Kong, henkan tokushū; opening (Asia as a Whole: "Ni hao" Hong Kong, Handover Special; opening)', June 30, 5:05 p.m.–5:55 p.m. JST.
2. *AERA* (1996–1997) 'Hong Kong Countdown', vol. 10, no.1, December 30 – January 6.
3. NHK Radio 1 (1997b) 'Marugoto Asia: "Ni hao" Hong Kong, henkan; shukenhenkan shikiten; radio yūkan (Asia as a Whole: "Ni hao" Hong Kong, Handover Special; radio evening edition), June 30, 6:00 p.m.–6:55 p.m. JST.
4. Based on exchange rate on June 30, 1997, 1 US dollar = 114.29 ~ 114.31 yen.
5. NHK Close-up Gendai (1997) 'Hong Kong Henkan: Hanei to Jiyu wa Mamoreru ka (Hong Kong handover: Can prosperity and freedom be protected?)' June 30, 9:30 p.m.–10:00 p.m. JST.
6. *China Times* (1997) 'Mr Qian does not recognise Taiwan as a political entity,' p. 4, July 1.
7. NHK Radio 1 (1997c) 'Marugoto Asia, "Ni hao" Hong Kong, henkan tokushu: shukenhenkan shikiten (Asia as a Whole: "Ni hao" Hong Kong, Handover Special: the Handover Ceremony)', July 1, 0:10 a.m.–01:30 a.m. JST.
8. *Guangzhou Daily* (1997) 'The 24 hours before the handover', p. 8, July 1.
9. BBC (1997) TV Bulletin, June 30.
10. NHK Radio 1 (1997d) News Bulletin, June 30, 7:00 p.m. JST.
11. Diane Stormont, interview with Alan Knight, June 19, 1998.

Self-Censorship in Hong Kong Media

1. Carol Pui-yee Lai, interview with Yoshiko Nakano, December 12, 1997.

Chapter Seven: The East Wind is Blowing

1. Government Information Services (1997) Press Releases, Brief on Government House departure ceremony, June 29.
2. *New York Times* (1997) 'China resumes control of Hong Kong, ending 156 years of British rule', July 1.

3. *South China Morning Post* (1997) 'Strain shows as Governor leaves home', July 1. *Ming Pao* (1997) 'Governor Patten full of emotions, as he leaves the official residence', A4, July 1. *Wen Wei Po* (1997) 'Britain bids farewell to Hong Kong: the end of colonial rule', B1, July 1. *Guangzhou Daily* (1997) 'The Last Governor Bids his Farewell to Government House', p. 6, July 1. *Straits Times* (1997) 'The last governor fights back tears', p. 6, July 1. *The Australian* (1997) 'Today is cause for celebration', July 1.

4. *Time* Magazine Asian Edition (1997) 'Playing by new rules', p. 25, July 14.

5. Feign's cartoon series, *The World of Lily Wong*, ceased to be published by the *South China Morning Post,* after it continued to represent Chinese Communist Party officials as cynical, corrupt and often violent opportunists. British administrators were meanwhile depicted as bumbling bureaucrats.

6. Lee Kuan Yew, then Singapore's Prime Minister, speaking on April 14, 1988, told the American Society of Newspaper Editors that:

> The media play a key role in the life of every country, but it is a role which differs from one country to another. When these differences are misunderstood or ignored; as frequently happens in the western media operating in developing countries, the result is friction.

7. The *South China Morning Post*, Hong Kong's largest circulation English language newspaper, was founded in 1903. It saw its readers as Hong Kong's educated elite. The group's afternoon newspaper, the *China Mail*, first appeared in 1845 as an official organ of the government. The *Mail* folded in 1973, as a result of falling circulation and one of Hong Kong's recurring stock market crashes.

8. Feng Xiliang, telephone interview with Alan Knight on April 16, 1997.

9. Ted Thomas, interview with Alan Knight, April 20, 1997.

10. *Mainichi Shimbun* (1997) 'Hong Kong no ichi-ryu hotel: nihon-jin dake ni hōgai ni takai ryokin o settei (Superior hotels in Hong Kong: Overcharging Japanese customers)', October, 11.

11. *South China Morning Post* (1997) 'Damage limitation', October 18.

12. Keith Richburg, interview with Alan Knight on April 30, 1997.

13. Y. Joseph Lian, interview with Alan Knight on July 1, 1997.

APPENDICES

Vox Pop from Guangzhou Daily

1. *Guangzhou Daily* (1997) 'The 24 hours before the handover', p. 8, July 1.

BIBLIOGRAPHY

BBC (1997) BBC-Online http://www.bbc.co.uk/home/today/index.shtml.

Chan, Anson (1997) 'Hong Kong and beyond', speech delivered at the Pacific Basin Economic Council, Manila, the Philippines, May 19.

Ching, Frank (1997) 'Misreading Hong Kong', p. 53–66 in *Foreign Affairs* 76(3).

Chua, Robert (1997) 'Advance Hong Kong', speech delivered at the meeting at Furama Hotel, Hong Kong, April 28.

Committee to Protect Journalists (1993) *Don't Force us to Lie*, New York.

Dayan, Daniel and Elihu Katz (1992) *Media Events: the live broadcasting of history*. Cambridge, MA and London: Harvard University Press.

Davies, Derek (1997) 'Two cheers for colonialism', paper presented at a Freedom Forum luncheon at Furama Hotel, Hong Kong, March 24.

Dimanno, Rosie (1998) 'Sayonara – and thanks', *Toronto Star*, February 22.

Dimbleby, Jonathan (1997) *The Last Governor*, London: Little Brown and Company.

Elegant, Robert (1990) Pacific Destiny: inside Asia today, New York: Crown.

Frcc, Brctt (1997) 'ISD in the media spotlight' *Civil Service Newsletter* Issue 39, Hong Kong, September.

Fung, Anthony Y.H. (1998) 'The dynamics of public opinion, political parties and media in transitional Hong Kong' p. 474–493 in *Asian Survey* May Issue, Berkeley: University of California Press.

Government Information Centre, Hong Kong SAR of PRC (1997) press conference by the Chief Executive in Tokyo, web site http://www.info.gov.hk, October 18.

Guangdong Provincial Government (1996) *Statistical Yearbook of Guangdong*, Guangzhou, China.

Hong Kong Alliance in Support of Patriotic Democratic Movements in China (n.d.) 'Organization, operation, and looking ahead', web site http://www.alliance.org.hk.

Hong Kong Journalists Association (1997) 'Thomas Chan: no orders from Beijing' *The Journalist*, Issue 1.

Hong Kong Journalists Association and Article 19 (1993) *Urgent Business: Hong Kong and Freedom of Expression and 1997*, Hong Kong: Hong Kong Journalists Association.

Hong Kong Journalists Association and Article 19 (1997) *The Die is Cast: freedom of expression in Hong Kong on the eve of the handover to China. 1997 Annual Report* 1997 Joint Report of the Hong Kong Journalists Association and Article 19, June.

Hong Kong Government Printer (n.d.) *A Career in the Government Information Services*, Hong Kong.

Hong Kong Government Publications (1966) *Hong Kong: Report for the Year 1966*, Hong Kong.

Hong Kong Government Publications (1997) *Hong Kong 1997: A Review of 1996*, Hong Kong.

Hong Kong Tourist Association (1998) Hong Kong Tourism Industry: year-end results, web site http://www.hkta.org/thisweek/tourism1997.html, February 7.

Hughes, Dick (1994) *Don't You Sing!: memories of a Catholic boyhood*, Sydney: Kangaroo Press.

ITN (n.d.) Web site http://www.itn.co.uk.

Japan, Prime Minister's Office (n.d.) Web site http://www.sorifu.go.jp/survey/gaikou-h9.html, Tokyo.

Knight, Alan (1997a) Reporting the Orient: Australian journalists in Southeast Asia, unpublished doctoral dissertation, University of Wollongong.

Knight, Alan (1997b) 'Dateline: Hong Kong', web site: http://www.geocities.com/Athens /Forum/2365/.

Lehrke, Gunter (1993) 'Radio and television in the People's Republic of China', in *Media Asia* 18 (4), Singapore: Asian Mass Communication Research and Information Centre.

Li, Tsze Sun (1993) *The World Outside When the War Broke Out: a comparative study of two Chinese newspapers of different systems*, Hong Kong: Hong Kong Institute of Asia-Pacific Studies.

Luard, Tim (1997) 'Being there' in *BBC On Air* May Issue, London.

Mak, Ying-ting (1996) 'Freedom of expression and the end of colonialism: Hong Kong press freedoms', paper presented at Intersections with Asia, the International Media Centre of the Department of Foreign Affairs and Trade, Sydney, November 12.

Morrison, David E. and Howard Tumber (1988) *Journalists at War: The dynamics of news reporting during the Falklands conflict*. London: Sage.

NHK Public Relations Bureau (1997) *NHK in Focus 1997*, Tokyo.

Patten, Chris (1997) Governor's address delivered at the Commonwealth Journalists Association Conference, Hong Kong, January 30.

Pedelty, Mark (1995) *War Stories: the culture of foreign correspondents*. New York and London: Routledge.

Rosenblum, Mort (1981) *Coups and Earthquakes: reporting the world for America*. New York: Harper and Row.

Scollon, Ron (1998) *Mediated Discourse as Social Interaction: a study of news discourse*. London and New York: Longman.

214

Scollon, Ron and Suzanne Wong Scollon (1997) 'Political, personal and commercial discourses of national sovereignty: Hong Kong becomes China,' plenary address to the Conference on Intercultural Communication and Changing National Identities at University of Tartu, Estonia, November 8.

Smith, Hedrick (1988) *The Power Game*, London: Collins.

Szeto, Wah (1997) Memorial speech delivered on the eighth anniversary of the Tiananmen Massacre at Victoria Park, Hong Kong, June 4.

Tannen, Deborah (1998) *The Argument Culture: moving from debate to dialogue,* New York: Random House.

Tsang, Tak-sing (1997) 'Hong Kong in Transition', speech delivered at the Commonwealth Journalists Association Conference, Hong Kong, January 30.

Welsh, Frank (1993) *A Borrowed Place: the history of Hong Kong*, New York: Kodansha America.

Zhang, Wei (1997) *Politics and Freedom of the Press,* Sydney: Australian Centre for Independent Journalism.

PROFILES

Alan Knight is a Professor of Journalism and Media Studies at Central Queensland University, Australia. He received his Ph.D. from the University of Wollongong examining the work of Australian foreign correspondents in Southeast Asia. While based in Hong Kong in 1993, his research on journalism took him to Cambodia, Indonesia, Singapore, Thailand, Vietnam, and Malaysia. A former Executive Producer at the Australian Broadcasting Corporation, he has been a journalist for more than two decades. He was an Honorary Research Fellow at the Centre of Asian Studies at the University of Hong Kong in 1997.

Yoshiko Nakano is a Research Assistant Professor in the Department of English at the City University of Hong Kong where she teaches intercultural communication. She received her Ph.D. in sociolinguistics from Georgetown University in the United States. Before she came to Hong Kong, she worked as a researcher on award-winning TV documentaries covering the Cuban Missile Crisis and the War in Bosnia. She has also contributed reports to Japanese radio and magazines in the United States and Hong Kong. Her next research project will examine how young Chinese people in Hong Kong, mainland China and Taiwan construct their image of Japan and its people.

Contributor

Barry Lowe is an Associate Professor in the Department of English at the City University of Hong Kong where he teaches journalism and video production. He also engages in media training work in the Asian region and is active as an independent documentary producer. He has a background in journalism and worked for newspapers and television in the Middle East, Southeast Asia and Eastern Europe. His research interests include reporting on conflict and ethics in journalism. He is also involved in research into the development of video archiving and digital image recognition systems.

INDEX

Tung, C.H. *see* Tung Chee-hwa
Tung Chee-hwa 8, 14, 35, 42, 43, 44,
    55, 63, 67, 82, 85, 97, 111, 118,
    126, 141, 155, 171, 186, 187, 195
  on PLA's arrival 107
  inaugural speech 199–201
  interview with CNN 71
  and media handling 39, 71, 155,
    178–9
  speech at the SAR establishment
    ceremony 201–6
TV Asahi 24, 142

Ueda, Yoshio 131–3, 136–8, 141, 142,
    143, 147–50, 152
United Nations
  and Cambodian election 17–8

Vietnam News Agency 93–96
Vines, Stephen 38–40
visual press release *see* press release
vox pop 95 *see also* BBC *and*
    Guangzhou Daily and ITN *and*
    NHK Radio

Washington Post 45, 46, 54, 56, 58, 60
Watanabe, Toshio 138, 139–40,
    143–4, 146–7
Welsh, Frank 120
Wen Wei Po 54, 55, 161
Wilhelm, Kathy 58, 62–4
wire services *see* foreign media; wire
    services
Wong Kar Wai 134

Xinhua (New China News Agency) 9,
    30, 36, 38, 77, 82–4, 95, 127–8,
    156, 178
  as diplomatic representation 4, 82,
    173
  web site 9

Yomiuri Shimbun 54, 55, 60
Yoshida, Ichiro 19, 24–6, 133, 140

Zhang Junsheng 82
Zhang Wei 72

DATE D

3 5282 00471 5523